Home, Heat, Money, God

**Roger Fullington
Series in Architecture**

HOME HEAT TEXAS MONEY AND GOD MODERN ARCHITECTURE

Text by Kathryn E. O'Rourke

Photographs by Ben Koush

University of Texas Press   Austin

This book is funded in part by the City of Houston through Houston Arts Alliance.

The authors gratefully acknowledge the support of

Fannie and Peter Morris
Anne Lewis and David Morris
H. Russell Pitman
Emily Todd
W. S. Bellows Construction Corporation

Publication of this book was made possible in part by support from Roger Fullington and a challenge grant from the National Endowment for the Humanities.

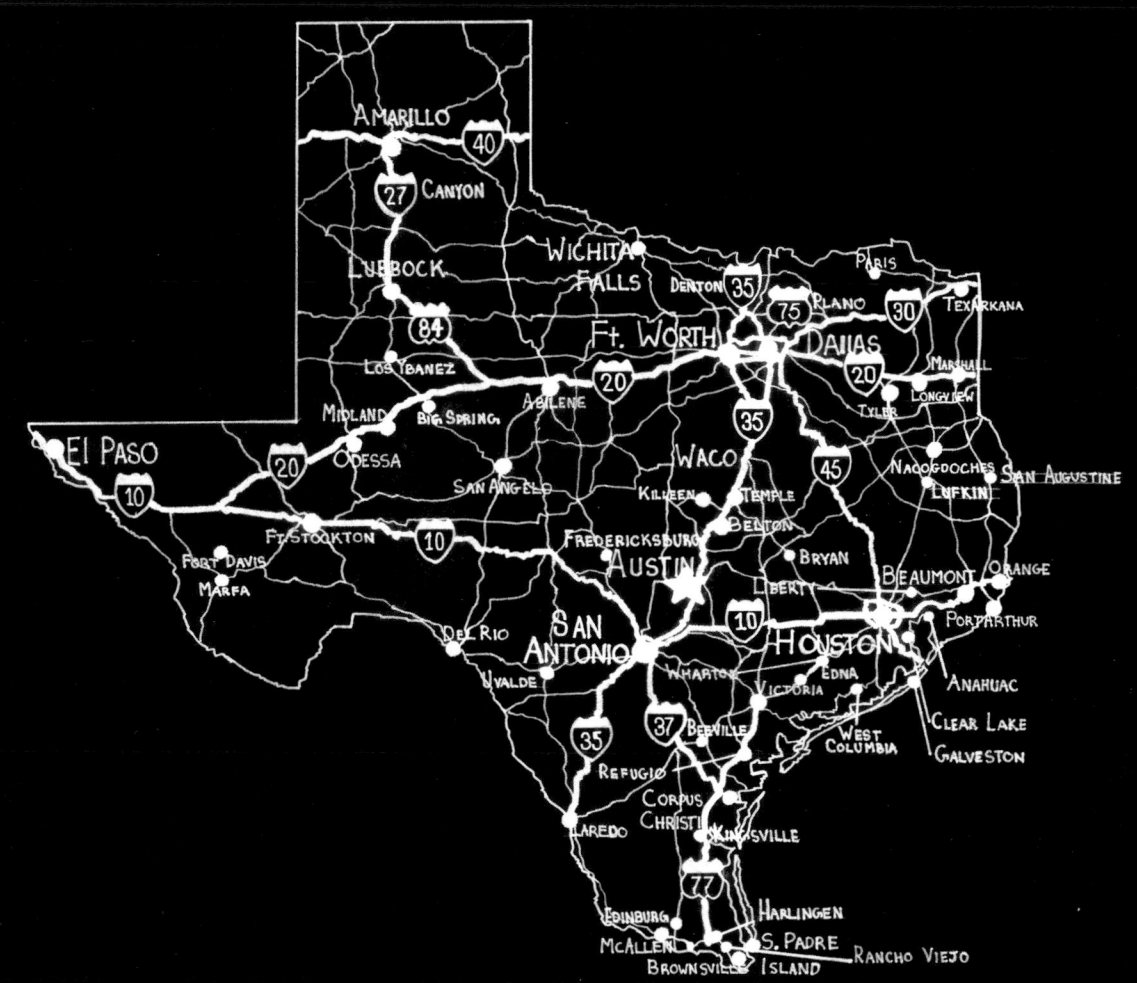

↑ Luke Leblanc, *Towards Texas*, 2022.

Contents

INTRODUCTION

History and Mythology in Texas Architecture
9

PART I PRIORITIES

1. Home — 53
2. Heat — 89
3. Money — 115

PART II PREOCCUPATIONS

4. God — 139
5. Government — 165
6. Care — 189

PART III R&R AND R&D

7. Sports & Leisure — 213
8. On the Road — 243
9. Knowledge & Power — 269

PART IV ASSEMBLAGE

10. Precious Objects — 295
11. Hearts & Minds — 315
12. Contact Zones — 335

CODA

What We Save and Why
361

ACKNOWLEDGMENTS — 376
NOTES — 378
FURTHER READING — 385
ADDRESS LIST — 388
INDEX — 393

INTRODUCTION

History and Mythology in Texas Architecture

Previous Spread: Kenneth Franzheim and
John F. Staub, Lamar High School, Houston,
1937. Relief map by Nino Lenarduzzi.

Above the entrance to the auditorium at Lamar High School in Houston is an enormous limestone map of Texas (see page 8). The work of stonemason Nino Lenarduzzi, the map rises three stories and is the only significant ornament on the severe, late–Art Deco building (1937). Long horizontal lines, a flat roof, and rounded corners accentuate the building's expanse across a grassy lawn. At the west end of the building, the auditorium juts forward from the main mass of the school, upending the expectation of symmetry that the main entrance introduces, with its sober formality (Fig. I.1). In 1939, *Architectural Forum*, a leading national architecture magazine, described Lamar as "imposing" and included it alongside new schools in Massachusetts, Connecticut, California, and Colorado as an example of the most forward-looking such buildings in the country, attuned to the needs of modern education and developments in modern architecture.[1]

→ Figure I.1
Kenneth Franzheim and John F. Staub, Lamar High School, Houston, 1937

Modern it was. The team of architects, led by Kenneth Franzheim and John F. Staub, was well versed in the major currents of 1930s architecture. While capturing the tone of moody modern classicism then dominant in public architecture in the United States, the architects integrated streamlined details with a rigorous composition of rectangular fenestration using concrete, brick, limestone, and steel on a plan in which expert audiences could easily recognize traces of the distinctive pinwheel plan of Walter Gropius's Bauhaus building (1926) in Dessau, Germany. Like Gropius, the Houston architects used their plan to show that different kinds of spaces, such as classrooms, an auditorium, and a gymnasium, lay within the building. But where Gropius was influenced by avant-garde painting and used asymmetry to express a set of ideas about twentieth-century technology and architectural education, Lamar's planners treated the wall plane of the auditorium as a canvas on which to remind all who entered and passed by that Lamar was in Texas. Almost like a brand on the rump of a cow, the map made a claim on the building, announcing that it was in and of the state, whatever else it might also be.

The map's chief audience, of course, was Lamar students. When the school opened, and for decades thereafter, they were all white, and many came from affluent families. On axis with the school's main entrance, River Oaks Boulevard runs north and terminates at the Club House of the River Oaks Country Club. East and west of the boulevard run some of the main residential streets of the neighborhood of River Oaks, which was built as a racially restricted enclave for the wealthy and was home to many Lamar students and their families.[2] How did the map read to them in the 1930s, 1940s, and 1950s? Mexico, Oklahoma, and New Mexico, along with a compass, a date, and lines of latitude and longitude, appear on Lenarduzzi's design in low relief. Louisiana and the Gulf of Mexico are implied. But it's clear what really counts: mountains, rivers, and selected cities: Houston, Austin, San Antonio, Fort Worth, Dallas, Wichita Falls, Galveston, Beaumont, Brownsville, Laredo, El Paso, Amarillo. Lenarduzzi merged political and topographical cartography in his composition, as if to acknowledge that much of the wealth in Texas cities came from the land, whether as oil pumped out of it, cattle grazed on it, cotton plucked from it, or goods moved through its ports and in trains across vast distances.

At midcentury, to a hypothetical Lamar student from River Oaks, the map might well have read as a matter-of-fact reference to life now and in the future—perhaps to further study at the University of Texas in Austin, where, having crossed into a new topographical region, she would meet students from other Texas cities like herself and be further prepared for a life of material ease buttressed by her family's own land-based wealth or that of one she married into. The map placed students, and particularly those arriving from River Oaks Boulevard, in the privileged position of the surveyor, suggesting that they could imaginatively claim the state and encouraging them to imagine themselves in terms of it.

Across that state, in eighty-two mostly rural communities not marked on the Lamar map, African American students learned in one-story, one- and two-room buildings that recalled vernacular houses in many parts of the United States. No maps or other sculptural decoration adorned them. They were made of wood, often raised on brick piers, with windows designed to maximize cross-breezes and light. Based on models and design guidelines established by architects Robert R. Taylor and William A. Hazel at Tuskegee Institute, they were built as part of the program funded by Sears and Roebuck president Julius Rosenwald, and conceived by Booker T. Washington, to build schools for African American students in the South.[3] Funds supplied by Rosenwald, along with local money and sometimes labor to build the schools, helped fill enormous gaps created by state educational systems that routinely spent far more money on schools for white students than on those for students of color.

Running from 1912 to 1932, the program helped fund the construction of more than five hundred buildings on nearly 470 campuses in Texas.[4] It was behind the construction of 5,357 schools throughout the South, and at its height served about one-third of Black students there. In the later years of the program, building materials and design varied more widely than they did early on. Many of the schools have been demolished or have not yet been documented. One that remains is the Columbia Rosenwald School, which opened in 1921 in West Columbia, Brazoria County (Fig. I.2). It operated until the 1950s, when centralization and consolidation, along with the *Brown vs. Board of Education* ruling of 1954, transformed the patterns and places of public education throughout the United States.[5] The building remains today, having been restored after years of neglect.

Figure I.2
Columbia Rosenwald School, West Columbia, 1921

Like Lamar, the Rosenwald Schools existed within national networks and patterns of architectural design, education theory, class, and race. But unlike Lamar, they did not appear in the pages of national architecture journals. Today, Lamar is a large, diverse, urban high school, and its campus has been expanded several times since the 1930s. The Rosenwald buildings that remain have been the subject of significant attention and preservation efforts since the 2000s as appreciation grows of their importance in the history of US education and within many communities. Seen together, Lamar and the Columbia Rosenwald School lay bare the ways architecture operates within, as well as reflects and often sustains, social and economic structures. Where local and state money and resources flowed freely to the school for wealthy urban white students, it was cobbled together through the marshaled forces of a national educational leader and Chicago-based corporate philanthropist for low-income rural Black ones. Where Lamar encouraged its students to see themselves as Texans and all of Texas as theirs, Columbia Rosenwald provided basic education to students whose rights as citizens were expressly denied by the state and who lived in places left off the Lamar map.

Home, Heat, Money, God: Texas and Modern Architecture documents and describes modern buildings in Texas, built from the mid-1930s through the mid-1980s. In this period, architecture and Texas grew and changed at an astonishing pace. The state became a significant force in national and international affairs, chiefly as a consequence of the oil industry and the presence of politically powerful Texans in Washington, DC. Major buildings, many designed by regionally and nationally prominent architects, followed the money in the state as the influence and image of Texas grew. Relentless ambition, a forward-looking attitude, and a strong sense of place combined to make Texans particularly receptive to modern architecture's implication of newness, its future-oriented image, and its capacity to reinterpret historical forms in novel ways. Modern architecture in Texas did not merely track that of the United States in multiple forms but contributed to it quantitatively and qualitatively, largely because of the substantial wealth of architectural patrons and their willingness to support innovative designs by Texan and non-Texan architects alike.[6] As the state grew in importance in national and international arenas, modern buildings were used repeatedly as signs and symbols of cosmopolitanism and of Texan readiness to take a starring role in any number of dramas.

Whether as the subject of fascination nurtured by mass-audience commodities like films and television shows about cowboys or the Alamo, or of horror—after the Kennedy assassination, for example—during the middle decades of the century, outside Texas's borders the state existed as fantasy almost as much as reality. Within its vast reaches, architects and their clients, and all the people who supported their enterprises, were at work transforming a rural state into an urban one. Texans tore down—sometimes only to rebuild in new guises—structures of many kinds that alternately bound and kept them apart as they collectively grew, becoming ever more diverse. The sheer size of the state made it impossible for them, and for most of us today, to know the entire place. For this reason, Texas necessarily exists in the mind as both present and past, fact and myth, its meaning repeatedly remade in words, buildings, landscapes, and images.

This book is intended to stimulate that imagination and fill in some gaps. *Home, Heat, Money, God* is a partial survey of extant buildings in big cities and small towns, selected from the state's large body of modern architecture. It unites recent photographs with brief analyses of buildings to help readers understand the architecture of the state as a consequence of and response to a wide variety of concerns and ideas. While the book identifies Texas architecture's continuities with the major strands of modern architecture internationally, it also underscores the variety within Texas modernism and moments when the forces of pluralism contended successfully with homogenizing and hegemonic pressures. The book's statewide, big city–small town scope is meant as a reminder that there are buildings and stories worth knowing about everywhere.

The focus on modern architecture reflects the author's and the photographer's interests and expertise, and is a response to the limited scholarship on modern buildings in Texas. Underrepresentation of the state in surveys of US architecture has more to do with the relative dearth, until recently, of academic architectural historians in the state than with the quality or quantity of modern buildings there. The size of Texas and the resulting self-sustaining capacity of its architectural culture, as manifest by the activities of the Texas Society of Architects and numerous chapters of the American Institute of Architects (AIA), for example, may also have contributed to a disinclination on the part of Texan architects to participate in a broader national architectural culture. At the same time, however, academic architects and historians have long labored under a cloud of imagined and real parochialism about the state.[7] Although there are numerous locally, state-, or regionally focused architectural guidebooks, historians have seldom organized modern architecture in the United States according to state boundaries. *Home, Heat, Money, God* at once relies on the a priori notion that Texas is a distinct, stand-alone place within the United States, even as it is implicitly experimental in its proposition that both modern architecture and the state can be better understood by reading the two together.

The book is a collaboration between Houston architect Ben Koush, who has taken approximately four thousand photographs of buildings throughout Texas, and architectural historian Kathryn E.

O'Rourke, who selected the buildings and photographs examined here and wrote the text. The result is a work of architectural history and the outcome of distinct curatorial processes on the part of the photographer and the author. The book is meant to be a readable distillation of the insights of an academic architectural historian and an alluring look at Texas's extant modern architecture seen through the eye of an architect. In a few instances, drawings and historical photographs are included to convey information not captured in the architect's photos or to underscore ideas. One of Koush's goals for the book was to draw attention to the role of professional architects in shaping the built environment, as different from the contributions to it made by people without formal training. His desire to emphasize the value of architect-designed buildings reflects a long-running concern within the profession about public misunderstanding of or indifference to the expertise and perspectives that trained architects bring to the world. (In 1857, the American Institute of Architects was founded to promote architects and architecture, a mission it pursues to this day.) Koush's ambition to make the case for the value of architecture using architectural history belongs to a current in twentieth-century modernism that courses through texts of many kinds authored by architects. It was present in writings compiled by Federico Mariscal that interwove Mexican colonial architecture, cultural nationalism, and professional expertise in 1910s Mexico City; in Le Corbusier's exhortations to architects in the 1920s to learn from classical temples and Gothic cathedrals (along with airplanes, ocean liners, and automobiles) in order to catch up with engineers and save the world from "revolution"; in Frank Lloyd Wright's apology in the 1930s for his own radical humanist organicism by way of Inca, "Mayan, Egyptian, Greek, Byzantine, Persian, Gothic, Indian, Chinese, Japanese" architecture; and even in Robert Venturi's "gentle manifesto" of the 1960s, in which he took readers on a marvelous journey through histories of mannerist and baroque architecture to situate contemporary works within a rapidly changing, pluralist society—one that was "black and white, and sometimes gray."[8]

Koush's focus on formally abstract buildings that eschew explicit allusions to the past reflects both his own preferences and the long-standing practice in most professional architecture programs to privilege such works and prioritize their formal and technical qualities. For decades, many academic architectural historians, particularly those whose primary disciplinary training is in art history, as O'Rourke's is, have endeavored to broaden understandings of architectural modernism by writing about the social and cultural contexts that inform architecture and within which architectural meaning is created, in addition to analyzing forms and structures. *Home, Heat, Money, God* reflects the coming together of these two ways of defining modern architecture. The text acts alternately as an explication of and foil to the images, and reflects O'Rourke's role in the project as historian, curator, and critic, simultaneously. (Architectural historians regularly play these three parts at once, if more covertly, in traditional single-author academic scholarship.) Her process of selecting the buildings that appear in the text was shaped by three goals: achieving geographical, typological, and chronological breadth and balance; identifying the state's major midcentury architects and firms; and, by telling little-known stories and grouping buildings across spatial and temporal lines, proposing a way of thinking about Texas, its history, and its buildings that invites readers to reconsider who Texans are and what it might mean to imagine Texas history in new ways.

The book's four parts—"Priorities," "Preoccupations," "R&R and R&D," and "Assemblage"—are meant to give shape to the body of buildings here and to suggest a framework for understanding why and how we build. The book's thematic structure (and title) suggests both the ways that architecture might be understood in general and how the buildings in the text reflect what is particular about Texas. This approach de-emphasizes stylistic, chronological, or evolutionary development and grounds architecture in social, political, and environmental contexts. The organization is inspired by the structure that architectural historian Dell Upton created for US architecture in his survey *Architecture in the United States*. To the extent that there is a narrative trajectory, it is one that follows the state's social and economic patterns during the twentieth century and is one of increasing openness to the world beyond its borders. As Texas brought the world to it and rose as a political, economic, technological, and cultural power, architecture was used repeatedly to express ambition and confidence as well as singularity. The book is informed by the conviction that who we are collectively is laid bare in what, how, where, and for whom we build, and in the meanings and associations we attach to buildings. As the most lasting and certain index of a society's values, and as the most practical of the arts, architecture illuminates places and pasts with special vividness.

Modern Architecture

In Texas, and internationally, modern architecture had many currents, and modern buildings took many forms, but they were linked by their architects' rejections of historical revival styles. Many modern buildings were intended to abstractly convey a sense of newness or an awareness of existing in "the present." In this way they revealed, unintentionally perhaps, their designers' acute concern with historical time. Consciousness of existing within history had defined Western architecture since at least the Italian Renaissance, but it began to intensify in Europe during the eighteenth century as architects studied the buildings of ancient Greece and Rome and as knowledge of them spread to elite architectural patrons and their architects.

Fascination with history often fused with evolving beliefs about the singularity of particular places or cultures and with a widening definition of the world. This was especially true in colonial Mexico, of which much of Texas was a part just one hundred years before our story begins. There architects and their patrons created an astoundingly rich and diverse collection of buildings from within an intense experience of cultural difference and geographical distance from the "center" of the Spanish empire. During the nineteenth century, in Mexico, Europe, and the United States, concern with history, culture, and place fused with an interest in style as a formal problem, which architects absorbed partially from art historical academic structures.

In the early twentieth century, Frank Lloyd Wright in the United States, along with avant-garde architects in several European countries, including Walter Gropius, Le Corbusier, and Ludwig Mies van der Rohe, consciously sought to shed style—which was by then widely understood as deeply bound up with history—as a category altogether in favor of designs that responded to the concerns of the early twentieth century. New construction techniques and the dramatic social and political transformations that the Industrial Revolution had engendered motivated their ambitions to design buildings that at once looked up-to-date, capitalized on yet helped discipline new technologies, and in some way advanced a wide variety of social causes. Interestingly, some of the sources that inspired the European avant-garde were American. They included plans and writings by Wright, and colossal grain silos, which could be found from rural South America to the US Midwest. The silos, like the magisterial example of the Harvest Queen Mill and Elevator in Plainview (1926) and, along Buffalo Bayou, the Houston Port Public Export Elevator

(1930) by John S. Metcalf Company (Fig. I.3), entered the European architectural imagination when Gropius illustrated them in publications and lectures in the early 1910s, and achieved canonical status when Le Corbusier published them in *Vers une Architecture* in the mid-1920s. By the end of the 1920s, knowledge of new European buildings began to spread widely throughout the world—in photographs, in architecture journals, and via the Bauhaus, whose graduates went on to work in many countries.

One of the most important transmissions of information about European modernism in the United States came in the 1932 International Style exhibition at the Museum of Modern Art in New

↑ Figure I.3
John S. Metcalf Company,
Houston Port Public Export
Elevator, Houston, 1930

York. Organized by architectural historian Henry-Russell Hitchcock and architect Philip Johnson, the show proposed that the new architecture be understood chiefly in formal terms and celebrated its rejection of historical allusions and classical planning principles. In naming what they had seen in several European countries (and four places in the United States) "international," Hitchcock and Johnson recycled an old art historical world ("international" was once used to describe a variant of Gothic architecture, for example) and reinforced the ambitions harbored by many modern architects to create "universally" relevant and meaningful forms that were seemingly unencumbered by troublesome nationalistic associations.[9] The highly influential exhibition helped establish the idea that there was an overarching, true modern architecture, and that it looked like the buildings represented in the catalogue and the museum. The formalism of the MoMA show was reinforced in the United States in the late 1930s when Mies van der Rohe immigrated to Chicago and began teaching at the Illinois Institute of Technology (then the Armour Institute) and redesigned its campus, and Gropius came to Harvard to lead the Graduate School of Design. In fact, this modernism was only one strand within a complexly woven fabric, as countless scholars, and this book, document.[10]

The at-times high-pitched debates about form and meaning in European modernism were of relatively little importance in the United States, where pragmatic concerns about cost, construction, and status-projection usually trumped theoretical ones. Here at least, money is the real scaffolding of architecture. No building is built without it, and many buildings are built to express it. In Texas, architectural modernism was used repeatedly to convey personal, professional, and civic prestige or authority, often within exclusionary social structures. Indeed, the long history of modern architecture that stretches back to the sixteenth century was built in many places on economic systems sustained by colonialism and slavery.[11] In Texas in the twentieth century, low-wage and uncompensated labor, themselves bound up with segregation; the denial of civil rights; and gender bias took their places alongside environmental exploitation and degradation to help fuel the creation of money that sometimes financed major works of architecture.[12] As uncomfortable as these histories may be to confront, and as invisible as they may seem, they are nevertheless parts of the history of modern architecture in Texas.

Introduction

Amid the Ugly and the Ordinary

Given that the vast majority of buildings in Texas (or anywhere) are not designed by architects, and that so many of the places and spaces of daily life—whether they are shopping centers, office parks, tracts of suburban houses, unimaginative apartment complexes, or seemingly endless expanses of concrete—are at best undistinguished, corrupted manifestations of the principles that defined great works, and often are painfully ugly, it is fair to ask why people bother looking at buildings and trying to understand them. Amid the mundanity, ugliness, and indifference that define so many buildings and landscapes in the United States, architecture endures as material evidence of the optimism that life might be made better through the marriage of ideas, actions, needs, and forms. It is distinguished from building by the thoughtfulness of its creators, attention to materials, suitability to purpose, craft, and, often, a willingness to prioritize values other than cost savings. Yet, to study architecture in Texas is often to confront baffling juxtaposition and to look in the eye raw devastation. So often, regard for scale and context is minimal (Fig. I.4). Outstanding, or at least interesting, works by major architects stand alongside reckless incarnations of consumer capitalism and the voids—vacant lots, gigantically scaled roads, deserted sidewalks, sweltering parking lots—it leaves in its wake (Fig. I.5). In West Texas, most notably in Midland, skyscrapers shoot up suddenly from the almost incomprehensible flatness of fields of oil and cotton, against expansive skies, and yet in a hauntingly frank relationship with the earth below, whose pillage and destruction they were built to support and by which they are sustained. The profound and disturbing intimacy between building, capital, and ecological rapaciousness contained in such visions concentrates the mind on the state's particular relationship to all three. Confronting these landscapes requires fortitude and patience. But it is worth it.

The problem of ugliness, decay, and minimal or nonexistent planning was a major topic for Texans in the mid-twentieth century. In the 1960s especially, it was discussed repeatedly in *Texas Architect*, the journal of the Texas Society of Architects, and during the group's annual meetings.[13] The August 1964 issue of the journal opened with an excerpt from a speech by President Lyndon Johnson in which he decried the physical and social consequences of sprawl and environmental degradation and declared, "We must act to prevent an Ugly America."[14] In Texas, and throughout the United States, city centers

↑ Figure I.4
Neuhaus and Taylor, One Moody Plaza, Galveston, 1971

Introduction

↓ Figure I.5
Durwood Pickle, American Bank, Bellmead, 1978
(demolished)

had begun to deteriorate largely due to the civic disinvestment that accompanied post–World War II suburbanization. The shift of private and public capital from cities to suburbs (via selective mortgage subsidies and infrastructure spending in the case of government monies), along with racially restrictive housing covenants, and, after 1954, widespread anxiety among whites about school integration, compounded to radically transform Texas cities and landscapes. The situation had become so dire that Texas Society of Architects president Arthur Fehr wrote in the journal in March of 1963 that "Yes, cities can be beautiful and that is not just a facetious statement." Alluding to the intimate relationships between city planning, social concern, and politics, he anticipated readers' doubts, writing, "You may ask how can [we] make any progress [toward creating beautiful cities] in a democracy?" The specter of Cold War ideologies hung heavily over such questions, Fehr suggested, noting that opponents of zoning readily labeled it "communistic."[15]

But before World War II, Texans had embraced monumental, integrated planning funded by public money. Fair Park, built in Dallas as the headquarters of the 1936 centennial celebrations of Texas independence from Mexico, entwined at city scale the stridency, stylishness, and characteristic integration of other arts in mid-1930s Art Deco and modern classical architecture (Figs. I.6, I.7, I.8). The fair helped codify for a broad audience a set of ideas, associations, and mythologies about Texas that shaped the image of the state far beyond its borders. In consultation with Philadelphia-based architect Paul Cret, who contributed to the planning of the campus of the University of Texas at Austin, the fair's chief architect, George L. Dahl, organized the fair's campus and coordinated the work of architects, including Donald Barthleme and Adams and Adams, as well as artists, among them Lynn Ford, Tom Lea, and Eugene Savage.[16] Murals, mosaics, and sculptures, along with the impressive modern buildings, presented Texas as a place of ever-striving heroic, rugged, determined individualism shaped by its often challenging landscapes.[17] This version of Texas papered over the realities of colonialism, slavery, secession, and the state's complicated relationship to Mexico before and after 1836. Buildings such as the Texas Hall of State Building, the Centennial Building, and the Tower Building anchored not only the Esplanade of State but a statewide network of historical markers and monuments. Texas history was thereby recorded in architecture and

↑ Figure I.6 , → Figure I.7
Texas Centennial Architects, Texas Hall of State, Dallas, 1936

History and Mythology in Texas Architecture

↑ Figure I.8
Texas Centennial Architects, Centennial Building (adaptation of a 1905 building by James Flanders), Dallas, 1936. Texas sculpture by Lawrence Tenney Stevens. Cameo reliefs by Pierre Bourdelle. Contralto, sculpted by David Newton in 2009 after the original by Lawrence Tenney Stevens (1936), is in the foreground.

27

landscape across a vast geography, reinforcing and enshrining fact with myth.[18] For rural, urban, and small-town Texans alike who became accustomed to seeing the monuments and markers as they traveled on the state's growing network of roads, the works of the centennial helped solidify the idea that Texas was a unique, distinctive, and unified place. The Lamar High School map, although not formally part of this program, belonged to it conceptually and visually.

Less than twenty years later, the ideal of Texas unity and the fantasy of Texan exceptionalism that such works expressed were literally crumbling, as if in acknowledgment of their conceptual tenuousness. The main story in the 1963 issue of *Texas Architect* in which Fehr pleaded for cities concerned Alfred C. Finn's San Jacinto Monument, which was then just twenty-five years old and deteriorating because of inadequate funding for maintenance (Fig. I.9).[19] The magazine reported that the monument, which was among the "most significant and important" in the state, was almost "certainly destined to abandonment unless immediate steps [were] taken."[20] The limited support for monumentality that the cracks revealed coincided with the fissures and fractures the country experienced as the movements for civil rights, workers' rights, gender equity, and the environment—all of which challenged the main narratives advanced in the works of the Texas Centennial—began.

At the same time, and in concert with the opening toward pluralism to which these movements were central, interest in historical and contemporary vernacular architecture and landscapes grew. This was reflected in *Texas Architect* and other publications, including Clovis Heimsath's 1968 book, *Pioneer Texas Buildings: A Geometry Lesson*. As early as the 1920s, Dallas-based architect David R. Williams, along with his protégé O'Neil Ford and Ford's brother, Lynn, had documented the "anonymous" architecture of (mostly) white settlers in Texas as part of their study of form, materials, and climate-responsiveness. Heimsath's work belonged to this tradition. It, like much research on vernacular architecture, emphasized building types, materials, and characteristic adaptations to site and context—such as porches—and offered a method of organizing and understanding Texas architecture to which this book has a familial relationship. Readers of Heimsath's texts were reminded of the formal similarities between vernacular architecture and major threads of "high" modernism in the foreword by Louis I. Kahn to *Pioneer Texas Buildings*,

→ Figure I.9
Alfred C. Finn, San Jacinto Monument, La Porte, 1938. Reliefs, bronze entrance doors, and crowning star by William T. McVey.

written while Kahn was designing the Kimbell Art Museum in Fort Worth. Rather romantically, Kahn cast vernacular buildings as the prehistory of US architecture, writing, "Later the Architect appears, admiring the work of the unschooled men, sensing in their work their integrity and psychological vitality."[21] As Heimsath's title suggested, Kahn and many other architects found in vernacular buildings evidence of the enduring importance of the basic geometries that, stripped of historical elements and ornament, defined their own work.

The tug and tussle of various strands of modernism invigorated architectural education in Texas as well. As the first director of the School of Architecture at the University of Texas at Austin, Harwell Hamilton Harris led a faculty that included Colin Rowe and John Hejduk.[22] At its height in the 1950s, Harris's program aimed to, as Alexander Caragonne described, "reconcile two divergent philosophies—the modernist insistence on technology, functionalism, and experimentation and the academic reliance on tradition and precedent—while simultaneously challenging the anti-intellectual tendencies of a pragmatic regionalism."[23] It was as theoretically rigorous and far-reaching as the major architectural programs on the coasts and in Chicago. That same decade, Howard Barnstone, Burdette Keeland, and William Jenkins shaped an ambitious new college of architecture at the University of Houston, where students were taught admiration for modernist titans in a program partially modeled on the one at Yale.[24] The state's oldest architecture program was at Texas A&M, where William Caudill and John Rowlett taught. In Austin in 1946, they founded one of the state's most innovative firms, Caudill Rowlett Scott, also known as CRS, which moved to College Station the next year, and to Houston in 1959.[25]

Capital "A" Architects and Architecture

Although interest in vernacular architecture coursed through Texas's architectural culture, the middle decades of the twentieth century were marked by clients' and architects' embrace of the major figures and forms of the main streams of architectural modernism. Nationally and internationally famous architects who worked here included Frank Lloyd Wright, who designed the Kalita Humphreys Theater in Dallas, and his student, Richard Neutra, the author of one of the state's most significant modernist houses, designed for George Kraigher in Brownsville in 1937 (Fig. I.10).[26] Houston was home to an extraordinary house by Bruce Goff and office buildings by Skidmore,

↑ Figure I.10
Richard Neutra, George Kraigher House, Brownsville, 1937

Owings and Merrill, and Welton Becket. Along with Kahn, Ludwig Mies van der Rohe, Edward Durell Stone, and Edward Larrabee Barnes all designed museums in Texas. Paul Rudolph's enormous Fort Worth house for Anne Bass is one of the masterpieces of his career and of Texas modernism, and one of several major buildings he designed in the state. I. M. Pei helped shape the skylines of Dallas and Houston. For nearly twenty years, William Wurster was a consultant in the development of the Trinity University campus in San Antonio. Félix Candela's pioneering work in thin-shelled concrete construction was influential in countless concrete "umbrellas," canopies, and vaults, as well as in buildings, including the Texas Instruments Semiconductor Component Division building, whose roof he designed.

But no internationally renowned architect left a greater imprint on Texas architecture than Philip Johnson.[27] Long favored by affluent private patrons and major commercial real estate developers, with his firms Philip Johnson and Associates and Johnson/Burgee, he designed office buildings, museums, churches, memorials, private houses, and academic buildings. Apart from his own mentor, Mies, Johnson was Texas's foremost link to both the early days of avant-garde modernism and its multiphased evolution into the language of corporate capitalism, labyrinthine bureaucracy, and what Alice T. Friedman has termed "American glamour."[28] Johnson's anti-Semitism and embrace of far right-wing political movements early in his career cast a long shadow over his work and, with his oeuvre's chameleon-like character, complicate any easy summation of his significance.[29] But it was precisely his flexibility and instinct for incipient shifts in the winds of formalism that made him so well suited to Texas clients who prized novelty, cosmopolitanism, and high fashion.

In the middle decades of the century, Texas was home to an impressive group of innovative architects and firms whose work has been overshadowed by that of nationally prominent architects. Among the major Texan architects were Dallas-based Howard R. Meyer, who over the course of his career designed some of the city's most significant buildings, and Howard Barnstone in Houston, whose stylistically varied body of work was marked by a keen attention to detail, materials, and context. The architects at Page Southerland Page and Lloyd, Morgan and Jones, in Austin and Houston, respectively, helped define corporate and governmental modernism in the state and beyond. The firm of Pratt, Box and Henderson in Dallas was a leader in urban planning and contextually responsive design. The large firms followed in the footsteps of Fort Worth–based Sanguinet and Staats, which was one of the first firms to establish offices in multiple Texas cities, and early in the century was one of the state's leaders in steel-framed skyscraper construction. Wyatt C. Hedrick bought their practice in the 1920s and went on to develop a booming one of his own that thrived into the 1960s, with offices in Fort Worth, Dallas, and Houston, and a national reputation. In San Antonio, Norcell Haywood, who had worked with O'Neil Ford, helped pioneer socially conscious community-oriented design practices in the 1970s. Garland & Hilles built numerous modernist houses in El Paso beginning in the 1950s, and Carroll and Daeuble and Associates (later, Carroll, Daeuble, DuSang and Rand) designed major commercial, religious, and civic buildings there. Tyler-based E. Davis Wilcox helped establish modernism as an important language in East Texas with rigorous and inventive compositions for houses, such as the Reitch House in Mineola (Fig. I.11), and on the campus of Tyler Junior College. The architects of Caudill Rowlett Scott (CRS) brought a highly collaborative, research-intensive approach to their work. As the baby boom made school architecture one of the most urgent and lucrative areas of design, CRS became a national leader in it. Their innovative spatial planning and heat mitigation strategies shaped schools across the state that looked altogether different from Lamar and the Rosenwald Schools.

Texas architects distilled the influences of major twentieth-century designers with varying degrees of originality, and their buildings contributed to the evolution of distinctive cityscapes. Mies's imprint was especially pronounced in Houston, where he and his protégé Johnson worked, and where Wilson, Morris, Crain & Anderson designed a building for the Bank of Houston that

↓ Figure I.11
E. Davis Wilcox, Reitch House, Mineola, 1961

Introduction

→ Figure I.12
MacKie and Kamrath, Phillis Wheatley High School, Houston, 1949

↓ Figure I.13
Wilbur Kent and Floyd Marsellos, Lufkin Federal Savings and Loan, 1962

↑ Figure I.14
Stone and Pitts, Tincy and Liggett N. Crim House, Kilgore, 1939

resembled the New National Gallery in Berlin.[30] But Wrightianism was also strong there and in East Texas. MacKie and Kamrath was Wright's major heir in the city, as is evident in their Prairie School–inflected Phillis Wheatley High School, built after desegregation to serve students in a predominately African American neighborhood (Fig. I.12). Wilbur Kent and Floyd Marcellos designed several buildings in Lufkin—the Lufkin Federal Savings and Loan Building among them—that reflected influences from Wright and his mentor, Louis Sullivan (Fig. I.13). On a gently sloping lakeside site in Kilgore in 1939, Stone and Pitts designed for Tincy and Liggett N. Crim a house whose play of planarity and materiality, carried in long white balconies, overhangs, rustic stonework, and an openwork exterior staircase to the dock, suggested they had closely studied Wright's famous Fallingwater, in western Pennsylvania, which was then just two years old (Fig. I.14). In 1940–1941, Chester E. Nagel, a student of Walter Gropius at the Graduate School of Design at Harvard, designed a house in Austin for himself and his wife, Lorine, that revealed deep understanding of the principles of Gropius's own house in Lincoln, Massachusetts, then just three years old. In 1937, O'Neil Ford built a hurricane-proof modernist ranch house for Sid Richardson on Saint Joseph's Island, a barrier island in the Gulf of Mexico.[31] With its clearly differentiated rectilinear volumes,

→ Figure I.15
Rittenberry and Carder, Panhandle-Plains Historical Museum, Canyon, 1932

↓ Figure I.16
Wyatt C. Hedrick, American Bank of Commerce, Odessa, 1960

↘ Figure I.17
Elizabeth Drane Haynsworth, mosaic on exterior of the American Bank of Commerce, Odessa, 1960

substantial glazing, and superbly elegant, slowly curving exterior staircase, the house could almost have been one of Erich Mendelsohn's English buildings of the same decade.

Yet, as the example of Lamar suggests, and perhaps precisely because of the weight of the Texas myth, the ambition to negotiate expressions of difference, sometimes coded as a distinctive cultural fusion, constituted an undercurrent in the state's architectural culture, alongside brash expressions of global worldliness and worthiness. For all the ways that some works of the 1930s seemed to express a particular Texan jingoism, such architectural assertions of self-importance lay firmly within a national and even international pattern of using symbol-laden but sober buildings to evoke feelings of national pride or to express nationalist sentiments, legible in countless works of federal architecture in the United States, as well as in Mexico and Germany, for example. At midcentury, architects and their collaborators used sculptures, reliefs, mosaics, architectural elements, and even building materials to localize and particularize buildings, often implicitly against the seemingly placeless forms of International Style modernism. In Texas architecture, such expressions frequently referred to and reinforced aspects of the state's history and its natural and cultural landscapes. At the Panhandle-Plains Historical Museum in Canyon, Macon O. Carder ornamented the doorway of an otherwise austere work of modern classicism with carvings of cattle brands, the head of a longhorn, and profiles of a cowboy and an Indigenous man (Fig. I.15). Any possible allusions to cultural coexistence were overwritten with the affirmation of colonialism above the door, which proclaimed that the building was "dedicated to the pioneers." Wyatt C. Hedrick's American Bank in Odessa of 1960 was a kind of hybridization of two Park Avenue skyscrapers: Lever House (Gordon Bunshaft and Natalie de Blois under the auspices of Skidmore, Owings and Merrill, 1952) and the Seagram Building (Mies van der Rohe and Johnson, 1958), enlivened at ground level by Elizabeth Drane Haynsworth's mosaic of pipelines, cattle, and agricultural fields (Figs. I.16, I.17).[32] Eight years later, for the front elevation of the theater at HemisFair '68 in San Antonio, Mexican architect and artist Juan O'Gorman created a mosaic depicting the fruits of European and Indigenous cultural convergence in the Americas, itself a descendant of his more famous work at the Central Library of the main campus of the National Autonomous University of Mexico in Mexico City (1952). O'Neil Ford's work of the

1960s provided a more subtle and profound challenge to the hegemony of mainstream International Style modernism. His close study of architectural history led him to repeatedly reinterpret and emphasize characteristic elements of nineteenth-century Texas architecture that also belonged to a long Western architectural history that stretched back to ancient Rome and wound through medieval Europe. His palette included segmental arches that recalled those framing windows and doors on nineteenth-century Central and South Texas commercial buildings, and detailed brickwork that evoked the boundary-crossing tradition of border brick in the Lower Rio Grande Valley.

↑ Figure I.18
Herbert Hunt and Harry Stoner, developers, Texas Pool, Dallas North Estates, Plano, 1961. Photographer unidentified.

Unsubtle and unconcerned about the theoretical or political implications of the International Style were projects of the opposite kind—those that traded on and extended popular understandings of the state to a wide audience, using architecture and its allied arts. One of the most astounding examples was the Texas Pool, a giant swimming pool shaped like the state and created in 1961 in a private neighborhood in Plano (Fig. I.18). A sort of aqueous map, it stretched roughly 100 feet from El Paso to Orange, and 90 feet from Dalhart to Brownsville; a diving board was anchored in Oklahoma, and slides shot out swimmers near Monahans and Del Rio. The pool was both an outlandish example of an insatiable popular appetite for all things "Texas" and, understood in terms of the racial segregation in housing and swimming pools that then governed the state, an expression of political privilege and power in the all-white neighborhood.[33]

↑ Figure I.19
From the opening sequence of Dallas, showing Neuhaus and Taylor, Campbell Centre, Dallas, 1972 and 1977

On the other hand, the abstract, high-gloss visual language of the International Style appealed to those eager to project urban cosmopolitanism and glitz, a phenomenon that was particularly notable in the (oil-)business-oriented cities of Houston and Dallas and their western poles, Midland and Odessa. By the 1980s, nothing typified the marketability and malleability of Texas's multifaceted character like the juxtaposition in the opening sequence of the television show *Dallas*, in which rolling aerial footage of the gleaming mirrored gold office towers of the Campbell Centre (Neuhaus and Taylor, 1972, 1977; Fig. I.19) was followed by that of cattle thundering across a dusty plain.

Architecture and Photography

Television brought Dallas, and at least some twentieth-century Texas buildings, to a mass audience, just as the 1960 film *The Alamo* transformed the ruined San Antonio mission into one of the country's most recognizable buildings, and the foremost symbol of a version of Texas history now widely recognized as incomplete.[34] But the medium on which twentieth-century architects depended most, and on which twenty-first-century historians rely, is photography. It has uniquely shaped understandings (and misunderstandings) of architectural history, helped canonize certain buildings, and trained viewers how to look at them. Photography bolsters architects' careers, and architectural historians' selections and judgments of their subjects can be shaped by photographs. Scholars have documented in detail the intimate relationship between buildings and photographs.[35] This book is about Texas architecture, but it is also implicitly about architectural photography. Its origins lie in Ben Koush's project, inspired by a sense of urgency in the wake of many demolitions, to create a photographic record of modern Texas buildings. His publication of many of his images on Instagram is similarly fueled by an ambition to help stimulate appreciation and conservation of these buildings.

Koush's fascination with major works of architecture—particularly the crisp compositions and disciplined vocabularies of modern architects, including Harlingen-based John York, Richard S. Colley of Corpus Christi, and Jenkins and Hoff of Houston—along with the ordinariness of the settings in which so many buildings stand, shapes his approach (Fig. I.20). Well aware of the nearly two-hundred-year history of architectural photography, Koush is also influenced by photographer Paul Hester, who has documented Texas architecture for many decades, and whose photographs were the subject of an exhibition at the Menil Collection in Houston in 1998–1999.[36] Like Hester, Koush has a discerning eye for detail and the visual power of juxtaposition, whether of building materials, textures, colors, or line, which he conveys using the tools of twenty-first-century digital photography and editing. His apparently neutral, objective photographs are marked by the most subtle hints that he—as photographer and spectator—is present. Even in the photographs most strongly marked by the characteristic techniques of the genre—oblique angles, details whose impact is magnified by close framing, a shot anchored by perpendicular alignment to a wall—he resolutely resists presenting his subjects as monumental on their own, or somehow entirely "clean"

↑ Figure I.20
Richard S. Colley, Ross L. Allen House, Corpus Christi, 1951

and sheered of context. There is never sentimentality, nostalgia, or irony. The more intimate photographs, such as the entry hall of Cocke, Bowman and York's Frank G. Parker House, with its rich palette of colors and materials, structural clarity, Christmas decorations, Ferris-wheel doorstop, and leather recliner, are marked by a restraint rooted in admiration for the architect and respect for the occupant (Fig. I.21).

Another influence on Koush are the photographs that resulted from the mid-1960s collaboration between architect Howard Barnstone, art historian and museum director James Johnson Sweeney, and photographers Ezra Stoller and Henri Cartier-Bresson. Published in Barnstone's book *The Galveston That Was*, and shown in an exhibition at the Museum of Fine Arts, Houston, the photographs captured the history and the present of one of Texas's greatest cities.[37] Koush is drawn to the ways the photographers' apparently "casual" compositions used juxtaposition to make Galveston "seem so special and the buildings seem extraordinary."[38] For example, he notes, their

↓ Figure I.21
Cocke, Bowman and York,
Frank G. Parker House,
Harlingen, 1950

Introduction

→ Figure I.22
Fred S. Stewart; Nicholas J. Clayton; N. J. Clayton and Company, Congregation B'nai Israel Temple, Galveston, 1871, 1887, 1890. Photograph by Ezra Stoller. © Ezra Stoller/Esto.

↓ Figure I.23
Jenkins and Hoff, 600 Building, Corpus Christi, 1964

three photographs of Congregation B'nai Israel Temple "considered together evoke not only the sculptural power of the building even in its diminished state but also the quiet and not a little harsh atmosphere of Galveston itself" (Fig. I.22).[39] Koush achieves something similar in some images, such as those of the 600 Building in Corpus Christi by Jenkins and Hoff (1964; Fig. I.23). Stoller's and Cartier-Bresson's photographs often included one or two people, not posed, but captured as part of the overall scene. They thereby rooted the buildings firmly in the realm of daily life and the Galveston landscape. We see the traces of the Galveston project in Koush's photographs that include evidence of human presence, whether in the empty metal chair on the deck at L. Brooks Martin's Searcy Medical Clinic in Bryan (Fig. I.24), or in the figure of the museum guard on his break, looking at the seam between Mies's Cullinan Hall and the original neoclassical wing designed by William Ward Watkin in the mid-1920s (Fig. I.25).

Very rarely, Koush himself appears in photographs, most often in reflections. His presence, along with those of other figures, unplanned and occasionally planned, are subtle reminders that for all the anonymous technology, the at-times tedious theoretical debates, and the crushing character of capitalism that undergirded modern architecture at midcentury, this architecture was also guided by a profoundly humanistic set of concerns and ambitions. In its implicit argument that what was built in the past matters for the future, and that architecture may be understood by considering the social contexts in which it exists, this book is a continuation of that humanist tradition. Koush's literal reflection is also a reminder that history is, first and foremost, a representation of the past—documented, organized, and written by individuals, who, for a variety of reasons, are granted authority to do so. Although camera phones and the internet have democratized photography and its dissemination to a greater extent than at any time in history, access to spaces and places is sometimes still governed by far less democratic practices and realities. Koush was able to photograph so many buildings, and move through so many spaces—in big cities and small towns, standing in busy streets, on desolate sidewalks, vacant lots, and alleys in residential neighborhoods and commercial corridors—more easily and securely than would most people of color and most women. While we wish that Texans everywhere were equally friendly to all, the reality is often otherwise, a fact that even the low-risk activity of architectural field research makes clear.[40]

↑ Figure I.24
L. Brooks Martin, Searcy
Medical Clinic, Bryan, 1950

→ Figure I.25
William Ward Watkin,
Museum of Fine Arts,
Houston, 1924; Cullinan
Hall addition by Ludwig
Mies van der Rohe, 1958,
altered by the Office of
Mies van der Rohe during
the construction of Brown
Pavilion, 1974

Concerning Absence

This book focuses almost exclusively on buildings designed by professional architects, even though there are any number of beautiful or historically significant buildings created by people who were not formally educated in architecture. Highly trained in technical and artistic matters, architects are accorded special status in the building process—above builders, contractors, interior designers, artists, technical systems specialists, and anonymous do-it-yourselfers who shape the built environment. Yet the term "architect" is not as straightforward as it might seem, owing to a variety of historical structures, strictures, and customs. Neither Wright nor Ford held degrees in architecture, but they have long been recognized among its leaders because of the number and quality of their buildings, which were supported by affluent, and sometimes fairly brave, clients. In Texas, calling oneself an architect was once much easier, but in 1937—the year after the centennial celebrations sought to define "Texas"—the state required "architects" to be licensed and registered, and therefore to have passed a series of formal academic and professional examinations.

↑ Figure I.26
John S. Chase in his office in Houston. MSS0113-PH0004, Houston Public Library, the African American Library at the Gregory School.

In a segregated, patriarchal state, this requirement helped narrow the potential pool of "architects" to those who could attend degree-granting universities, which seldom admitted applicants who were not white men. Given the state's history and demographics, the absence of Mexican Americans and Latino/as in the midcentury record thus far is striking, particularly given how many of them, along with Mexican immigrants, did the physical work of constructing, painting, and outfitting buildings, especially in South and West Texas. Although African American architects had worked in Texas since before the Civil War, it was nevertheless notable when Houstonian John S. Chase became the first African American to graduate from the School of Architecture at the University of Texas at Austin in 1952, the first to become registered as an architect in Texas two years later, the first to join the Texas Society of Architects, and the first African American from Texas to be elected to fellowship in the American Institute of Architects (Fig. I.26).[41] In 1971, he helped found

Introduction

the National Organization of Minority Architects (NOMA). Chase sought employment in twenty Houston architecture firms, all of which turned him down, before beginning his own firm in 1954 and going on to a long and very successful career.

↑ Figure I.27
Carolyn Peterson standing on the roof of Mission San José, San Antonio, late 1980s or early 1990s. Courtesy of Ford, Powell and Carson.

Victoria native Carolyn Peterson was among the very few women in her class in architecture school at the University of Texas. In 1964, immediately after she graduated, she joined the San Antonio firm O'Neil Ford and Associates, and she went on to become one of the foremost preservation architects in the country, entrusted with conservation of the San Antonio missions and the State Capitol in Austin, among other major buildings (Fig. I.27). In 2009, she became the forty-first person to win the Texas Society of Architects' Llewellyn W. Pitts Medal for lifetime achievement; the forty previous winners were all men. As a woman architect in Texas, Peterson followed in the footsteps of Mabel C. Welch, who came to El Paso in 1916 and during the 1920s and 1930s designed hundreds of buildings in West Texas, New Mexico, and Mexico, becoming one of the state's foremost practitioners of the Spanish Colonial Revival style.[42]

Unlike Welch, Ruth McGonigle, of Brownsville, was not a licensed architect, although she completed an architecture degree at Rice in 1924. Over the course of a long career, she designed houses in the Rio Grande Valley, including a modern ranch house for Professor Josephine Sobrino and her life partner, Kathryne Cherry. Sobrino, an expert on Indigenous languages and cultures in Mexico, taught at Texas Southmost College (where she helped found the Brownsville chapter of the American Association of University Women), and later at the University of Houston. She was also a pilot, and during World War II, trained US airmen in navigation and meteorology. Cherry worked for Pan American Airways and was a labor activist in Brownsville.[43] Organized in two wings, the two-bedroom Sobrino-Cherry house was designed to accommodate the needs of these busy, intellectual women: it included a large living room for entertaining, a barbecue pit, and a den, for which McGonigle designed built-in bookshelves and a pair of desks. With its fairly conventional one-story midcentury façade, the Sobrino-Cherry house would have been unlikely to draw much attention on a suburban street. Alice T. Friedman has identified this kind of modern house—in which the exterior resembles those of neighboring houses in style and scale, but the plan reflects the needs of households whose clients were not heterosexual couples with children—as "poker face" architecture. As she has shown, some of the most interesting and innovative houses in the history of modern architecture were shaped by clients who lived alone, were single parents, or part of same-sex couples.[44]

Among the absences in architectural history, those related to sexuality are some of the most difficult to redress, because private lives tend to remain private. Scholarship abounds on architecture's role (or complicity) in idealizing the white heterosexual nuclear family at midcentury and the consequent exclusion of households that did not fit the norm. Yet architectural historians and architects continue to grapple with homophobia as part of the social context in which modern architecture was shaped and practiced.[45] Reckoning with this aspect of architecture's past often requires reading between the lines of historical texts and inferring the meanings of archival absences. Among the gay architects whose work appears in this book, Philip Johnson and Paul Rudolph were the most famous, and although their sexuality was known to their colleagues and friends at midcentury, the architects did not discuss it widely, given the enormous professional and personal risks that being out entailed at that time.[46] By the late twentieth century, many architects felt freer than they had in earlier decades to come out, making it somewhat easier to read sexuality back into architectural history. Two of Johnson's last buildings, the Cathedral of Hope and its Interfaith Peace Chapel (chapel completed by Alan Ritchie Architects with Cunningham Architects in 2011) in Dallas, were designed for a congregation of the United Church of Christ, one of the nation's largest LGBTQ+ faith communities. Shortly before he died, Johnson said of the Interfaith Peace Chapel, "This is a building I've waited all my life to build. It will be my memorial."[47]

Acknowledging the historical prejudices that shaped architecture as a profession, whose ghosts still haunt architectural history writing, means that books like this one should be understood as presenting only part of the story of modern architecture in Texas.[48] The book is a partial account in other important ways as well, because of the constraints the authors set themselves. Few illustrations convey spatial planning, and limited access to private spaces has curtailed the number of interiors Koush was able to photograph. The innovative, influential interior designs of Sally Walsh, many of them now altered, for example, are not pictured. Information about many of the works not discussed here can be found in other histories, excellent locally focused architectural guides, and the two volumes on Texas in the Society of Architectural Historians' Buildings of the United States series, listed at the end.[49]

Many buildings that might be here are not because they were torn down to make way for new ones or, worse, for parking lots and freeways. The flipside of Texan ambition has been disregard for what doesn't fit (or generate enough profit) in the latest plan. The willingness to spend money, particularly on the part of commercial real estate developers (coupled with high interest rates that helped promote long-ish term approaches to development), which once fueled the creation of some of the state's great modern buildings, at times itself feels like a historical relic, especially when older buildings are demolished to make way for new, cheaply built ones that turn fast profits and contribute little to local landscapes. As was the case with the preparation and publication of *The Galveston That Was*, some of the buildings photographed for this book no longer stand. Regrettably, these losses echo those that occurred repeatedly in the twentieth century, when single buildings, large swaths of historic fabric, and even greater stretches of landscape were destroyed for new buildings and new car-oriented infrastructure. Yet historic preservation itself was also part of the story of modern architecture in Texas, and it was championed by architects, historians, conservationists, and ordinary citizens of many kinds. Today, it is taken up again by local, regional, and national organizations and offices, with an increasingly sharp focus on saving mid-twentieth-century buildings.[50] Particularly notable among these groups are the regional chapters of Docomomo International, an organization dedicated to the documentation and conservation of modern architecture. On an official, statewide basis, the staff of the National Register of Historic Places program at the Texas Historical Commission work tirelessly to document extant buildings and shape a more expansive and thorough history of Texas architecture.

Although understanding architects' intentions is critical to understanding buildings' meanings, some of those meanings and associations can change over time, if slowly. Lamar High School was named for Mirabeau B. Lamar, a president of Texas who supported slavery and Secession, and presided over the slaughter of Indigenous Texans. For most of its existence, the school's sports teams were called the "Redskins." In 1997, a student-led effort to change that name began. Nearly twenty years later, the mascot, although not the school's name, was retired.[51] This change had nothing to do with the architecture of the school, but it did signal an important opening to new ways of thinking about history and culture in the state's largest school district. Looking closely at buildings can open our eyes to aspects of ourselves and our histories that hide in plain sight. This book is offered in the hope that architecture might entice Texans and non-Texans alike, in cities, towns, and the country, to discover new places on the map, see the familiar in new ways, meet one another more often, and dare to reinvent Texas once again.

1. **Home** 53
2. **Heat** 89
3. **Money** 115

1. Home

Previous Spread: Associated Housing
Architects of Houston (Design Committee:
MacKie and Kamrath, Claude E. Hooton,
and Eugene Werlin), San Felipe Courts,
Houston, 1942, 1944

1. Home

In the United States, no building type rivals the dwelling as a locus of aspiration, anxiety, and association. "Home" takes many forms. It plays many roles simultaneously in private and public life: as the shelter of families and the theater of the profoundest relationships; as a touchpoint of memory and emotion; as the foremost outward symbol of status within capitalism. "Home" haunts social, political, and economic debates. Overtly and covertly, directly and indirectly, governments subsidize dwellings, or don't, and thereby participate in picking the winners in the "American Dream" sweepstakes, symbolized since World War II by the suburban house. Jeffersonian fantasies of agrarianism and the image of Monticello set amid a verdant lawn laid the groundwork for the invention, over many decades, of a vast national economy built on private control of land and homeownership and reliant on voracious appetites for filling homes with things. So entwined is home with national myth that at points it almost seems that the pursuit of happiness is coterminous with the pursuit of the perfect place to live.[1] Large Texas cities' gargantuan sprawl today reflects the fusion of the long-standing practice of transforming wilderness into real estate and the idea of home as a suburban house served by car-scaled infrastructure.[2]

Like architects in many places, Texans used the private house as the foremost type for experimentation. As early as 1927, small, detached houses, such as the Philip Taber House in Amarillo, began to reflect the influence of European modernism; it was followed by the Mayflower Investment Houses by Reynolds Fisher and Luther Sadler in Dallas of 1936 and 1937 (Fig. 1.1). Midcentury saw the emergence of high-rise apartment buildings and, of even greater significance, the proliferation of all manner of suburban ranch houses for the (mostly white) middle class. Significant among these are the houses of A. D. Stenger in South Austin built from about 1950 to 1960, or works by John G. York and Associates, such as the house designed for Dr. Rafael Garza in McAllen (1958), which, like other modern houses designed for prominent Mexican Americans in the city, stood just outside an elite white neighborhood (Figs. 1.2, 1.3).[3] Although it is related to the Prairie and Usonian houses of Frank Lloyd Wright, who grafted Jeffersonian and Transcendentalist ideas about land and individualism onto modern ones about family, cities, and daily life, the ranch house was invented in Southern California in the 1920s and given its

↑ Figure 1.1
Reynolds Fisher, Mayflower Investment House, Dallas, 1936

→ Figure 1.2
A. D. Stenger, Robert Howell House, Austin, 1950

↑ Figure 1.3
John G. York and Associates, Rafael Garza House, McAllen, 1958

romantic name to conjure associations with the architecture of settler colonialism in the west. From the 1930s into the 1960s, the image of the modern home was influenced by books, such as Emily Post's *The Personality of a House* (1930), and magazines, such as *House Beautiful* under the editorship of Elizabeth Gordon, that were dedicated to educating readers on domesticity, decoration, and style.[4] Yet the visual, psychological, and economic hegemony of the suburban house, whatever its style, often occludes the other forms of home and obscures its historical status as an anomaly in the history of human dwelling.

Apartment Life

For many, home is not a gabled-roof house isolated amid a lawn but an apartment rooted in a community. San Felipe Courts, which was built on the banks of Buffalo Bayou in Houston in 1940–1944, was one of the most important and innovative public housing projects in the United States (Fig. 1.4).[5] Designed by a team of twelve firms collectively called Associated Housing Architects, the apartments were notable for the quality of their design and execution, with exteriors by MacKie and Kamrath. Begun under the auspices of the Housing Authority of the City of Houston as affordable housing for workers in defense industries, San Felipe Courts originally included

→ Figure 1.4
Associated Housing Architects of Houston (Design Committee: MacKie and Kamrath, Claude E. Hooton, and Eugene Werlin), San Felipe Courts, Houston, 1942, 1944

eighty housing blocks and two multipurpose communal buildings on a 37-acre site.[6] In all, the complex provided one thousand homes of different sizes and configurations, ranging from one-bedroom apartments to four-bedroom duplexes. They were arranged in buildings organized on a campus informed by the principles of large-scale modernist housing and community planning that emerged in Germany and the Netherlands, both of which were world leaders in multifamily housing design in the 1920s. Individual buildings at San Felipe Courts were notable for their flat roofs, varied palette of materials, rigorous geometrical massing and detailing, and Wrightian articulation of horizontality.

From beginning to end, the project also typified the fraught dynamics of race, class, housing, and urbanism characteristic of many such projects in cities across the country. The courts were built for working-class white Houstonians, on the site of the city's historic Freedmantown in Fourth Ward, Houston's oldest African American neighborhood. Their construction displaced Black residents and destroyed nearly the entirety of the historic neighborhood. Unfolding in the shadow of a growing downtown, along the foremost artery connecting the central business district and River Oaks, the city's most affluent white neighborhood, the destruction of Freedmantown/construction of San Felipe Courts, as a late New Deal project, was one of the most vivid examples in the nation of the federal government's role in racialized urban reshaping and displacement. Until 1964, only whites could live there. Black Houstonians moved in in large numbers in the 1970s, the same decade that the city began its efforts to sell the increasingly valuable land. Today only 30 percent of San Felipe Courts remains, in altered interior condition. Despite having been listed on the National Register of Historic Places for its national significance, most of the buildings were destroyed and replaced by the Housing Authority with market-rate townhouses, apartments, and parking, disproportionately displacing low-income residents once again.[7]

Elsewhere in Texas, important housing complexes, typically consisting of low-rise, flat-roofed buildings, rose beginning in the late 1930s and, like San Felipe Courts, embodied the confluence of international ideas about modern architecture and US patterns of segregation. In San Antonio, the Alazán-Apache Courts (1939–1942), designed by N. Straus Nayfach and based in part on examples of workers' housing designed by Juan Legaretta in Mexico City, housed nearly five thousand working-class Mexican Americans on the city's Westside.[8] Funded by the federal government but maintained by a robust residents' association, they were considered a national housing model. Part of the success of the project lay in the thriving community that Alazán-Apache was home to. Community development was a central concern in other federally subsidized projects built through the 1950s, for example, in Tays Place (1941), designed by Trost and Trost and Frazer and Benner, and Ray Sherman Place (1953), by Louis Lloyd Mollinary, both in El Paso.[9] At Tays Place, white and Mexican American residents were segregated from African American residents in separate sections of the campus plan. Ray Sherman Place was built for veterans but was chiefly home to low-income Mexican American and white residents. In case after case, the visual economy of high modernism translated readily to limited public budgets.

Apartment buildings reflected changing styles and tastes while accommodating growing populations. In San Antonio, the two-story Lullwood Apartments by Ellis F. Albaugh (1937) typified the continuation of the low-rise, relatively low-density suburban apartment building that proliferated in cities throughout Texas in the 1910s and 1920s (Fig. 1.5). Designed in the jazzy language of Art Deco, the Lullwood Apartments, like other similarly scaled and sited buildings, proved that moderate multi-unit density, greenery, and cars could coexist harmoniously as development spread from cosmopolitan downtown cores. The Windsor Court Apartments in Galveston (1937), by Cameron Fairchild, is a somewhat less formally exuberant contemporary of the San Antonio building (Fig. 1.6). With its ground-level retail, moody modern details, and pronounced cantilevered balconies that wrap around the corners of the building and run along its long sides, the four-story T. W. Lee Apartment Building in Gladewater (1950; Fig. 1.7), designed by W. L. Kelly of Longview, was a strikingly cosmopolitan work for an East Texas town of about five thousand.

Austin's Rio House Apartments (1959) expanded on the courtyard apartment type popular in the 1920s and demonstrated the possibilities of adaptive reuse and stylistic fusion. Rio House consists of two wings that meet at a right angle: one built in 1959 of concrete block, and the other, a 1928 brick-clad building that originally housed St. David's Hospital, which was renovated at the time the new wing

1.   Home

→ Figure 1.5
Ellis F. Albaugh, Lullwood Apartments, San Antonio, 1937

↓ Figure 1.6
Cameron Fairchild, Windsor Court Apartments, Galveston, 1937

↑ Figure 1.7
W. L. Kelly, T. W. Lee Apartments, Gladewater, 1950

was built. Page Southerland Page connected the two buildings with long open-air walkways. These are framed in mauve-colored steel to function as balconies for individual units, but in concert with the concrete slabs that extend from the volume of the building, draw attention to the underlying structural rationalism (Fig. 1.8). Residents' plants and outdoor furniture in turn vernacularize and particularize a design that belonged to a broad international tendency in architecture. In 1959, the hospital's eclectic façade, with its Gothic Revival ornament and the pronounced would-be ogee arch door frame, was apparently too much to bear, but also too good to destroy. The architects covered it with a metal screen—a species of a slipcover—that remains today and is now itself a historic element (see page 63). They balanced the composition by screening an exterior staircase on the new wing.

1. Home

↑ Figure 1.8
Page Southerland Page, Rio House Apartments, Austin, 1959

Up and Out

Low-rise apartment buildings were in many ways well suited to the scale of residential neighborhoods on the edges of city centers, but in the 1960s, tall, suburban luxury apartment buildings began to rise. Most often, they were home to aging, wealthy refugees of large 1920s houses in neighborhoods such as River Oaks and Highland Park in Dallas, and to relatively cosmopolitan white-collar workers disinclined toward the bother of houses and yards.

Neuhaus and Taylor's Inwood Manor in Houston (1964) supported "gracious living" for the rich in 134 apartments, a two-hundred-car partially submerged garage, a restaurant, lounges, a private club, and a large rear garden designed by landscape architects Fred Buxton & Associates (Fig. 1.9). The stylish interior was the work of Wells Design. The architects articulated the building's off-white poured-in-place concrete frame in the language of restrained New Formalist rationalism. Large windows and balconies were framed by broad arches that subtly linked the tower simultaneously to a long tradition in Western architectural classicism and to the sophisticated glamour palaces of the day, from government buildings in Brasilia to halls for the performing arts at Lincoln Center in New York City. Collectively, these buildings communicated a Kennedy-era Cold War alliance of a tasteful and up-to-date elite across borders and typologies. Indeed, part of the appeal of an apartment at the Inwood Manor was the ease of leaving it to travel, an increasingly popular hobby for the affluent.

In 1964, the Inwood Manor appeared in *Architectural Record* alongside new high-rise apartment buildings designed by prominent architects throughout the United States, including in Philadelphia by Stonorov and Hawes and in Honolulu by Minoru Yamasaki.[10] Although somewhat less so in the case of apartment towers built in dense metropolises in the Northeast, the problem of parking was a central design challenge in nearly every project and was intimately related to questions of type and context. The Inwood Manor and many of its cousins throughout the country were significant not only as examples of scaled-up modernism for the domestic realm but as experiments in defining a building type that was still relatively new. Since the late nineteenth century, busy, pedestrian-scaled city centers had been the domain of tall buildings, but as early as the 1920s, the Parisian architect Le Corbusier had envisioned residential (and commercial) towers set in verdant landscapes that accommodated cars. Such schemes presented enormously complex questions about scale, context, and social dynamics that would be worked out with varying degrees of success after World War II in projects throughout the world addressed to people across a wide socioeconomic spectrum. The "success" of Inwood Manor and countless other modern luxury apartment towers, seen against the perceived "failure" of modern high-rise housing for the working class, powerfully illustrates the fallacy of attributing to architectural style and type causation of social problems.

In Dallas, two exceptional high-rise apartment buildings reflected both the growing popularity of the type and its potential as a locus of innovative design. A twenty-two-story luxury tower, 3525 Turtle Creek (1957), was designed by Dallas-based Howard Meyer, one of Texas's most important modernists, with grounds designed by Arthur and Marie Berger, the state's foremost landscape architects in the 1950s (Fig. 1.10). Meyer had briefly known Le Corbusier in Europe and worked with William Lescaze (with whom he designed the Magnolia Lounge in Fair Park in 1936). The famous 1931 PSFS (Philadelphia Savings Fund Society) office building in Philadelphia, one of the very few US buildings that Henry-Russell Hitchcock and Philip Johnson included in the International Style exhibition at MoMA, was the work of Lescaze and George Howe. The 3525 Turtle Creek tower reflected Meyer's astute

↓ Figure 1.9
Neuhaus and Taylor, Inwood Manor, Houston, 1964

↘ Figure 1.10
Howard R. Meyer, 3525 Turtle Creek Apartments, Dallas, 1957

command of the high modernist principles typified by PSFS and Le Corbusier's urban designs—the emphasis on taut geometries; deft manipulation of varied materials and textures; and, at high-rise scale, the priority placed on views, light, and abundant ground-level green space. Organized on a pinwheel-shaped plan, 3525 Turtle Creek is rigorously composed of sand-colored Mexican brick, concrete piers, and distinctive gridded precast concrete sunshades between them (Fig. 1.11). Meyer's building overlooks Turtle Creek Park, Turtle Creek Boulevard, and the creek for which they are named, all developed as part of the City Beautiful plan that George Kessler designed for Dallas in 1911, but which was only partially implemented.

In the 1980s, high-rise construction boomed (and busted) throughout Texas, both in city centers and along the shore of the Gulf Coast. That decade (when a combination of urban glitz and beach grit made *Miami Vice* one of the most popular shows on television) saw the construction of the Galvestonian, by Lloyd Jones Brewer and Associates (1983), a cool condo tower in Galveston, built to accommodate urban vacationers in comfort above the sand (Fig. 1.12). The curving line of the building's plan was an obvious sculptural allusion to the lines of waves and sand dunes, views of which denizens could enjoy from large windows. Typologically, and because of its seaside location, expressed concrete frame, and large balconies, the Galvestonian called to mind Le Corbusier's first realized large apartment building, the Unité d'Habitation in Marseille, which similarly had views to the water (the Mediterranean Sea rather than the Gulf of Mexico). The Galvestonian also had a familial relationship with other great serpentine-plan residential buildings: Alvar Aalto's 1949 Baker House dormitory at MIT, which overlooked the Charles River, and Affonso Eduardo Reidy's 1946–1951 cliff-clinging Pedregulho Housing Project in Rio de Janeiro, which looked out toward Guanabara Bay and included numerous spaces for social, recreational, and commercial activities. Built on East Beach, the Galvestonian could hardly have differed more from Galveston's historic nineteenth-century architecture, which was then receiving increasing attention from preservationists, and especially from Houston-based real estate developers George and Cynthia Woods Mitchell. As the Mitchells helped bring the Strand back to life to entertain visiting Houstonians, the Galvestonian gave them a place to escape from the expanding metropolis just up Interstate 45.

1. Home

↑ Figure 1.11
Howard R. Meyer, 3525 Turtle Creek Apartments, Dallas, 1957

↑ Figure 1.12
Lloyd Jones Brewer and Associates, Galvestonian,
Galveston, 1983

Party Like It's 1969

The homes of important architectural patrons, particularly those active in social, political, and philanthropic circles, often lead double lives as dwellings and stage sets upon which rituals of class and power are enacted, status and influence are cemented, and deals are done. The most interesting examples of such houses are those that challenge or reimagine architectural norms and expectations. Their owners' keen understanding of detail and nuance in architecture often translate into superlative command of the subtleties of soft social power, particularly when it is backed up by large checks. The patrons of the three houses examined here—John S. Chase, Patsy Steves, and Anne Bass—each made exceptional contributions to the arts in Texas (Chase as an architect, Steves and Bass as arts patrons) and regularly hosted gatherings that included the leading politicians and cultural luminaries, including John B. Connally, Lady Bird Johnson, Gregory Peck, and Van Cliburn. As works of architecture, their houses were nationally outstanding examples of the evolution of the large suburban house type.

The house that John S. Chase designed for himself, his wife, Drucie Raye Rucker Chase, and their children in 1959 in Houston's Oakmere neighborhood reflected his absorption of the principles of Frank Lloyd Wright's Usonian houses and his contribution to the evolution of the modern suburban courtyard house type (Fig. 1.13). Set back from the street on a large lot amid tall pine trees, with its long horizontal lines, flat roof, and orangey Roman brick laid in running bond, the house engaged with its site by simultaneously mirroring Houston's essential flatness and providing linear contrast to the tall, columnar trees on the lot. It was one of several notable Houston houses that reflected Wright's influence, including Karl Kamrath's second house for himself in River Oaks (1953). Seen with its western cousin, the Max Grossman House in El Paso (Fig. 1.14), designed by Garland & Hilles in a completely different climate and site, and with 1950s Wrightian houses in places as different as Dallas (Howard Meyer's Lipshy House, 1950), Pharr (Zeb Rike's Darby House, 1956), and Bryan (Merrill and Vrooman's Cunningham House, 1959), the Chase House belongs to an important body of buildings that reveal Wright's enduring relevance to modern architects in a variety of contexts, even as others diluted his form and disregarded his core principles, as ranch house suburbs rose, and as schools of architecture ignored him.

But unlike many architects who sought to emulate Wright, Chase designed his house around an enclosed central courtyard, which provided a fully private outdoor space for his children to play and which belonged to a broad tendency in midcentury residential design. The genetic ancestry of such spaces lay in the patios of villas and palaces of the ancient Mediterranean and was filtered through the designs of European avant-garde architects in the 1920s, but their popularity in the Cold War–era United States had everything to do with the availability of relatively large, inexpensive suburban lots, a national preoccupation with privacy, and the entwining of ideas about class and spaciousness.[11]

↑ Figure 1.13
John S. Chase, Drucie Raye Rucker and John S. Chase House, Houston, 1959, 1968

→ Figure 1.14
Garland & Hilles, Max Grossman House, El Paso, 1955

1. Home

↑ Figure 1.15
John S. Chase, Drucie Raye Rucker and John S. Chase House, Houston, 1959, 1968. Drawing by Luke Leblanc.

In 1968, Chase transformed his courtyard into a double-height "great room" when he added a second story to the house to accommodate his family's changing needs as his children grew up and, presumably, to make the house even more suitable for entertaining (Fig. 1.15). The story of the addition links the house to the stories of others in Houston, a city marked by the pronounced proclivity of its well-heeled upper-middle class to alter their homes. The most important part of the addition was essentially a great glass box placed atop the first floor. Light flooded the former courtyard, which was now accented by a dramatic staircase whose cantilevered treads endowed the interior with a swanky up-to-date elegance.

Chase's use of modernism to shape a home and assert class status was not exceptional; what was, of course, was that he did so as an African American architect working in a profoundly segregated city, in a state and society that repeatedly threw up barriers to his professional and financial success. For several decades, the Chase home was an important center of political activity in Houston. Its architect-owner's keen understanding of the potential of modern architecture to signal cosmopolitanism and even power, and his deft reading of the changing tastes within architecture—from disciplined Usonian privatism in the 1950s to the glassy glamour of a more complex section in the 1960s—is all the more significant when it is understood as a tool and symbol of the emergence of a powerful Black middle class in urban Texas. The two major eras of construction of the Chase House fell on either side of the years in which President Lyndon Johnson signed the sweeping civil rights bills that helped break some of the barriers that Chase and his family faced. The addition to the house was built during a period of transition for the civil rights movement—when much had been achieved but as its leaders discovered that even close allies would be unlikely to support the far-reaching economic reforms needed to continue the work they had begun.[12] Understood in this context, the renovation and second story, built to house important social and political gatherings, at once signaled arrival, uplift, and expectation.

71

Part I: Priorities

One of San Antonio's great party houses reflected not the influence of Wright but that of colonial Mexico. For Patsy Galt and Marshall Terrell Steves, Chris Carson, the youngest partner in O'Neil Ford's firm, oversaw the design of a one-story modern hacienda that unfolds across the top of a large sloping site in Terrell Hills (1965).[13] Here, too, privacy was prioritized, but in the traditional Mexican manner, with the living spaces enclosed almost entirely by a long, white stucco wall. As at the Chase House, the courtyard was a critical element of the plan, only here there were four: the first was expressed as a long entrance court opened to the south through a narrow break in the wall. Carson organized the house into three programmatically distinct wings that opened off a long central corridor, with bedrooms at the east end, public rooms and their ancillary spaces (including a servant's quarters) near the middle, and a game room and guest suite at the west end. At the rear of the house, a patio separated each wing and opened off the spinelike gallery. The pendant space to the entrance court on the front was a huge patio and large pool (Fig. 1.16). Stewart King, one of San Antonio's foremost landscape architects and a frequent collaborator with Ford, designed the gardens.

Fascination with Mexican art and culture on the part of affluent Anglos in the United States had begun at least as early as the 1920s, but it was heartily revitalized in the person of Patsy Steves, just as other affluent Texans began to "discover" San Miguel de Allende, and as major research on Mexican colonial architecture was being written by US scholars, including John McAndrew, George Kubler, and Elizabeth Wilder Weissman.[14] However, the Steves did have a direct connection to Texas's Spanish colonial history: Marshall Steves was a descendant of one of the fifteen families who emigrated to San Fernando de Béxar from the Canary Islands in 1731.[15] With O'Neil Ford, Patsy Steves traveled to Mexico, where they collected spolia of Mexican colonial buildings, including large wooden doors, stone columns, arcades, mantlepieces, a fountain, and sculptural and architectural elements that the architects reused in the Terrell Hills house. Fascinated by Mexican brickwork, Ford and Carson arranged for Mexican masons to come to San Antonio to build the structural brick vaults that cover the central gallery and dining room. Led by Mateo Avila, the masonry team included his son, Alfredo, and one of their relatives. Wooden beams support the bedroom ceilings and that of the living room, which includes a library loft reached by a spiral stone staircase. The arrangement and character of the rooms is evocative of haciendas, and the construction of the house as a whole was informed by field research on Spanish colonial buildings in Mexico undertaken by builder Bill Wolma. For the interior, designer Weldon Sheffield worked with Patsy Steves to fill her house with Mexican textiles, pottery, furniture, and folk art. Kitchen and bathroom surfaces were covered in painted tile.

As an expression of its patron's and architects' entwined fascination with Mexico, commitment to craft, and desire to create architecture reflective of history and context, there are few houses like it in the United States. In 1967, *House & Garden* magazine put the Steves House on its cover, named it the Hallmark House of the year, and described it as "exciting, yet comfortably intimate." It is one of the last truly interesting colonial revival buildings in the country, yet it is also paradigmatic of the diversity within and multistranded character of architectural modernism, having been built as architects increasingly sought to acknowledge local and regional traditions and at the same time when Robert Venturi wrote of the merits of complex, contradictory architecture that traded in fragments, incompleteness, and juxtaposition in *Complexity and Contradiction in Architecture* (1966).

In the ways that it celebrates colonialism and perpetuates the romantic image of "old Mexico," embodied by the San Antonio Riverwalk, in a city that mostly neglected the needs of the working-class Mexican Americans and Mexicans upon whose labor it relied, the house has a complex place in the history of San Antonio. Patsy and Marshall Steves were instrumental in the realization of HemisFair, the 1968 fair designed, ultimately, to cement connections between businesspeople in Mexico and San Antonio and encourage trade relationships between the two places. Construction of the fair buildings entailed the destruction of a significant, diverse, historic swath of downtown San Antonio and substantially advanced the association of San Antonio with Mexico for the purposes of tourism. The Steves helped bring Juan O'Gorman, one of twentieth-century Mexico's foremost architects, to San Antonio, where he created a mosaic, *Confluence of Civilizations in the Americas*, on one of the fair's major buildings. Patsy Steves went on to be a major patron of the San Antonio Museum of Art, home to one of the finest collections of Mexican art in the United States.

Few modern houses built in Texas rivaled the one Paul Rudolph designed for Anne Bass, her husband Sid Richardson Bass, and their two daughters in Fort Worth in 1970, thanks to a tremendous oil fortune, the

Part I: Priorities

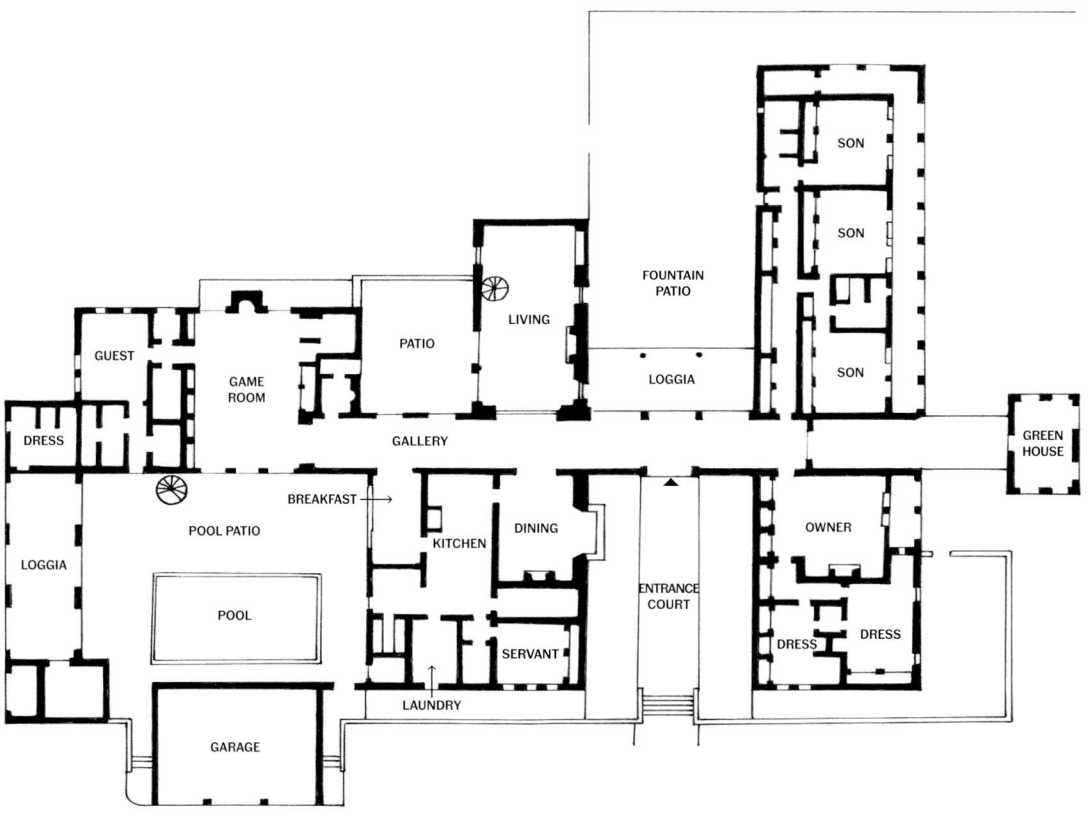

↗ Figure 1.16
O'Neil Ford, Chris Carson, architects; Bill Wolma, builder; Mateo Avila, lead master mason; Weldon Sheffield, interior designer; and Stewart King, landscape architect, Patsy Galt and Marshall Terrell Steves House, San Antonio, 1965, plan. Drawing by Olivia Bowness.

patrons' discerning eyes for architecture, and the Bass family's close ties to Yale University (Fig. 1.17).[16] Rudolph, who had been dean of architecture at Yale, was a nationally famous, if somewhat disliked, architect because of the foreboding formality and ponderousness of some of his buildings' exteriors, such as the architecture building at Yale. His first project in Texas was the Physical Sciences Building at Texas Christian University in Fort Worth (1970), which was funded by the Sid W. Ricardson Foundation. Rudolph was a master of materials and textures, and for his use of rough, often rather dark-colored concrete is sometimes associated with what is sometimes termed "brutalism." Rudolph's best works, such as the Jewett Arts Center at Wellesley College (1958), demonstrated a keen understanding of site and context, and his unrivaled sophistication in composing in section gave rise to some of architecture's most daring, complex, and provocative interiors.

1. Home

↑ Figure 1.17
Paul Rudolph, architect; Russell Page, landscape architect, Sid Richardson and Anne Bass House, Fort Worth, 1970. Drawing by Luke Leblanc.

The Bass House consists of a sophisticated play of interpenetrating white boxes and open-air terraces that push and pull outward across the crest of a hill on a secluded suburban site in the Westover Hills district in Fort Worth. Expansive glazing across the rear façade opens the interior to views of a large lawn and garden designed by landscape architect Russell Page. Rudolph's command of line, form, and volume places the house firmly in the lineage of de Stijl architecture—the Bass House is the sumptuous, expensive, expansive, yet more refined, and at times, precious descendant of the house Truus Schröder commissioned for herself and her children from Gerrit Rietveld in Utrecht in 1923. Where that client and architect admitted primary colors and wood, Bass permitted only white, offset by gray carpet and, on vertical surfaces, the smoothest of materials—glass, steel, and mirrors. Vibrant color comes from great works of modern art, including canvases by Morris Louis and

Frank Stella, a collection of cutouts by Henri Matisse, a group of portraits of Mrs. Bass and her daughters by Andy Warhol, and, occasionally, from rugs and the hues of nature seen through expansive windows.

Built as much for entertaining and fund-raising as for living, the Bass House is exciting in a way completely different from the Steves House. As in Chase's house, the treads of the main stairs are suspended, but here they lack a railing, endowing them with the quality of abstract sculpture and making them seem a little dangerous, a signature Rudolph device. The architect repeatedly used changes of elevation, and especially steps not joined to wall surfaces, to inject energy, drama, and a sense of risk to spaces. The main stairs lead to the master bedroom, which itself is cantilevered an astonishing 40 feet from the main volume of the house, and to a ballet studio. On the ground floor are guest quarters, mirrored changing rooms for day visitors headed to the pool, the kitchen, and a large family room with an embanked built-in couch, reached by several short steps and supported by an illuminated, mirrored base in an arrangement that vaguely calls to mind a nightclub.

The Bass House had two important predecessors in North Texas: Edward Durell Stone's Josephine Herbert and Bruno Graf House (1957) and Philip Johnson's Patricia Davis and John C. Beck House (1964), both in Dallas.[17] These houses spoke the language of money even more unabashedly than Rudolph's using an idiomatic formalism. The second story of the Graf House is defined by a long wall of concrete breeze block that

→ Figure 1.18
Edward Durell Stone, Josephine Herbert and Bruno Graf House, Dallas, 1957, plan. Drawing by Luke Leblanc.

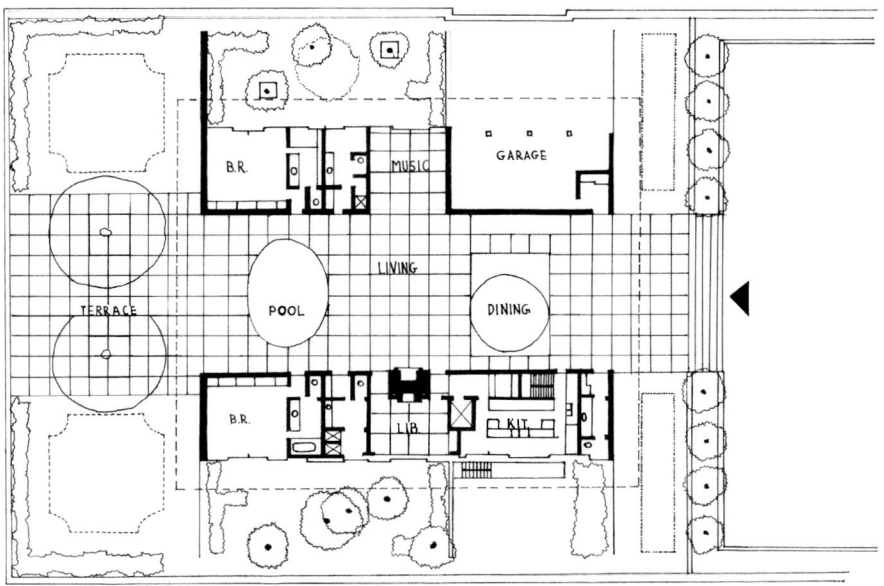

functions as a giant ornamental screen sandwiched between two concrete slabs. With the expanse of floor-to-ceiling glass doors and windows below, the effect of this arrangement is to give the house an almost institutional character. The building is quite obviously the cousin of Stone's US Embassy in New Delhi, which was under construction at the time. On the ground floor inside, a long central space runs from front to back and is partially subdivided by screens designed by T. H. Robsjohn-Gibbings. Stone included a circular white marble platform on which the dining table was placed and an interior oval-shaped swimming pool (which has been filled in; Fig. 1.18, 1.19). The architect apparently had in mind the courthouses of Pompeii when he conceived of this arrangement.

→ Figure 1.19
Edward Durell Stone, Josephine Herbert and Bruno Graf House, Dallas, 1957

With its sequence of segmental arches atop precast concrete columns forming arcades, the sprawling two-story Beck House is related both to ancient Roman buildings and to Inwood Manor. The building is a built-out, full-scale version of the folly that stands in the pond at Johnson's property in New Canaan, Connecticut. The double-height atrium is made dramatic by a pair of curving steel and bronze staircases, which are rather less sumptuous than those in the Metropolitan Opera, on which Wallace K. Harrison was at work at the same time.[18] With its attenuated white plaster columns supporting broad arches just in front of windowless but elegantly clad walls, the dining room partially reproduces the interior of Johnson's Guest House.

Auteurism

As singular as it is in many ways, the Bass House also belongs in a line of important Texas houses in which architects responded creatively to the ideas and forms of the European avant-garde of the 1920s, while enriching and complicating the language of architectural modernism. Beginning in the 1930s, as the formal and theoretical principles developed by Le Corbusier and architects associated with the Bauhaus spread around the globe, architects working outside of Europe experimented with a diverse palette of cladding materials, often in order to "localize" their buildings against the apparent placelessness of European avant-garde precedents.

In Austin in 1941, Chester E. Nagel built a house for himself and his family that typified this tendency and recalls the one Walter Gropius, Nagel's mentor at the Graduate School of Design at Harvard, had designed for his family in Lincoln, Massachusetts, in 1938. The Nagel House steps down its sloping, wooded site and is composed of interlocking volumes articulated in glass, white-painted wood, and rough-cut limestone (which abounds in Central Texas) laid in irregular courses. Metal railings, industrial windows, and a dramatic exterior spiral staircase, along with a prominent ground-level circular window, further punctuate the design and signal its architect's firm grounding in the principles of modernist composition (Fig. 1.20). The studied informality of the house, achieved using rigorous geometries, its prioritization of a partially covered terrace, and the staircase all echo Gropius's own house. On his hilly suburban New England site, the German architect ran wood sheathing vertically instead of horizontally, treated a screened porch as a major volume, and used industrial windows

1. Home

↑ Figure 1.20
Chester E. Nagel, Lorine
and Chester E. Nagel House,
Austin, 1941

→ Figure 1.21
R. Hood Chatham Jr.,
Cynthia Brants Studio,
Fort Worth, 1950

↑ Figure 1.22, → Figure 1.23
Anderson Todd, Anderson
and Lucie Wray Todd House,
Houston, 1961

and an exterior spiral staircase ornamentally. Nagel, who was born in Fredericksburg, Texas, returned to Cambridge in the mid-1940s to teach at Harvard and later joined Gropius's firm, The Architects Collaborative.

Even before World War II ended, architects began to consider the implications of the unprecedented scaling up of industrial production and manufacture undertaken by the country to support the war effort. One result was the influential Case Study House Program (1945–1962) initiated by John Entenza, editor of *Arts and Architecture* magazine. The idea was to test the efficacy of building modernist houses using prefabricated industrial parts, particularly steel and glass. Most of the houses built as part of the program were in California, and the most famous was the one that Charles and Ray Eames designed for themselves in Pacific Palisades in 1949. One year later, in Fort Worth, Hood Chatham Jr. designed a two-story, glassy, rectilinear painting studio for Cynthia Brants that, like the Eames House, made extensive use of exposed black-painted steel and nestles into its leafy site (Fig. 1.21). Brants was an important Texas modernist painter and part of the celebrated Fort Worth Circle of artists in the 1940s and 1950s.

The strand of modernism developed and honed by Ludwig Mies van der Rohe is exemplified exceptionally well in the house Anderson Todd designed for himself, his wife Lucie Wray Todd, and their two children in the Shadowlawn neighborhood in Houston in 1961 (Figs. 1.22, 1.23). With its clean, crisp planarity and play of brick, glass, wood, black-painted steel, and terrazzo floors, the one-story Todd House reflects its architect's thorough absorption of the principles and language of the German architect. Like the Chase House, this is a courtyard house, but unlike Chase, Todd pushed the courts (two, in this case) to the edges of the plan and enclosed them with brick walls. This made it possible to capture, with the use of window walls, exterior space as part of the visual space of the interior. The courtyard walls offered a noncomplicit response to a suburban context defined by large historicist mansions. Todd met Mies when he was a student at Princeton in the 1940s and was instrumental in securing for Mies the commission to design Cullinan Hall at the Museum of Fine Arts, Houston, and the later Brown Pavilion at the museum. As an architecture professor, Todd further embedded Mies in the fabric of Houston architecture in his courses at Rice.

Behind Closed Doors

One of the last houses pictured in *Planning Your Home for Better Living* (1945), a book written to help general readers who, in the words of the dedication, "look forward to the day when they can own their home," was the house that Mabel C. Welch designed for Norma Egg and Gladys Gregory in El Paso in the 1920s.[19] Egg and Gregory were a same-sex academic power couple at the Texas State University of Mines and Metallurgy (later renamed the University of Texas, El Paso). Egg was on the faculty from 1929 to 1954 and served as dean of women. Gregory, a political scientist, was the first woman to be promoted to the rank of full professor at the university and was well known for her research on the Chamizal Convention of 1963, the diplomatic agreement that resolved the dispute about the location of the US-Mexico border (which arose after repeated changes in course of the Rio Grande near El Paso in the late nineteenth century). The couple's one-story restrained Spanish Colonial Revival house gave no clue about either their professional achievements or their private life (Fig. 1.24). In its resemblance to other houses by Welch and to its neighbors in the Kern Place development, it was what Alice T. Friedman termed a "poker-face" house. Egg and Gregory welcomed to their home colleagues, friends, and prominent El Pasoans. In 1934, they hosted a tea there in honor of Margaret Sanger, who was in El Paso meeting with physicians, social workers, and representatives of the City–County Health Department to urge them to establish a clinic to distribute birth control and promote its use.[20] That the Egg-Gregory House was a landmark in the history of family planning and health care in Texas, appeared in a nationally available book on residential design, and was home to a same-sex couple by a woman architect raises fascinating questions about what other stories seemingly ordinary Texas houses might tell.

↑ Figure 1.24
Mabel C. Welch, Norma Egg and Gladys Gregory House, El Paso, 1920s. Photograph by Kathryn E. O'Rourke.

In the middle decades of the twentieth century, the prevailing image of domesticity in the United States centered on heterosexual couples with children. While the baby boom did increase the number of small children living in the country in this period, the hegemony of the norm owed much to the legacies of nineteenth-century ideas about gender, morality, and houses, and to Cold War–era advertising, television, and marketing that reinforced an image of domestic well-being centered on the white nuclear family and consumer goods in the suburban house.[21] The houses that sheltered the "typical" family projected middle-class "normalcy" through elements such as front lawns, driveways, windows (especially large picture windows), and, often, gabled roofs. The familiarity of these forms can blind us to their function as coded objects in a society in which sexuality was carefully policed. Two Houston houses built by gay architects for themselves illuminate the ways residential architecture was made to conceal difference and promote privacy at a time when being publicly "out" could end a career, or worse.

The house that Ralph A. Anderson Jr. built for himself (1960), where he lived with his partner, Gilbert Garcia, attracted attention almost as soon as it was completed in part because it differed from its neighbors so strikingly (Figs. 1.25, 1.26). Built around a courtyard that was glazed on three sides, the house was pointedly oriented inward. The front and side walls of the house were perforated only by narrow vertical slits, and read as nearly solid from the street. Piers, originally stained wood, gave the façade an almost classical rhythm. The off-center entrance was announced by a cantilevered canopy and two steps. The landscape design by Bishop and Walker helped visually nestle the house in its site, on a 50-foot-wide lot. A long carport, from which the house could be entered by a side door, ran along the west elevation. Organized around the courtyard, the rectangle-shaped plan was open, with its two bedrooms on the north end (the back of the house) and the living-dining area and partially enclosed kitchen at the other. The interior, designed by Herbert Wells, had a brick floor and white-painted brick side walls. Anderson's collection of art and modern furniture was illuminated by recessed lighting. In its plan, finishes, and carefully placed works of art, the house resembles Philip Johnson's Glass House for himself in New Canaan, Connecticut (1949–1950). On his own property, Johnson, who was also gay, built a nearly windowless brick guest house opposite the Glass House in an arrangement that similarly used contrasting wall surfaces to acknowledge sexuality architecturally, while pointing to the expectation of heterosexuality implied by the "typical" suburban house.[22]

In the ways the Anderson House literally screened its inhabitants from views from the street and then opened up spatially and visually on the interior, it pointedly materialized the dynamics of public concealment and private revelation that homophobic societies require of queer people. As striking as the house was the coded language used

← Figure 1.25, ↓ Figure 1.26
Ralph A. Anderson Jr., architect; Herbert Wells, interior design, Ralph A. Anderson Jr. House, Houston, 1960

by the architectural press in the 1960s to describe it. *Architectural Record* reported that although it was "planned as a bachelor house, the scheme is easily adaptable to the needs of a small family." The author repeatedly noted the building's "unusual degree of privacy" while stressing that the second bedroom was for guests.[23] The *Houston Post* went further in the caption of a photograph of the main façade, calling the building, "A House That Turns Inside Itself—And Not for Children."[24] A photograph taken from the courtyard and at night, and printed in *House & Garden*, showed heterosexual couples on the inside and was accompanied by a caption that read, "When Mr. Anderson entertains, [the] courtyard assures complete privacy."[25] By drawing attention to the architect-client's status as unmarried and childless, architectural writers invited readers to understand the house—and its occupant—as different from what was expected. The rhetorical emphasis on "privacy," something nearly everyone wants their home to provide, in a nonspecific way rather unsubtly suggested that privacy might be particularly important in this house.

John Zemanek, who was also gay, designed a house for himself (1968) whose interior spaces were also well shielded from view (Fig. 1.27). The house, which he called "Gaea I," was inspired by the planarity and proportions of traditional Japanese architecture, as well as by the rustic simplicity of rural Texas vernacular buildings. As if in anticipation of Frank Gehry's house for himself in Santa Monica (1978), Zemanek assembled ordinary, inexpensive materials, including corrugated steel and asbestos panels, timber beams and posts, plywood, and particle board, to create a building that reads almost as a collection of found objects. On the front façade, wooden slatted screens shield the door and upper-level window and contrast in texture and pattern with the windowless planes below and above them. The effect is one of pointed occlusion—the façade emphatically subverts expectations of transparency by offering blank walls and screens where viewers are accustomed to seeing windows and a door. Zemanek used concrete roof tiles to pave the space in front of the house, where a lawn would be, as if to draw attention to the usually unacknowledged coding of the lawn as a symbol of suburban heterosexual domesticity. Across the front of the property, in place of a low white picket fence, the architect erected a 5-foot, 6-inch unpainted slatted wooden one that echoes the screens on the façade and further reinforces the sense of the house as a private compound. The other sides of the lot were enclosed by 8-foot-high asbestos panels.

↑ Figure 1.27
John Zemanek, John Zemanek House, *Gaea I*, Houston, 1968

Inside, on the ground floor, the house consisted of an open-plan living room, a kitchen, and a library, each expressed as a discrete orthogonal volume on a three-part pinwheel plan and connected by a central entry hall. Within the site, these were experienced almost as separate pavilions set in nature. A small upper story contained the house's single bedroom, a dressing room, and a bathroom. Whereas the interior of Anderson House exuded a refined elegance carried in finishes and detailing, in the Zemanek House, materials were left rough and untreated, giving the building a rawness that existed in affecting dialogue with the landscape into which it was set, with its trees and small gardens. The house reads less as a cosmopolitan bachelor pad than as a rustic refuge built to accommodate solitary living and contemplation. *Progressive Architecture* stressed this quality, saying, "There are no doors in the house, which Zemanek designed for one-person occupancy: 'It's a house in which *I* will thrive,' he says."[26] The plan, program, perimeter fencing, and façade treatment made interior doors unnecessary. By manipulating the elements and conventions of the detached house, the architect created for himself a home in which he rendered the foremost symbol and instrument of privacy—the door—unnecessary, pointedly and poetically liberating space and self. Like other buildings in this chapter, the Zemanek House typified the home as a personal and collective priority, and as a site of architectural innovation and experimentation, whether as a secluded and shielded place for a single person or household, or as spatially and visually connected to a community.

2. Heat

Previous Spread: Bridges-Campbell and
Associates, Permian Building, Abilene, 1960

2. Heat

Heat is one of the central facts of life in Texas. The intensity of the sun, the duration of hot weather into months called "autumn" in other parts of the country, and the absence or superabundance of rain associated with hot weather shape not just daily life, but the physical, psychological, and cultural landscapes of the state. Everywhere, climate informs architectural decision-making. But in twentieth-century Texas, it provided particularly sharp contours to urban and architectural development. The power to make heat and humidity disappear, which arrived with air-conditioning in the mid-1930s and was wielded widely beginning in the 1950s, transformed the state and set it on course to be home to three of the nation's ten largest cities by century's end.

The story of heat in twentieth-century Texas architecture is also marked by a disquieting, circular irony: air-conditioning requires enormous amounts of energy and releases enormous amounts of heat into the atmosphere. Large air-conditioned buildings made possible the growth of an oil-based economy, whose capital was Houston, but which had major satellites in Midland and Odessa, along the Gulf Coast in the form of refineries and rigs, and into East Texas. Wealth from oil production and trade supported the building of several houses discussed in the previous chapter, contributed to the growth of the middle class, attracted top architects to Texas, and quite often underwrote the arts in urban centers as well as suburban sprawl. Yet all the drilling, refining, flaring, paving, flying, driving, and air-conditioning only made Texas, and the planet, hotter.

In 1965, President Johnson's Science Advisory Committee warned that increases in atmospheric carbon dioxide due to the combustion of fossil fuels could, by the end of the century, "be sufficient to produce measurable and perhaps marked changes in climate, and will almost certainly cause significant changes in the temperature and other properties of the stratosphere."[1] Temperatures were already rising when the report was published, and, even as they and their clients readily embraced air-conditioning, Texas architects developed a variety of strategies to mitigate the effects of heat and glare, particularly in buildings that were heavily glazed. Among the most interesting were exterior screening devices, which enlivened façades with texture and pattern and visually functioned almost as ornament.

Beaumont-based Pitts, Mebane and Phelps's Texas Tech Library (1962) was distinguished by one of the state's largest solar screens (Fig. 2.1). Set beneath façade-length colonnades and between narrow columns, it wraps around the building, which is only

Figure 2.1
Pitts, Mebane, and Phelps, Texas Tech Library, Lubbock, 1962. Western addition, pictured, by Atcheson, Atkinson Cartwright and Rorex; Stiles, Roberts, Messersmith and Johnson; and Schmidt, Tisdel and Associates, 1975.

partially glazed, helping reduce heat gain from the intense Lubbock sun and mitigate the visual mass of the building. The orangey-red color and circular perforations contrast with the beige tones of the bricks at the base and in the arches above, while horizontal courses denote floors and create a grid-like pattern with the columns. Built to accommodate a growing collection, the library was a major work of New Formalism in Texas and was published in a national survey of campus planning in 1964.[2]

On the other side of the state, in Beaumont, and under a different name, Pitts, Phelps, Mebane and White designed another monumental solar-screened building (1963). The screen of their First Security National Bank was designed by sculptor Herring Coe, who trained at Cranbrook Art Academy in Michigan and went on to create important sculptures in Houston and East Texas. (His work is included in the collection of the Metropolitan Museum of Art.) Coe's

→ Figure 2.2
Pitts, Mebane, Phelps and White, First Security National Bank, Beaumont, 1963. Solar screen by Herring Coe.

screen wrapped around nearly the entire building, covering all floors but the first, and consisted of a dense web of triangles inset with circles (Fig. 2.2). The all-over effect of the screen was checked by pairs of narrow vertical mullions that, with the overhanging roof slab, gave the building a restrained classical character. Even with the screen, floor-to-ceiling windows admitted abundant light to an interior fluent in the language of international corporate modernism (Fig. 2.3).

One of Texas's other great screens sheathed the addition to the Ector County Courthouse (1964) in Odessa, in the sun-soaked Permian Basin (Fig. 2.4). The building was originally designed by Elmer G. Withers in 1937. Nearly thirty years later Peters and Fields built a 60,000-foot air-conditioned addition and encased the entirety of the second story in a taut textile-like screen with a pattern of polygons that stretches between two slabs above a long portico. The building calls to mind the Graf House in distant, booming Dallas, even as it is

↑ Figure 2.3
Pitts, Mebane, Phelps and White, First Security National Bank, Beaumont, 1963. Solar screen by Herring Coe.

→ Figure 2.4
Elmer G. Withers, Ector County Courthouse, Odessa, 1937. Addition and solar screen by Peters and Fields, 1964.

an outstanding example of the embrace of an adaptive architectural modernism by the government of a county far from the cosmopolitan centers in which modern architecture flourished more abundantly.

The exterior sunscreen came to prominence in modern architecture in part due to commissions by European or US architects for government buildings abroad. They wrestled with the issue of how to adapt modernist forms to suit places that were not Western Europe or the northern United States, often by rather reductively settling on sunlight and heat as defining differentiators. The most famous such example was the Ministry of Health and Education Building in Rio de Janeiro, which had movable louvers on one glazed façade that made it possible to control light in the building. Le Corbusier, who served as an advisor on the design of the ministry building, called these "brises-soleil," a term that has been adopted as a catch-all means of describing heat mitigation devices installed on exteriors. Brises-soleil, and the ministry building, were catapulted to international fame when curators at the Museum of Modern Art in New York included them in the *Brazil Builds: Architecture New and Old, 1652–1942* exhibition and in the 1943 book that accompanied it.[3] Of course, people around the world had used louvers and screens for

→ Figure 2.5
Architect unidentified, San Felipe Cottage, 1868, now in Sam Houston Park, Houston. Rehabilitated by Harvin C. Moore, 1963.

centuries to control light and heat, as the example of the wooden lattice on a porch on a house at the Heritage Society in Houston's Sam Houston Park reminds us (Fig. 2.5). Screens like those by Stone, Coe, or Peters and Fields represent one significant, if somewhat underacknowledged, absorption of vernacular forms and typologies within architectural modernism.

Somewhat like the lattice pattern on the porch, some masonry heat-mitigating screens shaded exterior spaces as well. At the Ann Maddox Moore House in McAllen (1959; Fig. 2.6), Merle A. Simpson used decorative concrete breeze block to screen the entry. This exterior wall functioned with Martha Mood's multicolored, pierced ceramic light fixture, abundant vegetation, and a bed of pebbles to provide a pleasing contrast of pattern, rhythm, and texture to the building's articulated frame and concrete paving grid. At the Keith-Wiess Geological Laboratories building at Rice University (1958), by George Pierce-Abel

2. Heat

↑ Figure 2.6
Merle A. Simpson, Ann Maddox Moore House, McAllen, 1959

↓ Figure 2.7
George Pierce-Abel B. Pierce, Keith-Wiess Geological
Laboratories building, Rice University, Houston, 1958

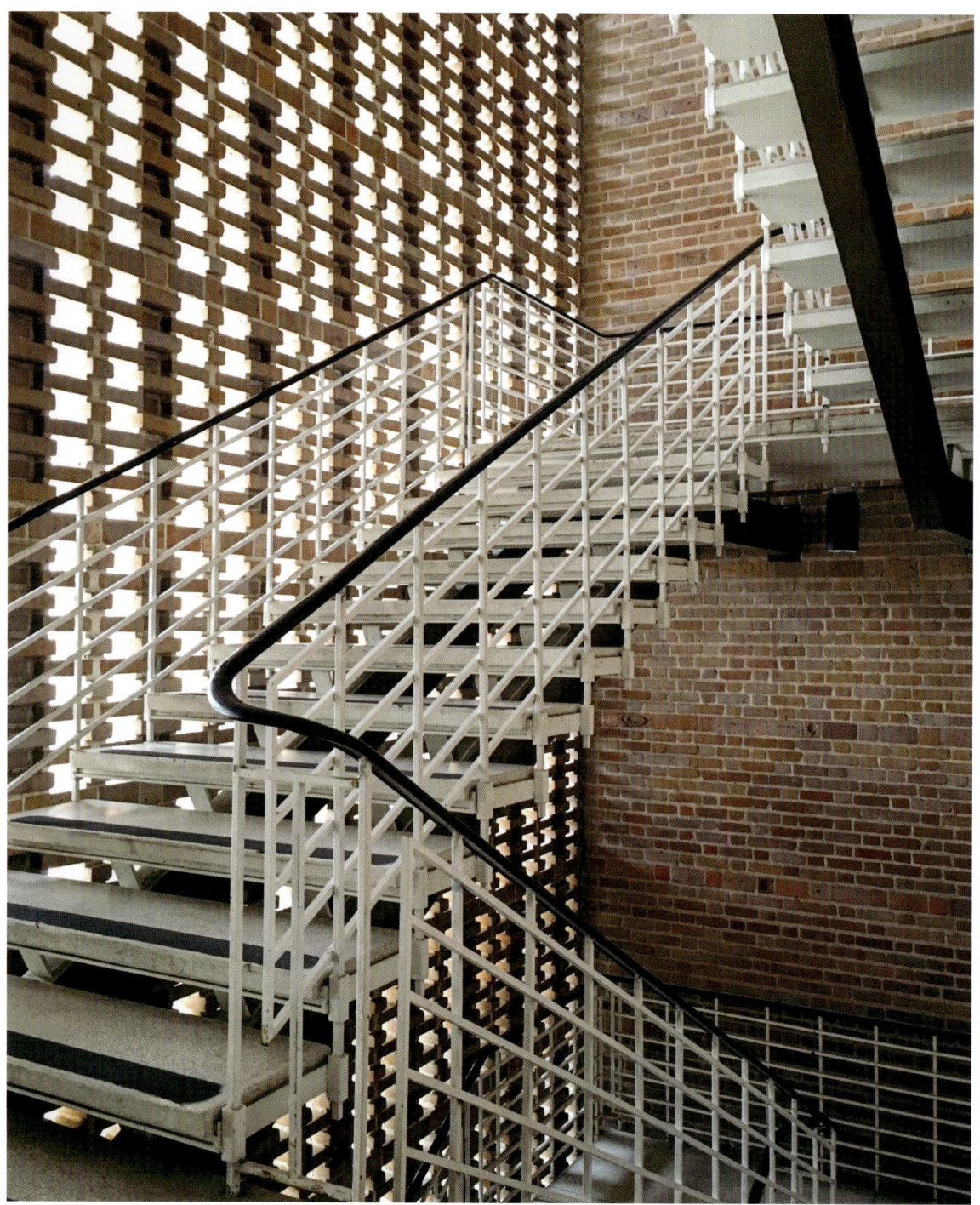

2. Heat

B. Pierce, multistory punctured brick walls screen staircases, enlivening an often-dreary spatial type with modulated natural light (Fig. 2.7). The openwork wall echoed slits between floating treads and the grilles of the railings in an arrangement that drew attention to the staircase as an almost sculptural object. The even more spectacular precedent for the Rice staircases was Carlos Raúl Villanueva's Plaza Cubierta at the Universidad Central de Venezuela in Caracas of 1953, which shields a giant ramp, steeply sloping concrete roof, and plaza-like interior space as it joins the exterior.

In the early 1960s, Texans developed all manner of brises-soleil —sometimes employed in concert with other sun-mitigating devices— for use on large low-rise commercial, professional, and civic buildings. In Laredo, the Cigarroa Medical Building (1960) by McAllen architect Max Burkhart Jr. has a dramatic concrete screen invigorated by a long series of parabola-shaped openings that drop from the cornice and rise from the base in front of tinted glass. One façade surface is decorated

↓ Figure 2.8
Max E. Burkhart Jr.,
Cigarroa Medical Building,
Laredo, 1960

Figure 2.9
Spicer, Bush and Witt, Waco-McClennan County Public Library, Waco, 1961

with tiny purple tile squares, further animating it (Fig. 2.8). Hundreds of miles north, Spicer, Bush and Witt took an entirely different approach to screening the Waco-McClennan County Public Library (1961). Tucked beneath a prominent concrete cornice defined by a jazzy band of pyramids in high relief, large granite panels sit between narrow bands of glass across much of the façade. At the corner, however, broad white slats positioned between base and cornice break the plane of the building and enclose a glazed volume in a notable, if understated, engagement with the latent classicism embedded in midcentury formalism (Fig. 2.9). At the Outlar and Blair Clinic in Wharton (1967), by Philip Willard and Associates of Houston, a nine-panel screen composed of concrete blocks with leaf-shaped perforations shields the long side of an asymmetrically composed façade and is balanced by a broad projecting canopy that shades the entrance and a plane clad in black stone set perpendicularly to the volumes. In his addition to

Figure 2.10
C. Gale Cook, Orange County Courthouse addition, Orange, 1964

the Orange County Courthouse (1964), C. Gale Cook anchored a metal screen to the wall and deep overhang of the roof to minimize heat gain and glare in a manner reminiscent of Paul Rudolph's use of metal screens at the Jewett Arts Center at Wellesley College (Fig. 2.10).

Equally as striking as the innovative approaches to the problem of strong sun taken by the architects of these buildings is the inventiveness of their compositions and command of varied materials, patterns, and form. While each of these buildings served important purposes in their communities, they were not monumental or terribly expensive works. They typify the high quality of design and execution that defined a great many fairly modestly scaled, and only moderately ambitious, buildings at midcentury. Easy to overlook when they are engulfed by parking lots or set back from the street in towns and cities where people rarely walk, the buildings sometimes look rather forlorn, but are reminders of an era when materials, construction, and arresting composition were more highly prized than they often are today.

Texans are expert at escaping the sun without going inside. When natural shade is in short supply, architects sometimes step in with inventive, vibrant, and even amusing solutions that imitate nature or depend on sophisticated engineering. At the Evelyn Motor Inn in Laredo, for example, guests could avoid sunburn under a giant mushroom-like umbrella whose columnar stand doubled as the support for a circular tabletop and called to mind candy canes (Fig. 2.11). In Bryan, the redesigned Holiday Inn used concrete "umbrellas" of the kind developed by Mexican architect Félix Candela to shelter guests arriving by car.

For young Texans, access to shade during the course of the school day enables the work of play and the learning that accompanies it. In 1951, at the entrance to West Columbia Elementary School, which served white students, Houston-based Donald Barthelme and Associates designed one of the state's most inventive shade structures, a car and bus drop-off pavilion formed of nine thin-shelled concrete arches that sloped to the ground on the short sides, was open to the air on the long sides, and was supported by narrow columns (Fig. 2.12). As little more than an understated, unbroken, undulating plane, the pavilion was an elegant and sophisticated response to the challenges of weather and climate. Modest though it was in scale and program, the pavilion was among the buildings in the vanguard of thin-shelled concrete construction, which Candela was developing in Mexico City. His diminutive, but revolutionary building at the National Autonomous University of Mexico, the Cosmic Ray Pavilion, was the exact contemporary of the one in West Columbia, but built on a much bigger campus, for much bigger people. The school district demolished the rest of Barthelme's internationally recognized West Columbia Elementary School in 2006.

Texas's foremost firm in climate-responsive school design in the 1950s was Caudill Rowlett Scott (CRS) of Bryan. Its founders began their climate research at Texas A&M and went on to design schools throughout the state that made extensive use of innovative shade structures and shaded exterior patios and were oriented to capture prevailing breezes. Most were one-story buildings with clearly articulated structural systems. The firm received attention in the national and international architectural press for schools in Edna, Laredo

2. Heat

← Figure 2.11
Architect unidentified, Evelyn Motor Inn, Laredo, 1960

↓ Figure 2.12
Donald Barthelme and Associates, car and bus drop-off pavilion, West Columbia Elementary School, West Columbia, 1951

↑ Figure 2.13
Caudill Rowlett Scott and A. A. Leyendecker, Blessed Sacrament School, Laredo, 1960

→ Figure 2.14
Caudill Rowlett Scott, Taft School, Port Arthur, 1965

(Fig. 2.13), Tyler, San Angelo, Andrews, Liberty, and Brownsville. CRS designed all of Port Arthur's public schools in the 1950s. Among their projects there were the Phillis Wheatley Elementary School (1953), which served Black students who lived in El Vista, near the Texas Company refinery, and Thomas Jefferson High School, built in north Port Arthur after the *Brown vs. Board of Education* ruling, whose pair of gymnasiums resemble Eero Saarinen's Kresge Auditorium at MIT (1955). With its broad gabled overhang and clerestory windows, the Taft School (1965) typified the firm's pragmatic approach to the challenges of heat and sensitivity to vernacular forms and patterns (Fig. 2.14). Many of the CRS schools have been radically altered, demolished, or permanently closed, reflecting the shifting fortunes of small cities, whose populations today are generally much smaller than they were when the postwar baby boom made school construction one of the most important topics in US architecture.

Summer in the City

Most Texans have never known life in the state without air-conditioning. But there was a time when it was new. The first air-conditioned buildings here were almost all office and commercial buildings or movie theaters. The rise of residential air-conditioning in the mid-1950s was among the factors that sped the growth of the suburbs and contributed to the dramatic change in the form of the detached house at midcentury. Eventually, central climate control made porches, cross breeze–maximizing plans, and exterior sunscreening devices seem unnecessary or merely ornamental, and it helped speed the adoption of houses with rather disinterested attitudes toward the street. But, difficult though it may be to imagine today, no one was certain exactly how central air-conditioning would work in suburban houses, nor how Texans would respond to it.

Austin's "Air Conditioned Village" was built as a kind of lifestyle experiment to test the new technology and to bring large machines by major US corporations, including Westinghouse, Frigidaire, Carrier, American Standard, and General Electric, directly into homes. From 1954 to 1956, under the direction of the architect Ned A. Cole, with Werner W. Dornberger, both of whom taught at the University of Texas, the National Association of Home Builders sponsored the construction of twenty-two centrally air-conditioned single-family houses on three streets in north Austin. The houses were each about 1,500 square feet, the size typical of middle-class suburban residences

↑ Figure 2.15
Fred W. Day, Chrysler Air Temp House, "Air Conditioned Village," Austin, 1954

at the time, and designed in a variety of styles by different builders. The walls and attics of many were insulated. As Fred W. Day's Chrysler Air Temp House suggests, the houses of the "Air Conditioned Village" reflected the technological and formal transition of which they were a part (Fig. 2.15). Even as they were cooled by conditioned air, the houses retained heat-mitigating elements like broad overhanging roofs; ventilated attics, kitchens, and bathrooms; and windows that were arranged to minimize passive heat gain. Day's building included a carport, a quintessential midcentury vernacular Texas type, which increased the shading of the houses and announced the primacy of the private automobile—to transport men to downtowns and women and children around expanding suburban landscapes—to the entire postwar project.

Brises-soleil had first been used on tall office buildings in the late 1940s, but they received renewed attention in Texas in the 1960s as glassy skyscrapers rose in city centers. In New York in the 1950s, Lever House and the Seagram Building had inaugurated the second wave of the International Style, which became the primary expression of corporate and governmental modernism. Glass curtain walls saved the expense of ornament and expressed sleek efficiency, but they also admitted tremendous amounts of light and were excellent conduits of passive heat. In Houston in 1963, Welton Becket and Associates, who specialized in practical glamour, with Goleman and Rolfe, George Pierce-Abel B. Pierce, and Bishop and Walker landscape architects, devised a way of communicating corporate sophistication without blinding executives and their clients. Ironically, or fittingly, their client was Humble Oil and Refining Company, one of the world's largest oil companies—therefore one of the major players in the collective warming of the planet in the twentieth century—which was eager to economize on air-conditioning. Forty-one of the building's forty-four floors are entirely wrapped in 7-foot aluminum shades that cantilever from the façade (Figs. 2.16, 2.17). The attic and cornice are articulated with vertically oriented fins, which, with the portico at the base, give the building a classical disposition. The Petroleum Club was originally housed on the upper two floors. From a distance, the sunshades read as a kind of gridded filigree and mark the building decisively as a modernist skyscraper in a sunny place. The building's cousin, built as the American General Building (now Wortham Tower) by Lloyd, Morgan and Jones in 1965, has tinted glass fitted into its brise-soleil. It stands on Allen Parkway, not far from what remains of San Felipe Courts.[4]

The Humble skyscraper belonged to an urban ensemble that included a rather narrow plaza and, fittingly, a parking garage, which stored both cars and the air-conditioning machinery for the tower. The six-story garage has its own distinct brise-soleil pattern—a densely patterned grille that visually is a kind of "solid" to the tower's "voids." Inside is a spectacular, rather thrilling multistory concrete ramp (Fig. 2.18). Parking garages such as this signaled the triumph of the automobile in the United States, on which Humble's business depended. It presaged the fundamental reordering of downtowns to accommodate them and the suburbs to which they were driven each evening.

The combination of high temperatures and abundant paving in downtowns can make them some of the most uncomfortable places to be during a Texas summer. Houston dealt with this problem, in part, by building an underground system of air-conditioned tunnels. In Fort Worth, with the help of a substantial private gift from the Amon Carter Foundation, the city used water to ameliorate the heat literally and psychologically on a 4.5-block site in the city center. The Fort Worth Water Gardens (1974) were also intended to appeal to conventioneers in the part of the city that had once been a red-light district, later

↓ Figure 2.16
Welton Becket and Associates, with Goleman and Rolfe,
George Pierce-Abel B. Pierce, Humble Oil Building, Houston,
1963

2.   Heat

↓ Figure 2.17, ↘ Figure 2.18
Welton Becket and Associates, with Goleman and Rolfe, George Pierce-Abel B. Pierce, Humble Building and Humble Garage, Houston, 1963, details of brise-soleil and parking structure

became known for its crime, and most recently had been cut off from more bustling parts of downtown by a large convention center.

For this urban water park, Philip Johnson and John Burgee designed an extraordinary sequence of pools, fountains, and terraces, creating spaces with dramatically different spatial, sonic, and psychological characters, from the "quiet" pool set in a deep canyon-like space framed by high walls and cypress trees, to the rather terrifying, and very loud "active," pool in which water plunges downward toward a collecting pool at high speed (Figs. 2.19, 2.20). Visitors can dangle their feet in the water and reach the bottom via a series of discrete, table-like concrete steps with no handrail to help them. Throughout the site, plazas, inclined walls, and stepped pyramidal forms evoke the monumental architecture of ancient Mesoamerica, used by its architects and patrons, like those centuries later in Fort Worth, to define urban space and connect people with nature under intense sun.[5] Johnson/Burgee's design was undoubtedly informed by Lovejoy Fountain Park (1966) by Lawrence Halprin and Keller Fountain Park

↓ Figure 2.19
Johnson/Burgee, Fort Worth Water Gardens, Quiet Pool, Fort Worth, 1974

2. Heat

(1970) by Angela Danadjieva, both in Portland, Oregon. In 1976 in Fort Worth, Halprin designed Heritage Park, a smaller and more tranquil project than the Water Gardens.

The Fort Worth gardens were the most spectacular of a group of significant late-midcentury downtown urban design projects in which architects used flowing water, changes of level, and vegetation to mitigate the effects of urban heat gain and dwindling pedestrianism, as cities poured ever more concrete and city centers all but emptied on evenings and weekends, when downtown workers decamped to suburban worlds. In Houston, Charles Tapley Associates designed Tranquility Park (1979), like the Fort Worth gardens, in part to help knit together disassociated pieces of urban fabric at the edge of downtown. In Dallas in 1986, also at the edge of the business district, landscape architects Dan Kiley and Peter Ker Walker created tranquil, verdant Fountain Place (originally Allied Plaza), a 5.5-acre terraced plaza at the base of the signature skyscraper in North Texas: Henry Cobb of I. M. Pei and Partners' 60-story prismatic blue office

↓ Figure 2.20
Johnson/Burgee, Fort Worth Water Gardens, Active Pool, Fort Worth, 1974

tower, Fountain Place (Fig. 2.21). Clad entirely in blinding blue-green glass, like innumerable such buildings around the world, and whatever the relative insulating properties of its panes, Fountain Place was the opposite of its brise-soleil predecessors insofar as it visually conveyed complete disregard for climate (Fig. 2.22). Yet it was highly suited to the hometown of Neiman Marcus, a place famous for delighting in elegant, extravagant, and expensive things. Like a giant diamond glistening in strong sunlight, the Fountain Place tower perfectly captured the Dallas elite's unrepentant love of shiny objects and exemplified one of the other chief priorities of Texas patrons and their architects: money.

→ Figure 2.21
Dan Kiley and Peter Ker Walker, Fountain Place, Dallas, 1986

2. Heat

↓ Figure 2.22
Henry Cobb, I. M. Pei and Partners, with Harry Weese and
Associates, and WZMH, Fountain Place, Dallas, 1986

3. Money

Previous Spread: Alfred C. Finn and
Campbell and White, People's National
Bank, Tyler, 1932

3. Money

Insofar as they reveal clients' ambitions, give clues about their budgets, and are bought and sold in the real estate market, all buildings are about money. The expression of affluence is easy to recognize in buildings such as Fountain Place and the Graf House. Corporate headquarters and banks are explicitly about money, and an unapologetic drive to increase it. What makes such architecture interesting is the wide variety of ways architects and patrons convey ideas about money to their audiences. Whether with skyline-defining towers or low-rise, suburban-scaled works, the creators of the architecture of money aim to inspire confidence, the emotion on which a money economy depends. In twentieth-century Texas, because of the state's near-total dependence on the fluctuations in oil prices and their corresponding effects on real estate markets, confidence—through busts as well as booms—was especially important. That cycle throttled Houston, Midland, and Odessa especially hard in the second half of the 1980s and 1990s, gave rise to uneven urban and architectural development, and left literally towering examples of (over)confidence. It also generated a colossal number of much smaller buildings dedicated to insurance and banking, which can be found in cities large and small.

High Hopes

In the 1930s, the most important skyline in Texas was Kilgore's. Approximately twelve hundred oil derricks, forty-four of them in one block, dotted the horizon of the small town by the end of 1931. Kilgore lies at the heart of the East Texas Oil Field, which stretches through parts of Gregg, Rusk, Upshur, Smith, and Cherokee Counties, and has produced more oil than any other site in the continental United States. Mostly small, independent operators began drilling there in 1930. In the rush that followed, townspeople and property owners tore down buildings to put up derricks, constructed them in their backyards, and drilled so much so fast that the price of oil plummeted precipitously. To stabilize the market, the governor sent the Texas Rangers and Texas National Guard to Kilgore to enforce an order to stop drilling. During World War II, oil from Kilgore traveled 1,400 miles to the East Coast, in what was then the longest pipeline ever built, to help meet the energy demands of the wartime nation at home and abroad. Oil derricks are rarely considered works of architecture. Yet in the case of Kilgore, they were far more important than any building or work of urban planning. Like monumental civic or commercial architecture, the derricks collectively operated symbolically as well as functionally, defining place, conveying character, and communicating purpose. Visually, and ironically, their closest relatives in the history of avant-garde architecture are the works of Soviet constructivist architects—one thinks of El Lissitzky's design for a tribune for Vladimir Lenin, or Vladimir Tatlin's giantly scaled Monument to the Third International, both of 1920—that mostly remained on paper, even as the derricks have obvious parallels to the grain silos beloved of Peter Behrens and Le Corbusier.

The most derrick-dense block in Kilgore, at Commerce and Main Streets, was known as the "World's Richest Acre." Production declines caused all but one of the derricks there to be removed by the early 1960s. But in one of the more unusual examples of historic re-creation and memorialization, since the 1990s, thirty-seven replica or relocated derricks have been installed in downtown, under the auspices of the Kilgore Historical Preservation Association (Fig. 3.1). In the twenty-first century, as windmills and solar panels provide ever more of Texas's energy, and climate change increasingly wreaks havoc worldwide, the re-created derricks read as discordant and pregnant with unintended meaning.

The derrick and the pumpjack represent just one part of oil's built environment. In an almost too obvious expression of the class differences between oilfield workers and the traders, lawyers, and bankers who oversee the turning of oil into money, the big-city

→ Figure 3.1
Kilgore Historical Preservation Association, replica and relocated oil derricks, Kilgore, completed in the 1990s. Original derricks built ca. 1930–1931.

3. Money

↑ Figure 3.2
Johnson/Burgee with S. I. Morris Associates,
Pennzoil Place, Houston, 1976

skylines of oil are altogether different from Kilgore's. Although it is not as tall as the state's tallest skyscraper, Texas Commerce Tower (now J. P. Morgan Chase), which soars seventy-five stories over downtown Houston, Pennzoil Place, just across the street, is one of its most important (Fig. 3.2).[1] The subject of national attention when it was completed, Pennzoil Place (1976) is both a giant pun on the "black gold" that was the company's raison d'être and an exceedingly clever response to the challenge that had preoccupied US architects since the 1870s of how to compellingly compose a tall office building. It was also a masterstroke of commercial real estate development by Gerald D. Hines, whose patronage of world-class architecture in the 1970s and 1980s helped reshape the image of Houston in the minds of locals and foreigners alike. Pennzoil Place, designed by Johnson/Burgee with S. I. Morris Associates and Sally Walsh as the interior designer for the lobby, consists of two thirty-six-story towers that occupy the northeast and southwest portions of the block and angle steeply downward from the 10-foot-wide radiant axial sliver between them. The towers are connected at the base by two indoor plazas such that the composition reads from the ground level as three great dark glassy prisms. The separation and angling of the volumes mitigate the sense of overwhelming scale that had long attended skyscraper design, and ingeniously transforms what might otherwise be a block-dominating dark mass into a monumental, crystalline urban sculpture that appealed to the tastes of high-end collectors of minimalist art and to high-dollar tenants. Johnson was aware of Ludwig Mies van der Rohe's 1921 proposal for a glass skyscraper on Friedrichstrasse in Berlin, which consisted of three leaf-shaped volumes connected at a central core, the tallest of which angled sharply downward. Although Mies helped revolutionize office building design with the Seagram Building in New York, the Friedrichstrasse project was never built.

    Johnson had helped bring Mies to the United States in 1937, just a few years after he and his MoMA colleagues curated the "International Style" exhibition. One of the only US buildings in that show was the skyscraper that William Lescaze and George Howe designed for the Philadelphia Savings Fund Society in 1931. Known as "PSFS," their building set a new standard for skyscraper design in its sleek articulation of program using cubist principles and distinct materials. Lescaze himself designed a building in Texas: the Magnolia Lounge, funded by the Magnolia Petroleum Company for the Texas Centennial Exposition at Fair Park in Dallas in 1936 (Fig. 3.3). Built to accommodate weary fair-goers in need of a break (and to advertise motor oil), the two-story building typified Lescazian modernism in its asymmetry, strong geometries, and varied palette. Its presence at a fair that was widely visited by Texas architects surely helped speed the spread of International Style modernism and its art moderne cousins in Texas in the 1930s.

Twenty-five years after Lescaze and Howe's Philadelphia building opened, Lubbock had its own version of PSFS, thanks to architect Daniel Boone, who worked in David S. Castle's office in Abilene. Built to house the Great Plains Life Insurance Company, the twenty-one-story

↓ Figure 3.3
William Lescaze,
Magnolia Lounge, Fair Park,
Dallas, 1936

↑ Figure 3.4
David S. Castle, Great Plains Life Insurance Company,
Lubbock, 1955

3. Money

↑ Figure 3.5
Thomas E. Stanley, First National Pioneer Building, Lubbock, 1968

building was once the tallest structure between Fort Worth and Denver and a radical intervention in Lubbock's urban core (Fig. 3.4). Stylistically, it was a first-generation International Style building built during the second generation of the style, a testament to the enduring capacity of Howe and Lescaze's building to convey cosmopolitanism, corporate presence, and money.

Down the street, Lubbock's other major midcentury skyscraper, built as the First National Pioneer Building, was somewhat more up-to-date insofar as it evoked the United Nations Headquarters (then only about sixteen years old) rather than a 1930s gem (Fig. 3.5). Composed as a thin slab entirely glazed on the two wide sides and raised on a base, First National typified the West Texas tower-on-podium skyscraper trend evident in works such as the Wilco Building in Midland (David S. Castle Co., 1958), American Bank of Commerce in Odessa (Wyatt C. Hedrick, 1960; see Figs. I.16, I.17), El Paso National Bank (George L. Dahl;

123

↑ Figure 3.6
Frank D. Welch, Forest Oil Company building, Midland, 1972

Carroll and Daeuble and Associates, 1963), and American National Bank in Amarillo (Kelly, Marshall & Associates, 1971).

Most striking about this group of skyscrapers—a family linked by money and typology but spread out over hundreds of miles across the South Plains, Trans-Pecos, and Panhandle regions of West Texas—is their essential incongruity in the flat, dusty, tornado-prone western landscape. The soaring towers of Houston and Dallas constitute recognizable clusters of capitalism, and whatever their particular architectural merits or acontextualism, as "skylines" they are instantly intelligible as exemplars of a global urban pattern. With the exception of the El Paso example, the towers of West Texas are, after pumpjacks, the foremost built manifestation of Permian Basin oil. That there are so few of them underscores that they do not in fact anchor cosmopolitan centers but are outcrops born of an upswing in the unstable, unsustainable oil economy, which has generated so much wealth so unevenly and left so much destruction in its wake.

In the 1970s, in a series of low-rise office buildings for oil companies in Midland, Frank D. Welch introduced a modern language altogether different from that of the towers. Cast-in-place concrete—unadorned, with the lines, plugs, and irregularities of formwork visible—was his chief material. At the Forest Oil Company building, Welch avoided a sense of heaviness by raising the building on piers (thereby creating covered parking at ground level) and building wide, sheltered walkways paved in brick and a glazed entrance. Lightness was further achieved with the inclusion of a beautifully scaled central courtyard (Fig. 3.6). It was the decade of brutalism in architecture, so termed in part to describe the "béton brut" concrete widely used by modern architects, but Welch's building was humane in its scale and acknowledgment of context. Here, in the intense sun and wind, Welch's concrete read not as an affront but as a sincere response to the brutality of the West Texas climate; a subtle, and even humble acknowledgment of the challenge of surviving in the landscape that his clients, like many West Texans, braved in the pursuit of wealth. The building reflected Welch's absorption of the lessons of his mentor, O'Neil Ford, and the master he admired, Louis I. Kahn.

One of Forest Oil's officers, John Dorn, was Welch's first client when he arrived in Midland in 1959. At Dorn's ranch in Sterling County, Welch designed one of Texas's great midcentury buildings, The

Birthday (1965), a modestly scaled retreat that was even more intimately bound to its site and reflective of the values of materiality, craft, and site sensitivity that permeated Fordian modernism than Forest Oil.[2] Like the Fort Worth Water Gardens, The Birthday typified the archaizing tendency in architectural modernism recognizable in works such as Taliesin West, Frank Lloyd Wright's winter home/studio in the Arizona desert. The Birthday was photographed by Ezra Stoller and appeared on the cover of *Texas Architect* in 1967. Thirty years later, the Texas Society of Architects honored it, together with Kahn's Kimbell Art Museum, with the Twenty-Five-Year Award. The house was effectively lost to the caprices of the real estate market in 1998, when new owners radically altered it and the site.

Bank On It

The history of banking is closely entwined with the emergence and growth of cities. At base an agreement within a group of people about the rules for the saving, lending, safeguarding, and recording of wealth, banking has taken many forms and been undertaken by collectives of many kinds to protect and promote individual and group interests jointly.

In San Antonio in 1922, twenty-five US Army officers formed an organization to spread the risk of insuring their cars. The city was (and is) home to major army and air force bases, and the small insurance collective quickly grew in membership, which was limited to those in military service. Over the course of several decades, it was transformed into the United Services Automobile Association (USAA) and became a huge integrated banking and financial services firm for members of the military and their families. In 1956, USAA built an eight-story headquarters at the corner of Hildebrand and Broadway in San Antonio (Fig. 3.7.) Growth was so rapid in the postwar period that the building was substantially enlarged just six years later. The work of Phelps, Dewees and Simmons and Atlee B. Ayres and Robert M. Ayres, it is a midcentury period piece of Texas corporate modernism. Set back from the street, the building's rectangular wings spread from a central core. Distinct fenestration patterns on the wings and projecting volumes, along with a vibrant contrast of gray-veined Georgia white marble and turquoise porcelain enamel spandrel panels, make it one of the city's boldest buildings. In Corsicana, in two iterations (1956, 1967), Preston M. Geren designed a similarly taut and visually compelling headquarters for the First

→ Figure 3.7
Phelps, Dewees and Simmons and Ayres and Ayres, USAA Building, San Antonio, 1956, 1962

National Bank, which moved into the new building from its original home in a 1915 building by Field & Clarkson. Like the USAA building, the bank in Corsicana, with its planar polychromy and asymmetrical but abstractly classical composition, signaled security and fitness for participation in a robust national financial system that was then being regularly rehoused in International Style buildings (Fig. 3.8).

    USAA's suburban site and siting reflect the full-throttle embrace of automobile culture at the company's heart in the 1950s. Built four years after USAA opened its first office abroad (and its first outside of San Antonio), in Frankfurt, Germany, to serve the legions of US troops stationed there, the building expressed an unbridled

↓ Figure 3.8
Preston M. Geren, First National Bank, Corsicana, 1957, 1967

confidence not just in the domestic economy but in the status of the United States in the world, as the nation took center stage in global affairs, due in large measure to USAA members and their colleagues throughout the military. USAA's Vietnam-era building in northwest San Antonio by Oklahoma City architects Benham-Blair and Affiliates (1975) is vastly larger, considerably less energetic, and seemingly never-ending. Best appreciated from the air, it stretches out in a serpentine form for one-third of a mile, across a 300-acre site, houses 3 million square feet of space, and sits atop a 2,600-car garage. It was a symbol of and a response to the increasing complexity of banking and insurance, and the growth of the US military, by the 1970s. Built beyond what was then the city's outermost freeway loop, the building acknowledged and helped advance the northward, car-centric sprawl of the city, a consequence, in part, of the expansion of a middle class that the US military had helped create in South Texas.

In Houston in 1963, John S. Chase designed a much smaller building for local banking needs. With its overscaled, overhanging jazzy, zig-zag cornice, the Riverside National Bank expressed optimism in its energetic use of line, form, and pattern in a sequence of elongated diamonds (Fig. 3.9). But its importance extended far beyond architecture. Built in Third Ward, a neighborhood whose residents in the postwar period were predominately African American and which was then in the early stages of disinvestment, Riverside National was the first bank in Texas owned by African Americans. Discriminatory lending practices and restrictive real estate covenants compounded four centuries of unequal access to capital and unequal (or nonexistent) wages to make it extraordinarily difficult for Black Texans to attain wealth comparable to that of white ones. The opening of a purpose-built Black-owned bank designed by a Black architect to serve Black Houstonians the year before the major civil rights legislation of the decade was passed was a landmark event in the state's history. Beneath a diamond-profiled roof canopy (now heavily altered), Riverside National Bank's expansive glazing—a hallmark of high modernism with its myriad associations with transparency, openness, and futury—metonymically conveyed a connection between the institution and its neighborhood, as well as the confidence that money, and with it power, would soon be more equitably distributed—the

↑ Figure 3.9
John S. Chase, Riverside National Bank, Houston, 1963. Still from KPRC-TV news footage of the bank's opening, broadcast August 16, 1963. Footage courtesy of KPRC-TV, and provided by Texas Archive of the Moving Image, www.texasarchive.org.

Part I: Priorities

← Figure 3.10, ↙ Figure 3.11,
↓ Figure 3.12
Wisznia and Peterson,
Mercantile National Bank,
Corpus Christi, 1969

prescription that Dr. Martin Luther King Jr. outlined four years later in *Where Do We Go From Here: Chaos or Community?*, his visionary analysis of US history, politics, and race.

Perhaps the most whimsical of Texas's midcentury banks is the Mercantile National Bank by architects Wisznia & Peterson built in Corpus Christi in 1969. With a design that cleverly integrated allusions to waves and clouds and symbolically fortified the bank against both robbers and hurricanes, the building's delightful contextualism and superb interior details—from stair rails and black tile wall surfaces, to wooden screens, to sinewy patterns in turquoise and gold mosaic—made it one of the decade's most architecturally lively places to do business (Figs. 3.10, 3.12). The building's most distinctive element is its roof. It consists of nine staggered broad, pillowy triangles that appear to float above the building and together act as a colossal, discontinuous but light-hearted cornice, uniting the main, enclosed portion of the bank with four giant drive-thru lanes, undoubtedly the most monumental of their kind in Texas, and perhaps in the world (Fig. 3.11). The two stories of the enclosed portion are articulated in elongated oval windows set between narrow vertical ribs. The solemn association with classicism discernible in the glazed "pediment" (which recalls the profile of the Riverside National Bank's roof canopy) is defused by a playful geometric pattern on the intercolumnar walls. The sense of security against weather and other threats that the concrete clouds convey is heightened by virtue of its difference from the void of the vehicular space at one end of the building.

Inside, the clouds part to make way for clerestory windows that are protected from the ravages of hurricane winds but admit ample Gulf Coast sunlight into the banking lobby. Mosaics also link the interior and exterior. In these, languid lines in tropical colors appropriate to the slower rhythms of coastal life first appear outside as cladding on the tall columns that support the drive-thru canopy and continue inside on columns and wall surfaces (see Fig. 3.12). Since its founding in the nineteenth century, Corpus Christi had been a city unafraid of risk; in the twentieth century, that confidence helped give rise to energetic modern buildings such as the Mercantile National Bank.[3]

Long a center of trade and commerce in East Texas, Tyler boomed economically and architecturally after the discovery of oil in East Texas. Among its thirteen notable Art Deco buildings is the People's National Bank, designed by Alfred C. Finn and Campbell

↑ Figure 3.13
E. Davis Wilcox Associates, People's National Motor Bank, Tyler, 1966 (foreground); Alfred C. Finn and Campbell and White, People's National Bank, Tyler, 1932 (distant)

3. Money

→ Figure 3.14
Alfred C. Finn and Campbell and White, People's National Bank, Tyler, 1932, interior

and White. Just down the street stands People's National Motor Bank of 1966, designed by Tyler's premier midcentury architect, E. Davis Wilcox Associates (Fig. 3.13). The rather sober fifteen-story office building calls to mind the severe towers of Rockefeller Center of the same era, and, like many New York skyscrapers of the 1930s, retains its sumptuous Art Deco interior (Fig. 3.14). In contrast, the motor bank is a low-rise concrete building whose pronounced trabeation and projecting beams reflect the enduring influences of both French rationalism (Wilcox was trained at the École des Beaux-Arts and at Yale) and traditional Japanese architecture in US modernism.

Although it was not quite as large as the Astrodome, like that iconic building, the American Bank in Bellmeade was circular in plan, easy to spot from a distance, and had plenty of parking (as well as a drive-thru option; see Fig. I.5). Lest it be confused with a small stadium

133

Part I: Priorities

↓ Figure 3.15
Neuhaus and Taylor, Campbell Centre, Dallas, 1972; second tower by HKS, 1977

or concert hall, its owners had its name positioned in large letters atop the cornice, a distant echo of the giant "PSFS" sign that Lescaze and Howe put atop the roof of their building. American Bank was nearly windowless and composed of 25-foot-high fiberglass-reinforced concrete panels. In its shape and materials, it bore a familial relationship to another great circular building, the more disk-like Administration Building at Lamar State College of Technology (today the Otho Plummer Building at Lamar University), a work of exceptional pizazz in Beaumont by Pitts, Mebane and Phelps (1959). Its continuous concrete screen, composed of broad zig-zagging, up-down trapezoidal frames, animates and opens the building visually.

No chapter on money in Texas architecture is complete without mention of the Campbell Centre in Dallas, a spectacular cluster of mirrored gold buildings (see Fig. I.19; Fig. 3.15). In 1972, the first structure of what became a group of office buildings, designed by Houston-based Neuhaus and Taylor, rose at a 45-degree angle to the North Central Expressway. Set in a giant-scaled, anti-urban landscape, the gleaming, rounded-corner rectangular form's dual associations with Narcissus and the quintessential material embodiment of wealth perfectly captured the essential selfishness on which capitalism is built. And it was well suited to a city famous for its affluent residents' love of large, shiny trinkets. A second tower, by HKS, Inc., appeared late that decade, when *Dallas* was on the air, and helped cement the city's image as a capital of unscrupulous consumerism internationally. The Campbell Centre exuded confidence and paved the way for Fountain Place's comparatively restrained homage to diamonds. The group today includes two low-rise connector buildings and a hotel building between the first two towers.

Inspired in part by reflective lenses in aviator sunglasses, architectural gold glass emerged from research begun in the mid-1950s by Kevin Roche and John Dinkeloo in the architectural office of Eero Saarinen, and was embraced by architects and clients in part because of its heat-reflecting properties.[4] Mirror glass began to be used in the late 1950s, on buildings ranging from Bell Telephone labs in New Jersey to the campus of Oral Roberts University in Tulsa, Oklahoma, in the 1960s. The first Campbell Centre tower, however, was in the vanguard of buildings clad entirely in gold glass. It helped popularize the material for architecture and anticipated the 1980s vogue for wraparound mirrored eyewear, which likewise used opacity to convey cool self-assurance in the sunshine, another priority for many Texans.

PART II   PREOCCUPATIONS

4.	**God**	139
5.	**Government**	165
6.	**Care**	189

4. God

Previous Spread: Howard R. Meyer and Max Sandfield, William W. Wurster, consulting architect; mosaic by György Kepes; textile by Anni Albers, Temple Emanu-El, Dallas, 1957

4. God

Nearly everyone has an opinion about god. Whether understood as an anthropomorphic omnipotent savior, as a constellation of distinct deities and forces, as a descriptor of plentitude rooted in empathic connection and labor, or as an idea invented and manipulated to serve unholy aims, god preoccupies. In some regions of Texas, cultural expression and social life center on religion. Faith helps bind distinct communities within the state's large, pluralist cities and exerts outsized influence on politics.

In the mid-twentieth century, the challenge of creating modern sacred space was one of the foremost topics in architecture.[1] Some architects hewed closely to traditional forms and spatial arrangements, even as the façades they designed became increasingly sober and unadorned. Such works appeared in many countries and belonged to a vein of church design marked by formal stridency that often conveyed a certain conservatism. Examples in Texas include First Presbyterian Church in Raymondville (1949) by San Antonio architect Henry Steinbomer, a building whose combination of austere planarity and sculpture (depicting John Knox) calls to mind the larger and more expressionistic 1930s churches, townhalls, and slaughterhouses Francisco Salamone designed in the Argentine pampas (Fig. 4.1).[2] In First Baptist Church in Longview (1951), by Wilson, Morris & Crain, with sculptures by Richard M. Hetrick, the abstract play of mass, volume, and pattern in brick is interrupted by the descent of three quite upright angels (Fig. 4.2). But for many people, the horrors of genocide, fascism, and atomic warfare, coupled with the rise of science and abstract art, seemed to suggest that if God exists, meaningfully housing spaces for ritual and prayer would have to look considerably different than they had historically. And yet, unlike new building types that appeared in the wake of the Enlightenment, such as museums, office buildings, and train stations, there was nothing new about God. In fact, the sense of religion as ancient, the repetition of ritual across generations, the idea of universal relevance—across centuries and oceans—were central to many people's engagement with the divine.

Particularly thoughtful architects recognized that although the old forms would no longer do, old needs remained. How to support the kinds of rituals and practices that had long sustained individuals and cultures, but do so without outmoded forms, and in spaces that could awaken in modern people the same kinds of feelings that the great religious

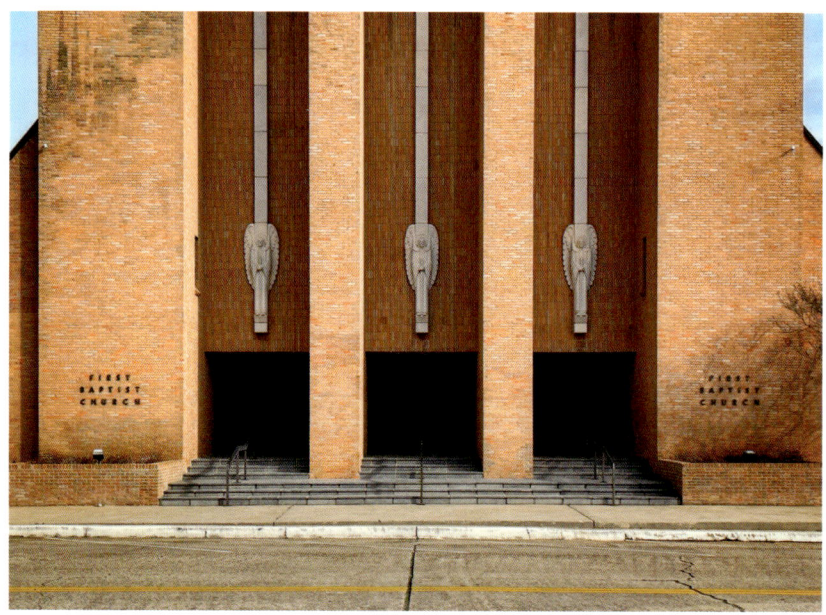

↑ Figure 4.1
Henry Steinbomer, First Presbyterian Church, Raymondville, 1949. Sculpture attributed to Charles Umlauf.

→ Figure 4.2
Wilson, Morris & Crain, First Baptist Church, Longview, 1951. Sculpture by Richard M. Hetrick.

buildings of the past had?³ For those architects who had clients willing to try new things, religious commissions offered exceptional opportunities. A house of worship might test the limits of abstraction as well as architects' imaginations in and against a long history of architecture in which religious buildings played a leading role. In designs for religious buildings in Texas, architects turned repeatedly to two forms: the triangle and the curved line, whether as arched profile or rounded volume. Often used at huge scale but balanced with elements, details, and works of art of much smaller proportions, and often seen in carefully modulated lighting schemes, the triangle and the curve associatively linked new buildings to Romanesque and Gothic structures while affirming modernist commitments to clearly articulated constructional geometry. High ceilings created a sense of spaciousness that similarly recalled the soaring structures of the medieval period and acknowledged the primacy given to space as an architectural element in many postwar architectural debates. Architects often devoted special attention to interiors, which were routinely enriched by restrained works of art and detailing.

A history of Texas architecture that continued past the mid-1980s would include purpose-built mosques, Hindu and Buddhist temples, Sikh gurdwaras, Quaker meetinghouses, and evangelical megachurches. The expansion of religious architectural typologies in the state (at least in big cities) corresponded to Texas's increasing diversity, even as religious affiliation declined overall. During the period covered in this book, the outstanding buildings for religion were most often Christian churches, nondenominational chapels, or Jewish synagogues. A disproportionate number of significant such works were built on college campuses, but many also stand in the midst of suburbs.

Faith and Reason

At its best, college teaches students to ask questions. Doubt, contemplation, and discomfort are essential to learning. They also attend belief. College campuses were propitious sites for innovative religious architecture because they were the places in Texas where experimentation and inquiry were most likely to be tolerated.

One of Texas's greatest buildings is a chapel so small that it is called the Little Chapel in the Woods (Fig. 4.3). Built on the campus of Texas Woman's University in Denton in 1939, it is an extraordinary work of collaboration whose landscape, materials, scale, works of art, and story harmonize as an exquisite and exceptional whole.⁴ Funded with private donations and a grant from the Public Works Administration,

→ Figure 4.3
O'Neil Ford and Arch B. Swank Jr., Little Chapel in the Woods, Denton, 1939

its architectural design was led by O'Neil Ford and Arch B. Swank Jr., but it was built by unemployed and underemployed local men at the end of the Great Depression. The building's stunning interior is a result of the coordinated work of undergraduates, led by art professor Dorothy Antoinette LaSelle. The chapel's chandeliers, woodwork (including pews, pulpit, and altar), and, above all, its stained-glass windows that honor historical and contemporary women and their labors were designed and executed by students, all of whom were women.

Evidence of the human hand is everywhere throughout the building. Indeed, the Little Chapel is one of the finest examples anywhere of the entwined effects of the Arts and Crafts movement and industrialization on modern architecture. On the exterior, the masonry of the stone courses becomes more exact as the walls rise, and as the masons became more expert. Brick, stone, and wood each contribute their distinctive textures and colors inside and out. Visitors enter beneath an abstract "rose window" inspired by the colors of Texas wildflowers and move through a nave whose sequence of parabolic arches at once calls to mind medieval building traditions and oft-reproduced images of the parabolic hangar at Orly Airfield, beloved of

4. God

↗ Figure 4.4
Beatrice Paschall and Billie Marie Culwell, Signature Window, detail, Little Chapel in the Woods, Denton, 1939

both Ford and Le Corbusier. For the vestibule, the students created a "signature" window in which they depicted the people who contributed to creating the chapel. From bottom to top appear the trustees and president; the architects and builders; and LaSelle and the students (Fig. 4.4). Eleanor Roosevelt dedicated the building in 1939.

For his alma mater, Rice University, Houston architect Harvin C. Moore designed the Rice Memorial Chapel of 1958 (Fig. 4.5). The challenge of designing at Rice, as at so many campuses with monumental historic cores, was how to acknowledge existing (and in many cases, beloved) buildings while creating a modern space. The highly eclectic, broadly eastern Mediterranean vocabulary that Ralph Adams Cram and William Ward Watkin had established at Rice in its first decades had in certain respects provided a ready-made starting point, insofar as the campus's very general Byzantism could conjure a place and period in which religion was presumably more intensely observed than it was on the campus of a math- and science-intensive college campus during the Cold War. But the Rice chapel, like many other collegiate chapels of the mid-twentieth century, was intended as a nondenominational space. It therefore required a design that was minimally prescriptive as it accommodated ritual and liturgy, and was restrained in its allusions to the divine. Moore was well versed in fusing historical allusions and modern needs, having designed numerous historicist houses in Houston with his partner Harmon Lloyd.

For the chapel, Moore developed a limited formal palette, keyed to the patterns and geometries of Rice's existing buildings. Like the designers of the Little Chapel, he used contrasting materials, including brick, wood, marble, and glass, to great effect. With its enormous concave floor-to-ceiling gold mosaic apse, gold mosaic-clad columns, and elevated white marble cylinder in lieu of an altar, the chapel's interior stands on the knife's edge of earnest religiosity and midcentury glamour kitsch, making it perfect for Houston in the 1960s (Fig. 4.6). Moore's design also firmly embedded the chapel in an international network of modern, not-too-devout chapels. Abstract golden screens were popular in these because they alluded to a long tradition of gilt altarpieces, keeping the aura generated by shimmering color while discarding the specific formal references to religion. Eero Saarinen and Harry Bertoia took a similar approach in 1955 at Kresge Chapel at MIT (another school for math and science whiz kids), where Bertoia's gold-leafed screen frames a simple marble altar elevated on a circular platform.

↑ Figure 4.5, ↗ Figure 4.6
Harvin C. Moore,
Rice Memorial Chapel,
Rice University,
Houston, 1958

Distinct from but in close proximity to Houston's Catholic university, the University of St. Thomas, stands the extraordinary Rothko Chapel, a building known internationally for its art and an institutional commitment to promoting human rights (Fig. 4.7). Influenced at midcentury by a worldwide ecumenical movement, the modernization and opening of the Catholic Church that followed the Second Vatican Council, and the potential of modern art to support sacrality and prayer, the Rothko Chapel's patrons, Dominique and John de Menil, made Texas home to one of the most ambitious and challenging religious buildings in the United States. Silence and light—elements that Louis I. Kahn identified as central to architecture—lie at the heart of the Rothko Chapel, which was designed by Philip Johnson, Howard Barnstone, and Eugene Aubry to house paintings by Mark Rothko. Clad in rose-colored brick, with a modest entrance marked by black steel doors, the windowless chapel stands on one side of a small plaza facing a rectangular reflecting pool and Barnett Newman's *Broken Obelisk*, which the Menils dedicated to Martin Luther King Jr. Visitors pass through a small, dark antechamber before entering the chapel, an octagonal space lit by a large skylight and dominated by Rothko's fourteen enormous canvases. Each is an abstract composition in deep

↑ Figure 4.7
Philip Johnson, Howard Barnstone, and Eugene Aubry,
Rothko Chapel, Houston, 1971

purples, browns, and black. Nine of these are arranged as triptychs; the remaining five are hung singly. They are meant to be absorbed, as much as seen, over time, in the changing light beneath Houston's sky of fast-moving clouds. Encountered in an atmosphere of silence and stillness, the paintings function as objects of meditation.

By design, the Rothko Chapel is unlike the city that was rapidly rushing up around it when it opened in 1971. Just five years later, *New York Times* architecture critic Ada Louise Huxtable declared Houston "the American present and future" and called it "an exciting and disturbing place."[5] Ironically, perhaps, the Rothko was built from the proceeds of a fortune rooted in oil exploration to be a spiritual and psychological refuge amid the chaotic, commercial, crass world outside. The darkness, size, and abstraction of the canvases that surround the visitor are intentionally difficult; they demand concentration and invite confrontation—with doubt, uncertainty, loss, fear, pain, complicity, and plentitude. The god of the Rothko is a god of questions, not answers. The building proposes that communion with the divine and with one another lies in a never-complete process of disconnecting and reconnecting with the outside world and an inner self.

An architectural and artistic offspring of both Le Corbusier's church of Notre-Dame du Haut (1955) in Ronchamp, France, and Henri Matisse's Rosary Chapel at Vence, and as a keeper of the tradition of the human rights movements that shaped the era when it was founded, in twenty-first century Texas, the Rothko Chapel seems more important than ever. At a time when many people find it hard to be still, silent, and attentive, and as the fabric of democracy frays, the chapel provides space for desperately needed solace and, in its own quiet way, implores visitors to rediscover a common humanity. Dominique de Menil summarized the building's mission by saying that "the Chapel must go beyond opening its doors to those who are already united. It must provide a common place where men and women of different traditions can meet."[6] Robust programming harnessed the de Menils' vision to the architecture in supporting visits to the chapel by international social justice leaders, including Rigoberta Menchú, Archbishop Desmond Tutu, the Dalai Lama, and Nelson Mandela. Yet combined with the austerity and difficulty of Rothko's work, and the complex cultural coding of abstraction, the chapel is a case study in the limits and potentials of modern art to reach wide audiences and communicate shared values.

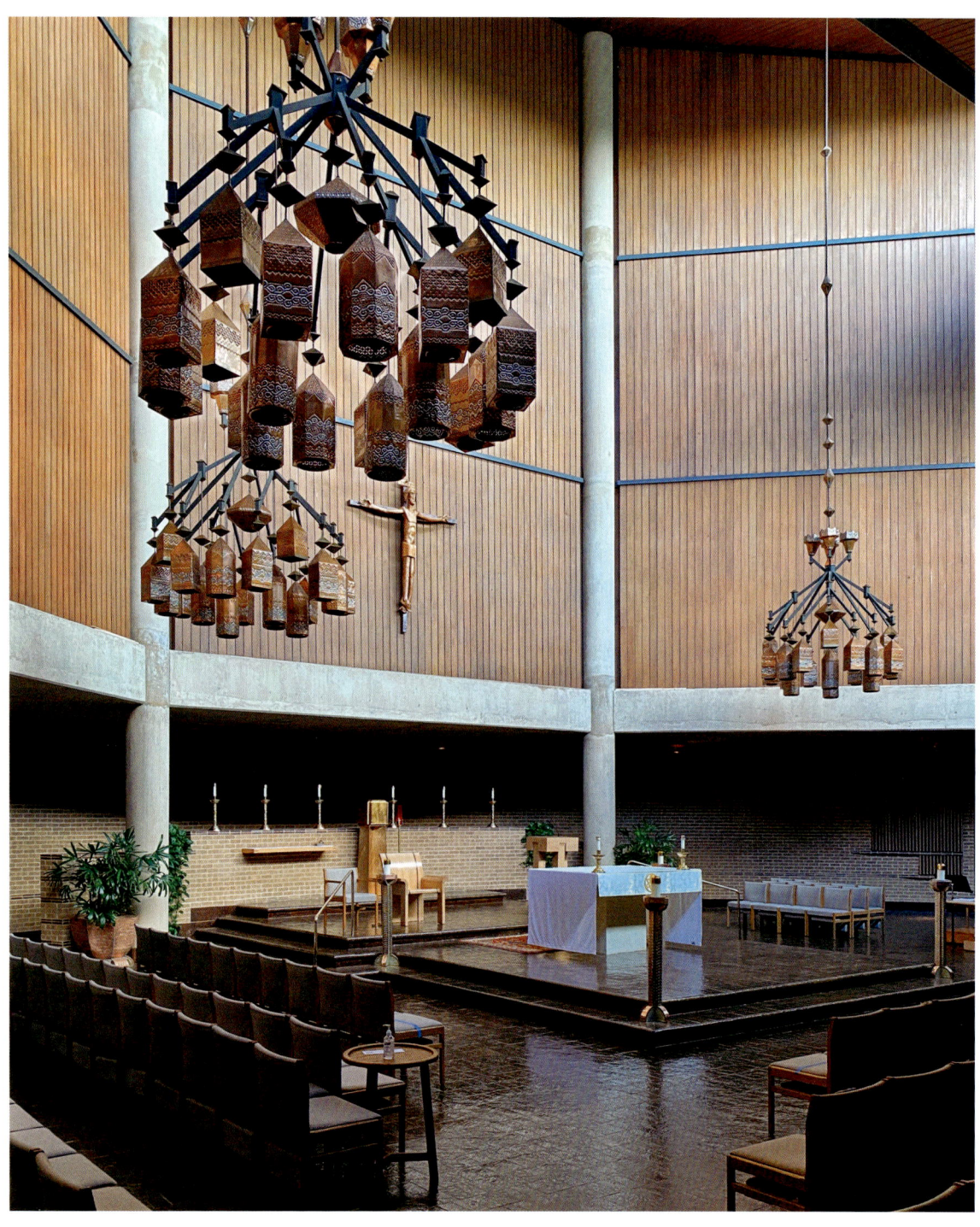

↑ Figure 4.8 :
Jane Landry and Duane Landry, Church of the
Incarnation, University of Dallas Irving, 1985

Like the Rothko Chapel, the Church of the Incarnation on the campus of the University of Dallas in Irving (1985), designed by Jane Landry and Duane Landry, is shaped to direct attention inward and to spatially emphasize equality rather than hierarchy, and shared rather than individual experience (Fig. 4.8). Faceted in plan, with interior walls that frame the altar in an octagonal space capped by a stepped-section lantern lit with clerestory windows, the church reworked ancient forms for the post–Vatican II world. Landry and Landry nestled the church into its sloping, wooded site. They used scale differentiation and a limited materials palette—concrete, brick, wood, and steel—to maintain continuity with the surrounding campus buildings while architecturally signaling the building's singularity. Punched copper light fixtures designed by the San Antonio craftsman Isaac Maxwell enrich the interior and exterior. The Landrys (a wife and husband team) worked in the office of O'Neil Ford, and in its scale, attention to craft, and careful siting, the Church of the Incarnation has a familial relationship to the Little Chapel in the Woods, in nearby Denton, and is also emblematic of the substantial body of religious architecture they designed together.[7]

Heavenward and Here

Ford's influence in Texas religious buildings was pronounced. In 1957, he returned to Denton with his colleague Howard Wong to design another church, this time the First Christian Church. Here, the parabolic arches of the Little Chapel were exchanged for an even more sophisticated roof structure, formed of tilted hyperbolic paraboloids in thin-shelled concrete engineered by Félix Candela. By this time, Candela was world famous, thanks to works such as the Church of the Miraculous Medal in Mexico City (1955), in which he responded to the problem of the modern religious building by radically updating the medieval tradition of daring formal and structural innovation in vaulting. In Mexico City and in Denton, the results were sensuous and moody interiors that ingeniously played with mass and lightness in ways that might be abstractly associated with the divine (Fig. 4.9). Wong closed the church's entrance front with a subtly detailed wall of buff brick that rises to a pronounced triangular gable (Fig. 4.10). Carved wooden doors by Lynn Ford enriched the scheme. The First Christian Church embodies Ford's characteristic interest in history and design integrity in the deepest sense, and his intense engagement with the challenges of modern religious architecture. Writing informally about the project in 1957, he remarked, "Must study ways to soften the dull triangle that

↑ Figure 4.9, → Figure 4.10
O'Neil Ford and Associates, Howard Wong, associate in charge; structural consulting by Félix Candela, First Christian Church, Denton, 1959

4. God

← Figure 4.11, ↓ Figure 4.12
Shelton and Associates,
Zion Lutheran Church,
Abilene, 1963

makes a façade. Modern clichés are so much more objectionable than traditional tidbits—such as brickwork variations.... Our precedent is so strong and so good—Finland—Sweden—Italy. Modern churches are so trivial and arty."[8] At St. John's Episcopal Church in Dallas, Ford and Swank configured half cylinders and a sweeping elliptical form to create a powerfully sculptural composition reminiscent of Sigurd Lewerentz's St. Mark's Church in Björkhagen, Sweden, of 1956–1960.

Triangular forms, however, were favored by architects for religious buildings throughout the state, from Shelton and Associates' Zion Lutheran Church (now Galilee Baptist Church) in Abilene (1963; Figs. 4.11, 4.12), with its extraordinary series of ground-to-peak telescoping volumes and almost prismatic interior, to MacKie and Kamrath's Congregation Rodef Shalom in Waco (Fig. 4.13), with its equally dramatic roofline, to the comparably restrained First Baptist Church in Bandera (Ed Nicholson, 1965). Four triangles define the façade of the Samaria Missionary Baptist Church in Waxahachie (Fig. 4.14). Here, the strong geometries of architectural modernism meld with allusions to vernacular typologies (particularly houses) to abstractly express the idea of church as shelter for those within who direct prayer heavenward. The present building sits across the street from the site where the congregation was founded in 1864, when enslaved Texans gathered under an oak tree for a prayer meeting. Shortly thereafter, the present lot was acquired for the church, and a building was built. The current church reflects multiple renovations, the most recent undertaken in 1967, to a 1915 structure that replaced the original building after a fire.

Norcell Haywood's Antioch Missionary Baptist Church (1974) in San Antonio also has a steep triangular gable, but rather than wood, it is clad in beige brick (Fig. 4.15, 4.16). Haywood worked in Ford's office in the 1960s and was only the second African American student to graduate from the architecture school at the University of Texas at Austin.[9] In 1965, he founded a firm under his name, and in 1971, was a founding partner of Haywood Jordan McCowan, which had offices in Houston, San Antonio, and Dallas. At Antioch Missionary Baptist, Haywood used a timber roof whose rafters run the length of the nave. Between the points where they meet the short end of the building, narrow rectangular leaded windows with abstract patterns run vertically almost the entire length of the wall. This rigorously geometrical composition simultaneously heightens the viewer's awareness of the triangular form of the roof, links the building to medieval precedent, and creates on

4.　　　　　　　　God

← Figure 4.13
MacKie and Kamrath, Congregation Rodef Shalom Temple, Waco, 1960

↓ Figure 4.14
J.M. Harris, original architect, 1915; remodeled by M. D. Barrington, contractor, Samaria Missionary Baptist Church, Waxahachie, 1967

↑ Figure 4.15
Norcell Haywood, Antioch Missionary Baptist Church,
San Antonio, 1974

→ Figure 4.16
Norcell Haywood, Antioch Missionary Baptist Church, San Antonio, 1974

the interior a rich play of materials, color, and light. Antioch Missionary Baptist was one of several buildings Haywood designed on the city's East Side that served African American San Antonians. The church has hosted the city's major interfaith religious celebration held in conjunction with San Antonio's annual Martin Luther King Jr. march, one of the largest in the nation.

To suggest religious dynamism, mystery, or archaic ritual, some architects revisited the architectural expressionism associated with the 1920s, with its attenuated forms, sweeping lines, and fulsome volumes. St. Paul Presbyterian Church in San Angelo (1968), by Donald

R. Goss Associates, is among such works. Here, two low wings, at right angles to each other, radiate from the circular church to frame a terraced garden. Rising above the roof of the church is a semicylindrical pylon, its upper rim scooped out with a deep, curved incision. The entire building is clad in white stucco, but in its spatial organization and fenestration has parallels with Frank Lloyd Wright's Dallas Theater Center of 1959. At St. James United Methodist Church in Beaumont (1960), a building clad in red brick and blue, green, and gray mosaic tiles, John S. Chase cleverly merged the Gothic Revival style and New Formalism to create a work that conveyed continuity with long-standing traditions in Christian architecture even as it called to mind early twentieth-century architecture in northern Europe. The most extraordinary neoexpressionist work was California-based architect Sidney Eisenshtat's Temple Mount Sinai in El Paso (1962). Photographed by Julius Shulman shortly after it was completed, this outstanding building is grounded on a ledge in its desert site while soaring dramatically upward in dialogue with the mountains. The composition powerfully suggests continuity between the terrestrial and the heavenly, continues the multimillennia tradition of using architecture as a linking device between the human and natural realms in settings for ritual, and invites viewers to imagine continuities between the West Texas desert and the landscape of the Sinai Peninsula where the story of Moses's reception of the Ten Commandments is set.

    Offering contrast to the divine drama created by the works of Eisenshtat and Goss are three smaller buildings, each notable for their play of materials and textures. Least prepossessing among these is Ruth Young McGonigle's All Souls Unitarian Universalist Church in Brownsville (1950, D. L. Mullen and Co., contractor; Fig. 4.17). Constructed of large orange bricks laid in the manner of adobe blocks and built around a courtyard, with its simple forms and earthy materiality, the single-story building evokes the vernacular architecture of Spanish colonists farther west. With a porch supported by wooden posts and exposed end beams on the main façade, the church has a pleasing rusticity and simplicity that contrasts markedly with the monumentality common to many religious buildings. Roughly 240 miles up the Gulf Coast, in Victoria, Milton A. Ryan, of San Antonio, designed First Church of Christ, Scientist (1953; Fig. 4.18). The building's sloping roof overhangs a wood and glass volume housing organ pipes, which itself slightly overhangs a brick wall. Although it is in obvious

4. God

→ Figure 4.17
D. L. Mullen and Co., contractor, All Souls Unitarian Universalist Church, Brownsville, 1950

↓ Figure 4.18
Milton A. Ryan, First Church of Christ, Scientist, Victoria, 1953

↓ Figure 4.19
Harwell Hamilton Harris and Charles Adams, St. Mary's Episcopal Church, Big Spring, 1960

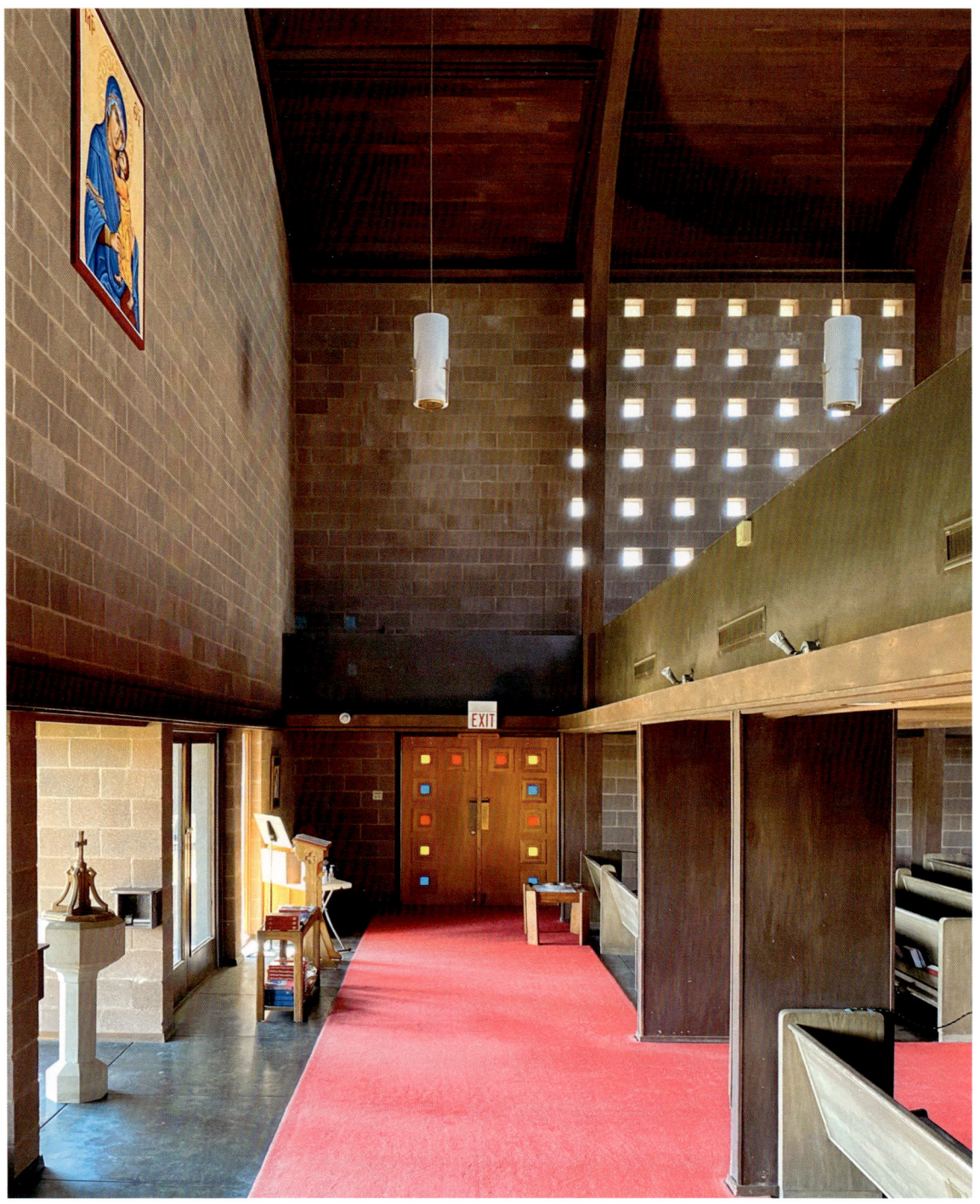

dialogue with the tradition of using soaring rooflines on religious buildings, Ryan's church is modestly scaled and well suited to its site in a residential neighborhood of gabled roofs and porches. Pronounced gables also distinguish the exterior of St. Mary's Episcopal Church (1960) in Big Spring by Harwell Hamilton Harris and Charles Adams (Fig. 4.19). On the inside, the architects used concrete block walls, cast concrete pews, wooden beams, and geometric glazing patterns to create a luminous space that balances associations with industry and nature, and sensations of rawness and warmth.

Temple Emanu-El in Dallas (1957), by Howard R. Meyer and Max Sandfield, with William W. Wurster as consulting architect, combines monumental geometric volumes and exquisitely detailed craftsmanship with works of art (Fig. 4.20). Significant in the religious and architectural histories of Texas, it houses the oldest Reform Jewish congregation in North Texas (founded in 1875), is the largest such congregation in the southern United States, and powerfully exemplifies the kind of artistic collaboration that marked some of the best buildings of midcentury. At Temple Emanu-El, leading Texas architects worked with nationally and internationally prominent designers and artists. The synagogue was among the major projects associated with the northward expansions of the Dallas suburbs and had among its patrons Dallas's Nasher and Marcus families. When it was completed, the temple was published in *Architectural Forum* and *Life* magazine and represented a significant addition to both an impressive group of modern synagogues and temples in the United States built in the 1950s and 1960s (including Eisenshtat's) and the rich field of religious architecture internationally in the 1950s.[10]

Before hiring Meyer and Sandfield, the congregation considered a scheme by Erich Mendelsohn for a different site. On the advice of Wurster, who was then dean of the architecture school at UC Berkeley, the architects integrated programmatic clarity and monumentality by articulating the sanctuary as a giant central cylinder and housing programmatically subordinate spaces, including a chapel, offices, and a school, in a rectangular volume around the perimeter. The vast sanctuary rises to a dome 90 feet above ground. The building's primary geometries are articulated by concrete frames with pinkish brick infill and enclosed by covered walkways and verdant courtyards designed by Marie Berger and Arthur Berger. As a whole, the temple is defined by a rich play of solid and void, mass and space, and shifts in scale

→ Figure 4.20
Howard R. Meyer and Max Sandfield, William W. Wurster, consulting architect, Temple Emanu-El, Dallas, 1957

that support different aspects of religious practice and community life. Inside the sanctuary, artist György Kepes, founder of the program in visual design at MIT, created a luminous mosaic in the brick wall behind the ark with bits of glass inlaid in mortar (Fig. 4.21). In concert with this wall, the tiny clerestory windows that puncture the wall above narrow slats of teak and the cylindrical chandeliers suspended at different heights create a dazzling staccato of shimmering lights. (A similar vocabulary defines the smaller rectilinear chapel.) These elements shape the setting for the focal point of the space—the doors and curtain of the ark woven by Bauhaus artist Anni Albers, who taught at Black Mountain College in the 1930s and 1940s. Sculptor Richard Filipowski created menorahs and lights for the congregation as well.

  The remarkable group of buildings discussed here illustrate the potential of architecture and the allied arts to create affecting spaces of lasting meaning. In the relative diversity of practices and beliefs they accommodate, they also remind us of the sacred separation of church and state that underpins the rule of law and democracy, which government—another preoccupation—is charged with safeguarding.

4. God

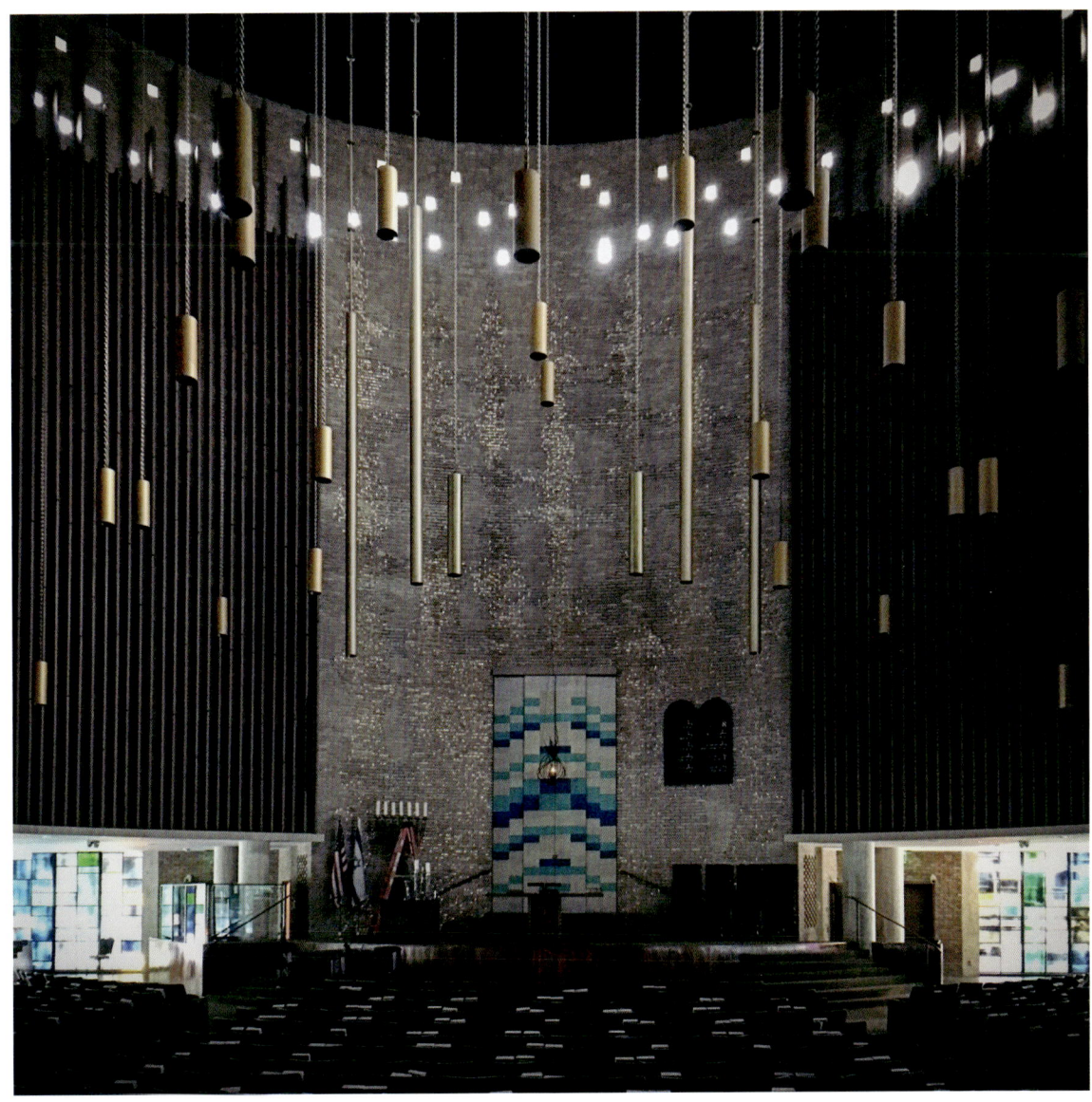

↑ Figure 4.21
Howard R. Meyer and Max Sandfield, William W. Wurster, consulting architect; mosaic by György Kepes; textile by Anni Albers; metalwork by Richard Filipowski, Temple Emanu-El, Dallas, 1957

5. Government

Previous Spread: Wilbur Kent, Angelina
County Courthouse, Lufkin, 1955

5. Government

Along with religion, Texans are famously preoccupied with government. A preference for limited government is one of the central strands of Texan identity as it has been historically imagined and propagated. Yet this supposed tenet of Texanity looks less convincing when it is judged against the scope and scale of public architecture and infrastructure projects in the state, and considered in light of a long history of governmental efforts to support certain private interests, on the one hand, and limit broad political participation, on the other. Seen relative to the state's abundant and high-quality governmental architecture, anti-government rhetoric is used to discourage democratic participation so as to keep the levers of power securely in the hands of the few. Unease with government is perhaps most voluble and familiar when it is expressed by landowners worried about private property rights. But apprehension can run deep as well in those excluded from the wealth and power that property ownership confers. Among the first uses of government in Texas, in 1836, was as a tool to establish slavery and enshrine the rights of a minority with respect to property ownership. Architecture's relationship with land and real estate, and its long-standing use as a means of conveying governmental power, inevitably make it part of this story.

In Texas, government plays a particularly important role because the size of the state demands enormous coordination of services, bureaucratic processes, and resource management. Notably, in the 1930s—the decade when the idea of Texan singularity and heroic individualism became firmly enshrined—federal money poured into the state to buttress its economy and support collective labor. Evidence of this abounds today in public park projects and bridges built by the Civilian Conservation Corps and the Public Works Administration, and in the state's impressive collection of 1930s courthouses, city halls, and post offices, the decorative programs of which, whether as sculpture or frescoes, did so much to perpetuate images keyed to economic and political interests of certain landowners framed as "Texan." The manufacturing of a distinctively Texan image and the fomentation of a feeling of state pride often relies on public money, whether for the buildings of the Texas Centennial Exposition in Fair Park, or classrooms, laboratories, libraries, and football stadiums for public school systems and public colleges and universities throughout the state. Government is manifested architecturally and spatially in many ways. The buildings examined in this chapter generally do one of three things: convey authority emphatically, communicate accessibility to the services and benefits that government delivers, or suggest the increasingly fine line between government and corporate capitalism at midcentury.

Modern Classicism for Growing Cities

In the late 1920s and 1930s, the dominant architectural language of government buildings in the United States was modern classicism, typified by public buildings designed by architects Bertram Grosvenor Goodhue, of New York, and Paul Cret, of Philadelphia. Axial symmetry, heavy massing, sober, sometimes even severe façades, with restrained abstract and figural decoration—or occasionally none at all—were used to express control, stability, and permanence. Depending on their locations, these buildings, which included city halls, county courthouses, and central libraries, were clad in brick, concrete, terracotta, or fossilized limestone. Texas has an outstanding collection of such works. They include the Eastland County Courthouse in Eastland (1928), by Dudley Green for Lang and Witchell; the Cottle County Courthouse in Paducah (1930), by the Wichita Falls firm Voelcker and Dixon, who specialized in courthouse design; and the former central branch of the San Antonio Public Library (1930), by Herbert S. Green, which now houses the Dolph and Janey Briscoe Western Art Museum.

One of the finest low-rise modern classical buildings was the Chambers County Courthouse in Anahuac (1936; Fig. 5.1). Here Austin-based Corneil G. Curtis created a sober two-story (plus basement) building that stands, like many nineteenth-century Texas courthouses, in the middle of a square. Fittingly for a building built the year after the enormous Anahuac Oil Field was discovered and the Humble Oil and Refining Company began to drill there, an oil well is among the objects depicted in the small circular reliefs on the main façade.

Representations of local sources of wealth and vegetation were commonplace in modern classical public buildings, whose decorative programs often advanced historical narratives. Such buildings reveal a typically underacknowledged economic alliance between government and certain private interests, combined with a shared ambition to shape public understandings of a region's character and history. Few buildings embody this as thoroughly as the Potter County Courthouse in Amarillo (1932) by Townes, Lightfoot and Funk, with Page Brothers of Austin as consulting architects. The region's

5. Government

→ Figure 5.1
Corneil G. Curtis, Chambers County Courthouse, Anahuac, 1936

economy was historically rooted in ranching, which grew up only after bison were systematically exterminated (in part to feed eastern appetites for hides), and the US Army forcibly seized land controlled by the Comanche and displaced and killed Comanche people. This story—told from the perspective of the white minority that came to prominence after 1875—is naturalized and sanitized on the façade. Atop the outer piers of the central mass are reliefs of a gun-wielding white colonist and an Indigenous man. Below, the main entrance is framed by large reliefs depicting nopales. Above the doors a dedication runs across three panels: "To the early settlers of this county this building is respectfully dedicated" / "Their efforts were tireless" / "Their courage was undaunted." A longhorn head appears above the central door.

The blocky, eight-story courthouse in Amarillo stands at one side of a city block, presiding over a short, grassy mall. This arrangement was repeated, at larger scale, in Houston, where Joseph Finger's taller City Hall comes up to the street on one side of a block while dominating a long mall on the other (Fig. 5.2). City Hall, with its three tiers and decisive setbacks at each change of level, calls to mind the stepped composition of so many 1930s New York skyscrapers, giving the building a decidedly more cosmopolitan character than its cousin

169

Part II: Preoccupations

↓ Figure 5.2
Joseph Finger, Houston City Hall, Houston, 1939.
Reflecting basin and landscape by Hare & Hare.

5.   Government

Figure 5.3
Haynes and Kirby, Lubbock County Courthouse, Lubbock, 1950

in Amarillo. Commercial skyscrapers were already rising nearby in Houston, which the would-be urbanity of City Hall acknowledges. The building's character as part tall office building anticipated an even more pronounced confluence of the languages of corporate capital and government by midcentury. The impulse to create civic space by positioning a government building at the end of a mall or, as in the case of Trost and Trost's dramatically sited and superbly composed San Angelo City Hall, at the end of a wide street, reflected the absorption of City Beautiful planning principles in Texas. Modern classicism remained the preferred vocabulary in some places well into midcentury, as the example of the Lubbock County Courthouse (1950), by Haynes and Kirby, reveals (Fig. 5.3).

    But in many cities in the 1950s, Texas architects filtered the formal principles of classicism and rationalism into modernist idioms that conveyed authority and sobriety with varying degrees of vitality and invention. At the Angelina County Courthouse in Lufkin (1955), Wilbur Kent relied on rectilinearity, deployed in varied scales, orientations, and materials, to communicate monumental governmentality (Fig. 5.4). The façade is dominated by a colonnade-like pattern of limestone piers that partially shade the windows and link the building to classical tradition. Kent avoided the suffocating effects of axial symmetry in what is otherwise a fairly severe but compellingly composed building by advancing the east end slightly, cladding it on the south façade in concrete panels, and enlivening it with raised metal letters reading "ANGELINA COUNTY" and an abstract clock face. Wyatt C. Hedrick took a similar approach in his 1952 renovation of the Coleman County Courthouse in Coleman, which was originally designed by W. W. Dudley in 1884 (Fig. 5.5). The sophistication of Kent's design (and the compositional value of asymmetry) can be appreciated by comparing the Lufkin building to its contemporary in Hempstead, the Waller County Courthouse (1955). There, Herbert S. Voelcker similarly articulated the fenestration on the main façade in tall narrow bays, but organized the building axially, emphasizing compositional and governmental centrality by framing the central entrance bay with a massive advanced block.

↓ Figure 5.4
Wilbur Kent, Angelina County Courthouse, Lufkin, 1955

5. Government

↑ Figure 5.5
W. W. Dudley; Wyatt C. Hedrick, Coleman County
Courthouse, Coleman, 1884, 1952

→ Figure 5.6
Phelps, Dewees and Simmons, with Davis, Foster, Thorpe and Associates, Federal Reserve Bank of Dallas, El Paso Branch, El Paso, 1956. Sculpture by Heinz Warnecke and Harold Buzz depicting "Frontiersman, conquistador, and Indian of Southwestern history."

↓ Figure 5.7
Rustay and Martin, Calhoun County Courthouse, Port Lavaca, 1959

Other inventively composed buildings for government that decade were the El Paso Branch of the Federal Reserve Bank of Dallas (1956) by Phelps, Dewees and Simmons of San Antonio, with Davis, Foster, Thorpe and Associates, and the Calhoun County Courthouse in Port Lavaca (1959) by Rustay and Martin of Houston, successors to Joseph Finger (Figs. 5.6, 5.7). To varying degrees, these buildings reflected acceptance on the part of architects and their clients of the formal principles of International Style modernism that Hitchcock and Johnson articulated in 1932: a preference for regularity rather than symmetry, an avoidance of applied ornament, and an emphasis on volume rather than mass. In both, visual vitality is a consequence of the careful arrangement of planes—in a particularly Miesian manner in the case of the bank, and more volumetrically in the courthouse—and of the contrasts of color and texture in the materials. The rather anemic and incongruous relief on the upper left of the main panel of the bank balances the lettering on the lower right; its presence is a symptom of the anxiety that total abstraction provokes in some architects and clients.

Cold War Monumentality

In 1962, in response to the perception that the nation's buildings were poorly designed, the US General Services Administration adopted the "Guiding Principles for Federal Architecture." This Kennedy administration document applied only to federal buildings, but it had a far-reaching effect because the US government was a major architectural client, and the sheer number of buildings it commissioned helped define the language and tone of bureaucratic architecture at state and local levels. The guidelines called for buildings that reflected "the finest in contemporary architectural thought," acknowledged local and regional building practices, were enriched by works of art, and whose planning began with close consideration of site and context. Importantly, the authors located the power to dictate form with architects, rather than clients, and specifically discouraged the "development of an official style."[1]

In midcentury Texas, the most important federal building (in terms of its association with governmental power) designed under the guidelines was by Page Southerland Page and Brooks, Barr, Graeber and White, and is now known as the J. J. Pickle Federal Building. Built in 1963–1964 in downtown Austin, the restrained eleven-story slab, with its tripartite façade composition and cage-like grille of subtly tapered concrete piers and spandrels, embodies the cool balance of transparency, aloofness, and monumentality that came to define so many public buildings built in the 1960s and 1970s. That Page Southerland Page was, at the same time, designing and building the Office Products Division of IBM in North Austin, and would soon design the US Embassy in Mexico City, is a vivid reminder of the close alliances between government and industry during the Cold War, as well as the friendship between architect R. Max Brooks and Lyndon B. Johnson. The Pickle building was most famous in the 1960s as the site of the official local office of the Chief Executive of the United States. From his office, dining room, or sitting area, President Johnson could gaze onto the Texas Capitol, the University of Texas, and the Hill Country.

Fueled by the twin engines of capitalism and bureaucracy, the evolution of International Style modern architecture in the 1960s coincided with the steady erosion of reliable formal distinctions between government buildings and corporate office buildings. The highly Miesian Harris County Family Law Center Building in Houston (1969), by Wilson, Morris, Crain & Anderson, is based on the design of the American Republic Insurance Co. Building in Des Moines, Iowa, of 1965 by Skidmore, Owings and Merrill (Fig. 5.8). Above a prismatic lobby (the most readily recognizable Miesian space) hovers a giant cube containing six glazed levels set within a highly articulated concrete frame, which recalls Mies van der Rohe's 1923 design for a concrete office building. The building's insistent orthogonality and banded pattern of solid and void convey abstractly the balance, reason, and impartiality on which the judicial system depends, with no hint of the human drama that enfolds within and the messy irrationality and trauma that attend it.

The visually massive elements of the Family Law Center anticipated even more forceful sculptural expressions in concrete in the 1970s—a decade whose architecture has yet to be fully appreciated, in part because it has never been widely loved. The term "brutalism," often used to describe works such as the Nueces County Courthouse (1977) by Kipp and Winston; Smyth and Smyth; Bennett, Martin and Solka; and Wisznia and Peterson, or even Dallas's City Hall (1978) by I. M. Pei and Partners and Harper and Kemp, is both telling and misleading. Derived from the French "béton brut" (meaning "raw concrete"), the English word "brutalism" tends to suggest as much about some viewers' emotional

5. Government

→ Figure 5.8
Wilson, Morris, Crain & Anderson, Harris County Family
Law Center Building, Houston, 1969

↑ Figure 5.9
Tittle, Luther, Loving, Lee, Taylor County Courthouse, Abilene, 1972

→ Figure 5.10
Kipp and Winston; Smyth and Smyth; Bennett, Martin and Solka; and Wisznia and Peterson, Nueces County Courthouse, Corpus Christi, 1977

response to buildings as it does architects' treatment of materials. Yet this phase of modernism was essentially like that of the avant-garde modernisms of the 1920s, Art Deco, and modern classicism insofar as materiality and abstract façade composition remained central preoccupations for architects. What was "brutal" about architecture in the 1970s was the scale of buildings and the gargantuan plazas and parking lots adjacent to them, and perhaps viewers' associations with large institutions like governments, rather than forms or materials.[2]

While buildings such as the Taylor County Courthouse in Abilene by Tittle, Luther, Loving, Lee (1972) suggested their architects' capacity to assimilate disparate precedents—in this case, medieval fortresses and Le Corbusier's famous Villa Savoye—the quality of foreboding ponderousness conveyed by the nearly windowless upper floors likely overwhelmed any prospective curiosity about the work's architectural lineage on the part of most citizens (Fig. 5.9). On the other hand, with its tiers of oval frames inset with elongated hexagonal panes of gold mirrored glass, the rather fabulous Nueces County Courthouse demonstrated that it was possible for even county government to make you smile (Fig. 5.10). The courthouse's massive cylindrical forms mark the building as a hurricane-ready cousin of John Portman's glassy 1974–1976 Bonaventure Hotel in Los Angeles.

Even though its domain is limited to Dallas, I. M. Pei's City Hall belongs to an international network of sculptural, top-heavy, concrete buildings (many associated with governmental clients), and to a constellation of works with pronouncedly inclined planes (Fig. 5.11). In the latter category are the London and South America Bank Headquarters in Buenos Aires (1959–1966) by SERPA and Clorindo Testa, the College Life Insurance Building in Indianapolis (1967–1972) by Kevin Roche John Dinkeloo and Associates, and the Gulf Oil Building in Midland (1983) by CRS Sirrine. The opposite of Pei's glass pyramid at the Louvre, City Hall is a descendant of Le Corbusier's major buildings at Chandigarh (1950–1953) and has a familial relationship to Kallmann, McKinnell and Knowles's Boston City Hall (1968). Bounding the long south edge of Akard Plaza, Pei's building continues a long urban tradition of juxtaposing large-scale open spaces with massive government buildings so as to spatially and visually intensify statist symbolism.

↑ Figure 5.11
I. M. Pei and Partners, with Harper and Kemp,
Dallas City Hall, Dallas, 1978

5.   Government

For the People   Many people experience government and the services it provides chiefly locally and at small scale. Texas has a rich collection of small buildings designed to accommodate the very ordinary activities required by society. Three particularly energetic and even inviting examples are the Edna Police and Fire Building (1947) by Williams, MacKie and Kamrath; the Texas Department of Public Safety Building in Austin (1952) by Kuehne, Brooks and Barr, with its turquoise screen and square reliefs in limestone (one of which resembles a fingerprint, as if to remind citizens that they leave traces everywhere); and the Post Office in Saint Augustine (1960; Figs. 5.12–5.15). The façade of the Post Office is invigorated by an abstract mosaic with a rapidly repeating wavy line pattern, which suggests a familiarity with avant-garde art unexpected

→ Figure 5.12
MacKie and Kamrath, Edna Police and Fire Department, Edna, 1947

↑ Figure 5.13
Kuehne, Brooks and Barr,
Texas Department of Public
Safety Headquarters,
Austin, 1952

→ Figure 5.14
Kuehne, Brooks and Barr,
Texas Department of Public
Safety Headquarters,
Austin, 1952, detail

5. Government

→ Figure 5.15
Architect unidentified, US Post Office, San Augustine, 1960

(unfairly, perhaps) in small-town East Texas. The Edna and San Augustine examples are vivid reminders of the reach of modernism far beyond large urban centers, its acceptance by people outside of them, and a capacious view of architectural patronage on the part of governmental clients, even before the "Guiding Principles" were written.

We, the people—as individuals and as embodied by governments—live up to our ideals imperfectly and inconsistently, and sometimes fail to do so altogether. Since public torture and execution went out of fashion with the spread of Enlightenment ideals, prisons have been important building types, as exemplified by George Dance's Newgate Prison in London (1765–1768) and the panopticon form of John Haviland's Eastern State Penitentiary in Philadelphia (1821–1836). Two examples in Texas suggest not so much an engagement with the latest theories of incarceration and reform, as an impulse to design architecturally up-to-date jails that coexisted more or less harmoniously (unlike the famous buildings named above) with their contexts. Whether façade designs reflected ambitions to reintegrate inmates into society, or were intended as frank admissions of the fact of incarceration as one activity among many in a city, or were simply means of conveying architects' command of style, the examples here read now as almost quaint reminders of a time before the United States had the highest incarceration rate in the world and Texas led the nation in executions.[3] Originally just three stories tall, the Lubbock County Sherriff's Department and Jail (1931) by S. B. Haynes is an excellent example of Art Deco architecture and could as easily have housed office workers as inmates. The Hockley County Jail in Levelland (1938) by the Butler Company of Lubbock is a superb streamline moderne building built with a grant from the Public Works Administration.

Education can help prevent incarceration, and one of the happier tasks of government is supporting the vital work done by and in public libraries, many of which were among the first major institutions created and sustained using public and private funds together. Along with schools and infrastructure, libraries form the backbone of a well-functioning society. The history of architecture is filled with magisterial libraries (most of which were closed to all but the most elite readers), but there is something equally affecting about the well-designed small public library, particularly when it is also a beacon for a community.

Programmatically, the Gregg County Community Building in Gladewater (1939), by C. H. Leinbach, reflected the idea that reading, government, and civic life unfold together and in dialogue (Fig. 5.16). The late Art Deco building had a library and county offices on the

→ Figure 5.16
C. H. Leinbach, Gregg County Community Building, Gladewater, 1939

ground floor, with spaces on the upper floor for community meetings and social events. Its two wings opened out toward a small yard and the street, as if beckoning Gladewater citizens. Across the state, the jazzy Ector County Library (1942), by J. Ellsworth Powell with Haynes & Strange of Lubbock, was the first purpose-built library in Odessa. Clad in yellow brick laid in alternating courses, the building acknowledges its corner site with curved volumes and an entrance canopy that sweeps around the corner and serves as the transition point between two distinctly articulated volumes. Glass block and steel-sash picture windows further invigorate the main elevation, and as a whole, the design suggests its architect was conversant with European expressionism. An expression of the wealth pumped from the surrounding landscape, the building's formal exuberance on the outside was matched on the inside not by form but by luxuriously low temperatures. Unusually in 1942, it was air-conditioned.

The Dennis M. O'Connor Public Library in Refugio (1961) by Charles P. Donnelly was animated differently: by a roofline formed of folded-plate concrete in repeating triangles, above a series of brick planes aligned at angles like so many books on a shelf (Fig. 5.17). The strong geometries give the building a formal rigor while also suggesting refuge from strong sun and heavy rain, phenomena that Corpus Christi–based Donnelly knew well.

→ Figure 5.17
Charles P. Donnelly, Dennis M. O'Connor Public Library, Refugio, 1961

↑ Figure 5.18
Ray Bailey Architects, Carnegie Branch, Houston Public Library, Houston, 1982

5. Government

By the 1980s, International Style modernism was at once historical and enshrined as the language of the twentieth century. Consciously or not, some architects revisited the technophilic expressions of the 1920s avant-garde as they shaped buildings for the MTV decade, even those intended for reading. Expansive glazing, a clear-span space topped by an exposed truss, and a zig-zag form defined the main volume and one façade of the Carnegie Branch Library in Houston (1982) by Ray Bailey (Fig. 5.18). Built east of Interstate 45, on the city's north side, the library frames one end of a green would-be quadrangle partially enclosed on two other sides by Marshall Middle School and Northside High School. Spatially, this arrangement recalls the historic role of libraries as community cornerstones.

Houston's first library—the Houston Lyceum and Carnegie Library—opened in 1904, having been launched by a gift from Andrew Carnegie, the famous endower of nearly 1,700 libraries nationwide. That institution, however, was closed to the nearly 40 percent of Houstonians who were Black. A second (much smaller) grant from Carnegie supported the creation of the Colored Carnegie Library, which opened in 1913 and received national attention as one of the first libraries built west of the Mississippi River to serve African Americans.[4] De jure library segregation ended in Houston in 1953. Four columns from the 1925 Carnegie Branch Library (the third Carnegie library in the city, and the one Ray Bailey's building replaced) stand in front of the library today.

Architectural history is rich in examples of buildings constructed at the behest of governmental patrons who understood architecture as a means of expressing state power and grandeur. Texas, like the United States as a whole, has yet to live up to that tradition in proportion to its population and economic power. By contrast, for example, governments in Mexico and Brazil were among the leading patrons of modern architecture in the Americas in the twentieth century. The reasons for this difference are many, but the reluctance on the part of governments in the United States to be great architectural patrons is perhaps analogous to the collective decision to leave so much that pertains to the public, such as care, in private hands.

6. Care

Previous Spread: Wilson, Morris & Crain,
Childress Optometrists, waiting room,
Longview, 1951

6. Care

Hospital construction moves forward at a determined if somewhat ponderous pace. . . . The primary motivation here is improvement—improvement in facilities themselves as well as in availability, in medical programming, in over-all attention to health needs. A prosperous nation, we "just ain't done right" by our people. **—Emerson Goble, Architectural Record**

So began *Architectural Record*'s special issue on hospital construction in 1955. Among nonresidential building types, schools constituted the single greatest area of growth in US architecture in the postwar period. But buildings for health care followed as the population grew, spread, and gradually began to live longer, in tandem with astounding advances in medical science and treatment—from vaccines to antibiotics to ever more complex surgeries. Today, Houston is famous as the site of one of the largest medical centers in the world, but Texas has long had an important place in the history of medicine. In 1952, smallpox was eradicated worldwide, the first smallpox vaccination mandate in the (future) United States having been executed in San Antonio in 1830. When nationwide trials of Jonas Salk's polio vaccine opened in 1954, children in Nueces County were the first Texans to receive the shots. In 1968, one of the world's very first human-to-human heart transplants took place at St. Luke's Hospital in Houston. Then and now, in an age shaped by a pandemic induced by a new virus, health and health care—whether for individuals or a wide public—preoccupy us all and shape often-wrenching conflicts over policy and politics.

But care is not just health care. A chapter on the architectures of care could be filled with playgrounds, day-care centers, and nursing homes, each with their distinct programmatic requirements and problems of formal expression. It might center on dwellings—where most caretaking occurs—or religious buildings, built as many are to nurture the spirit, or include park pavilions and nature centers, meant to help connect people with the earth in ways that can help sustain both. The buildings in this chapter remind us of the breadth of care-oriented architecture and the ways that modern architectural ideas about space, form, and planning fused with evolving approaches to the giving and receiving of care.

→ Figure 6.1
Wade, Gibson and Martin, Mercy Hospital, Laredo, 1957

Mercy Hospital in Laredo, by Corpus Christi architects Wade, Gibson and Martin, not yet completed then, was among the buildings that *Architectural Record* profiled in its 1955 hospitals issue (Fig. 6.1). Planned for a ridge northeast of Laredo's historic downtown, and about a ten-minute drive from the nearest bridge across the Rio Grande, Mercy Hospital typified modernist designs for large hospitals. With the rise of bacteriology and modern surgery in the nineteenth century, the overwhelming focus of hospital architecture became air circulation and spatial segregation. The imperatives to avoid cross infections, keep operating spaces clean, and, as medicine improved and more people survived procedures, accommodate recovering patients and their visitors made hospitals among the most programmatically complicated of all building types. Spaces for hospital staff to work (and rest) apart from patients were also required, as was planning for vehicular access and transitional zones to accommodate ambulances, mortuary vehicles, and private cars. With its essentially L-shaped plan (a typically modernist configuration), a surgical suite isolated from other spaces but easily accessed from the emergency room, spatial accommodation of discrete departments, and ample parking, Mercy Hospital typified up-to-date hospital planning. Critics were particularly impressed with the architects' handling of spaces for labor and delivery, and noted the utility of the L form for isolating the delivery room and newborn nursery, both for the security and health of the babies and the rest of mothers in separate rooms.

With its long wings, flat roof, bands of windows, and minimal ornament, Mercy Hospital reflected patterns in modern hospital design internationally. The attention to program and spatial planning, along with the imperatives of efficiency and cleanliness that are particularly evident in such buildings, shaped the entwined histories of medicine and architectural modernism, especially in the first half of the twentieth century.[1] The foremost example of the co-evolution of modern care and modern architecture was Alvar Aalto's tuberculosis sanatorium in Paimio, Finland (1929–1933), which, like Mercy, had spatially and programmatically distinct wings and long bands of windows, and whose balconies, like Mercy's sunshades, were both practical and formal devices. But the Laredo hospital's internationalism extended beyond its forms, even as it occupied an important place in local history and daily life. It was run by the South Texas branch of the Sisters of Mercy, an order of religious women founded in Ireland in 1827. The Laredo sisters established the first hospital in the city in 1894. In the 1950s, their building was considered a large hospital and was built to serve people coming from as far as 150 miles, on both sides of the border.

The conventionality of Mercy Hospital's modernism is striking when the building is compared to the much smaller, L-plan Victor Keidel Memorial Hospital in Fredericksburg (1938) by Edward Stein (Fig. 6.2). Built to serve a small town rather than a bustling international metropolis, Keidel Memorial embodies in a single building distinct formal impulses in twentieth-century architecture. Its larger main volume thrusts forward from the site to meet the corner with a triangular gable and classical formality in the vein of Fredericksburg's nineteenth-century commercial vernacular architecture. Meanwhile, the façade of the short wing of the L is defined by a moody, nearly moderne classicism punctuated by an inset concave glass-brick window, with comparably narrow rectangular casement windows and a small porch topped by an almost neoformalist canopy supported by neobaroque cast-iron balusters. In its tone, formal tautness, and fundamentally astylar character, this façade of the Keidel Memorial anticipates the sobriety and tension of some buildings of the 1940s.

→ Figure 6.2
Edward Stein, Victor Keidel Memorial Hospital, Fredericksburg, 1938

The Keidel Memorial Hospital was named for Dr. Wilhelm Victor Keidel, a physician and German immigrant who treated white and Indigenous patients. Keidel seems to have understood care as extending far beyond the realm of medical attention for individuals to include human rights and collective welfare. His views may be deduced from his political activities: Keidel was vice president of the State Convention of Germans in 1854 that adopted a platform calling for the abolition of slavery; pay equity; direct election of the US president; free, secular, public education; and the abolition of capital punishment.

6. Care

For many, medical care occurs in small medical offices, which abound in small cities and suburbs in Texas. A particularly interesting and cogently executed example of the type is C. Gale Cook's Park Avenue Medical Center in Orange (1960), a meticulously detailed low-rise building (Fig. 6.3). It is enlivened by a restrained play of gray-blue asymmetrically composed planes in a varied palette of materials that includes brick, glazed tile, and an advanced metal sunscreen somewhat like the one he designed for the addition to the Orange County Courthouse.

Also among the state's notable small clinics was the one that Raiford Stripling designed in Nacogdoches in 1952 for Dr. James G. Taylor, who was a dentist, and Dr. W. B. Allen, a general practitioner. Stripling's building is pronouncedly horizontal and defined by a flat, overhanging roof, an orange brick base separated by a continuous course from redwood panels above, and an advanced volume on one end, with a distinct fenestration pattern and a porch. Meticulous detailing at doorways and corners makes the work particularly satisfying when seen up close (Fig. 6.4). The building is significant as an example of modern design in the oeuvre of an architect best known for

→ Figure 6.3
C. Gale Cook, Park Avenue Medical Center, Orange, 1960

195

Figure 6.4
Raiford Stripling,
Taylor and Allen Clinic,
Nacogdoches, 1952

his historical preservation work, particularly in San Augustine and in Goliad. Stripling's projects in these places especially helped shape an image and idea of Texas history that foregrounded religious, political, and settler colonialism. But he also designed new buildings of multiple types in a modern idiom, including the Taylor and Allen clinic, which spatially reinforced racial inequalities in health care. Although the building has been modified, it originally included a space labeled on the plan as the "colored waiting room." As that plan (Fig. 6.5) makes clear, Black patients entered through a different door, at the back of

6. Care

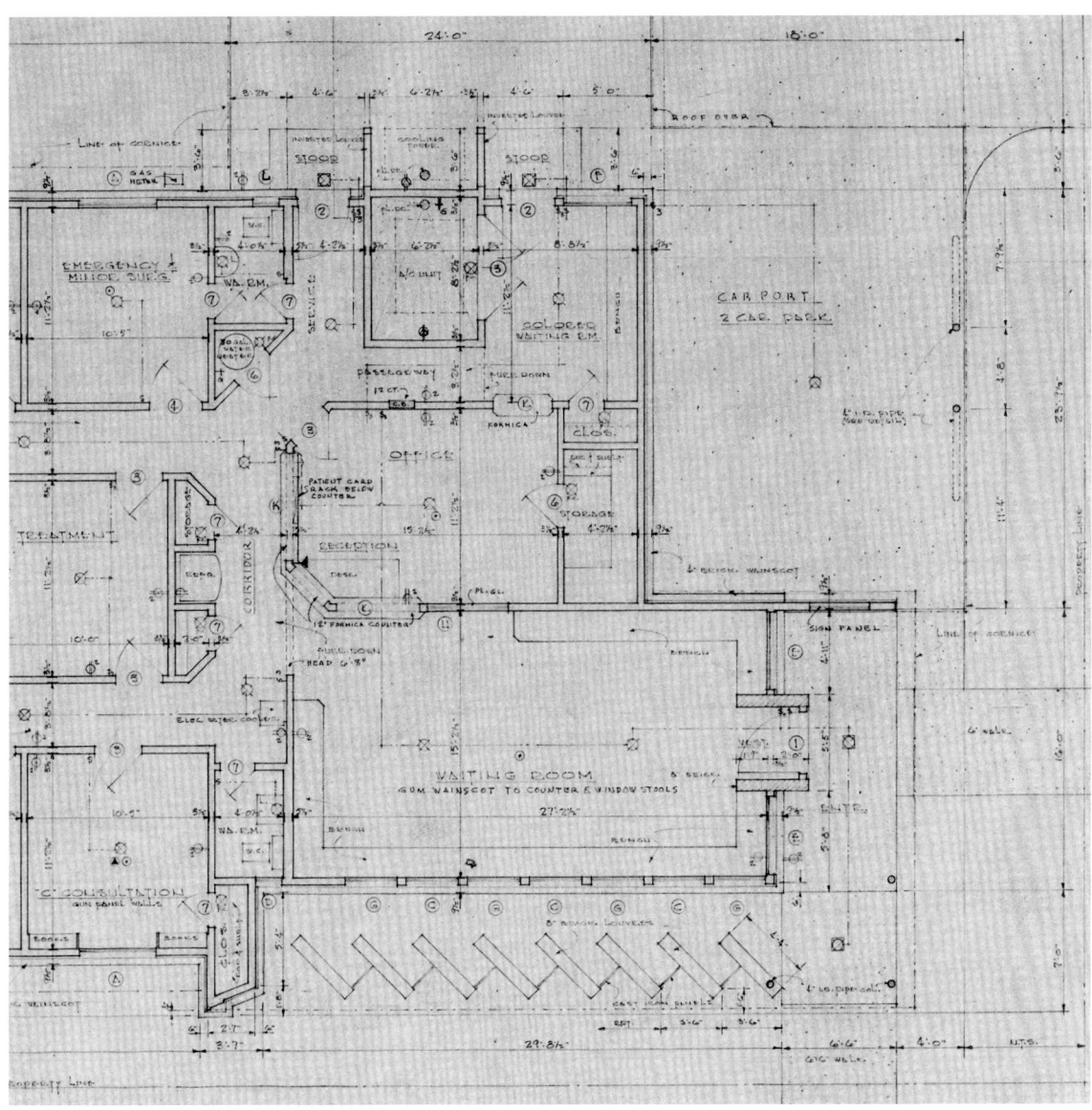

↑ Figure 6.5
Raiford Stripling, Taylor and Allen Clinic, Nacogdoches, 1952, plan. "Colored" waiting room is to the left of the carport, entered via a "stoop." Courtesy of Perky Beisel and Judy Kugle.

the building, than white ones did. Before seeing the doctor, they were accommodated in a space less than one-quarter the size of the white waiting room. While segregated waiting areas were commonplace in railroad stations starting in the 1890s, and continued to exist in buildings associated with transportation into the twentieth century, the purpose-built space for segregation in a new building dedicated to health care in the 1950s starkly revealed the depth and extent of racial prejudice and architecture's role in perpetuating it, even as desegregation efforts in Texas were underway in earnest.[2]

With its expressed cast-in-place concrete roof slabs, piers, and beams; its pinkish-orange brick; and simple plate-glass windows, the Harris County Center for the Retarded (1966) by Howard Barnstone and Eugene Aubry may have looked insignificant and undistinguished from the outside (Figs. 6.6, 6.7). In fact, its design and planning, which went hand in hand with an innovative institutional philosophy, placed it at the forefront of care centers for people with intellectual disabilities in the United States. At a time when many people with such disabilities were still sent "away" from their families and communities to live permanently or semipermanently in self-contained facilities where they had little contact with the rest of society, the Harris County Center for the Retarded helped prepare people with intellectual disabilities to hold jobs and live independently. In 1967, *Architectural Forum* characterized it as "the country's most comprehensive" such facility, composed as it was of spaces for preschool through high school classes, recreation, therapy, a workshop, and research.[3] There were no residential facilities, in accordance with the principle that the days of those who learned there should follow the typical pattern of living at home and going out to school or work, and the conviction that they and their families were best served by living together.

Working with a very tight budget, Barnstone and Aubry organized the center as a campus of six main buildings, grouped programmatically. Circulation occurred via open-air covered walkways, small gardens, and a patio. From the beginning, the architects strove to create a humane sequence of spaces that supported the work—on the part of caregivers and the cared for—of preparing to live in a larger world. Long before the Americans with Disabilities Act was signed, the Harris County Center was designed with ramps as well as stairs. Other pragmatically specific designs included having bathrooms in each classroom, a shallow swimming pool, and a model apartment, where people could practice the habits of independent daily life.

When the center opened, critics praised it immediately for its visual warmth, scale, and careful site planning, which Barnstone and Aubry achieved in collaboration with interior designer Sally Walsh and landscape architect Ralph Ellis Gunn. The *Houston Post* recorded that it was widely viewed as "the outstanding institutional building complex in Houston. And remarkably, there is nothing institutional about it."[4] *Architectural Forum* noted that "because the center is a prototype

6. Care

↓ Figure 6.6
Howard Barnstone and Eugen Aubry; landscape design
by Ralph Ellis Gunn; interior design by Sally Walsh,
Harris County Center for the Retarded, Houston, 1966
(demolished)

199

↑ Figure 6.6
Howard Barnstone and Eugen Aubry; landscape design by Ralph Ellis Gunn; interior design by Sally Walsh, Harris County Center for the Retarded, Houston, 1966 (demolished)

↑ Figure 6.8
Paul Rudolph and Wilson-Doche, Harrington Cancer Center, Amarillo, 1981

for a new kind of treatment, and because it is an architectural solution of distinction, hardly a week goes by without visitors."[5] The complex further fulfilled its patrons' ambition to build community within and help people connect with communities without by itself serving as a kind of community center. The center's auditorium was regularly rented to private groups, the school system used the center for various activities, and it served as a polling place.

The Harris County Center for the Retarded was also remarkable as a collaboration between some of the leading lights of Houston architecture. Early in his career, Barnstone was instrumental in introducing the formal language of Miesian modernism to Houston, his designs becoming ever more attuned, as his career continued, to the distinctive patterns and particularities of the city. He was also instrumental in writing early architectural histories of the area, which appeared as *The Galveston That Was* (1966) and *The Architecture of*

John F. Staub: Houston and the South (1979). Walsh, who had worked with Hans Knoll, was the city's premiere interior designer at midcentury, and she helped speed the adoption of modernist furnishings and fittings in corporate buildings. Gunn was among the first landscape architects to practice in Texas. He created designs for over two hundred residential landscapes in River Oaks and the grounds of the city's Shamrock Hotel. Regrettably, it and the Harris County Center for the Retarded have been demolished.

With its expressed concrete frame, brick facing, and covered walkways, the Don and Sybil Harrington Cancer Center in Amarillo (1981), by Paul Rudolph and Wilson/Doche, was akin to the building in Harris County (Fig. 6.8). A later work of Rudolph's, the Harrington Cancer Center has signature Rudolph elements, including raking angles, a sophisticated sectional play, and exquisite brick and concrete detailing. In plan, it consists of four parallel bars that terminate in angled edges and step down the sloping site. The front elevation is defined by overlapping inclined planar canopies and a pair of staircases with sharp turns that frame a polygonal forecourt. Although it is not considered a major work in Rudolph's oeuvre, the Harrington Center is an excellent example of the sculptural character of his buildings and his manipulation of texture and color to great effect, all of which are almost impossible to appreciate without seeing the buildings in person.

Rudolph's handling of the site and dramatic expressions on the exterior of changes of level, along with the materials, recalled his first important building, Jewett Arts Center at Wellesley College in Wellesley, Massachusetts (1958). The Harrington Cancer Center followed Rudolph's most significant building dedicated to care, the monumental Mental Health Building at the Boston Government Services Center (1962–1971).[6] This earlier building was scaled and massed to form part of a dramatic urban complex on a relatively flat site, while the Amarillo project was a stand-alone building on a suburban hill overlooking the Amarillo Botanical Gardens. Like the Boston building, the Harrington Center was marked by Rudolph's scenographic massing and circulation patterns. Although they were not universally admired, Rudolph's buildings embodied his fascination with form, materiality, and spatial drama, and powerfully proclaimed the importance of design in health care and healing. Today, offices occupy the Harrington Center, which is part of a large medical complex.

6. Care

Communities of Care

Also built as part of a medical campus, not for patient care but as a dormitory for student nurses, was the Josephine Traylor Brooking Memorial Nurses Home in Wharton by Fehr and Granger (1954). It typified low-rise 1950s modernism, with its flat-roofed, overhanging second story, asymmetrically placed entrance, and balanced but varied geometrical façade composition (Fig. 6.9). The thirty-one residents, who were students at Wharton Junior College and trained in local hospitals, lived in shared rooms on the second floor, where there was also a snack bar and sitting room. A large lounge, classroom, and apartment for the "house mother" occupied the ground floor.[7]

The architects clearly articulated the programmatic differences between the two floors on the exterior and provided the students with a long balcony and jalousie windows, which helped make the warm months bearable before the installation of air-conditioning. As a two-story building with articulated slabs, exterior staircases, and a long balcony, the Brooking Memorial Nurses Home resembled the dormitories O'Neil Ford designed on the new campus of Trinity University in San Antonio, which were widely published, and which the Austin-based architects surely knew. In the 1950s, when nursing was one of the few professions readily open to women, the nurses' home powerfully represented the prospect of independence and self-care for the women who lived there, even as it was dedicated to preparing them to care for others. Living apart from their families, the students could look forward not just to professional mastery but to a reliable, independent income that would provide them a degree of autonomy and security unavailable to most unwaged women. Named for the donors' mother, Josephine Traylor Brooking, in this project the forward-looking impulses of architectural modernism fit the program perfectly.

Few projects in Texas revealed the confluence of modern architecture and the theories and practices of care as thoroughly as the Roseville Apartments in San Antonio (Fig. 6.10). Built to house and provide services for low-income elderly people on the city's East Side, Roseville is a leafy, pedestrian-scaled residential campus that embodied architect Norcell Haywood's community-centered design. It also reflected the values of its institutional patron, Alpha Tau Omega, the San Antonio chapter of Alpha Kappa Alpha, which was the first sorority created by Black women in the United States, in 1930. In the mid-1960s, the sorority focused its service projects on the needs of seniors, and in 1965, under the direction of sorority president

↑ Figure 6.9
Fehr and Granger,
Josephine Traylor Brooking
Memorial Nurses Home,
Wharton, 1954

→ Figure 6.10
Norcell Haywood, Roseville
Apartments, San Antonio,
1972

Zudora McCoy, began planning Roseville. In 1952, with segregation still deeply entrenched in Texas, as a leader of the San Antonio Girl Scouts, McCoy had spearheaded the creation of Camp Mira Sol near Waring. It was the first camp for African American Girl Scouts in a state where going to summer camp in the Hill Country was a rite of passage for many affluent white girls.

Haywood and his colleagues at Haywood Jordan McCowan grouped the apartments into small nuclei of one-story beige-brick buildings that open onto a central sidewalk flanked by small front yards. The roofs slope toward the backs of the buildings, giving the profile of each nucleus a typically suburban residential character but also, by leading the eye upward and toward the communal spine of the group, reinforce a sense of shared space and shared life. Haywood said of the arrangement that the shared space "allows the tenants to develop their own environment collectively. Yet at the same time, they have privacy in their own dwelling units. In a way, it lets them watch over one another."[8] Roseville residents had on-site access to sewing, typing, and shop classes, as well as a variety of services. Alpha Tau Omega continues to run the apartments today according to their founders' vision of humane housing and care.

The Roseville Apartments were just one of a series of large projects Haywood designed to support community life and well-being for the predominately African American residents of San Antonio's East Side. Among these were the Carver Branch of the San Antonio Public Library and the Claude Black Community Center. Haywood believed in the importance of a community-focused approach to architecture that engaged and enhanced its urban context and called on minority architects to embrace what he called the "community architect concept."[9] Haywood founded and led Minority Architects, Inc., a nonprofit whose members were Texas- and Louisiana-based Black architects who focused on urban design and development.

Death is not among the themes in this book, but because death sometimes follows and precedes caregiving and the need for care, this chapter concludes with two works created to support mourning and remembrance. In the first decade of the twentieth century, Kansas City landscape architect Sid J. Hare laid out Greenwood Memorial Park and Mount Olivet Cemetery in Fort Worth. In 1960, Harwell Hamilton Harris designed mausolea for both, which Harris's former draftsman,

Charles Adams, oversaw the construction of after Harris went to Dallas to work for real estate developer Trammell Crow. The mausoleum at Greenwood is an engaging work of funerary architecture. The long, low, nearly windowless pavilions are organized around a central courtyard. Eternity is evoked materially in the fossilized limestone panels that face the pavilions, while low-slung Richardsonian arches, discreetly enlivened with Wrightian voussoirs, introduce a somber tone (Fig. 6.11). The interiors are midcentury glamour boxes, restrained by taut geometries and gridded patterns in the marble floors and wall vaults (Fig. 6.12). Small interior gardens, illuminated by skylights, contrast with all of the hard surfaces and call to mind Harris's innovative use of interior landscaping at the Dallas Trade Mart.

Philip Johnson's memorial to John F. Kennedy in Dallas (1970) spatializes collective reckoning with the death in Texas that towered over all others—and placed the first Texan in the White House

↓ Figure 6.11
Harwell Hamilton Harris and Charles Adams, Mausoleum at Greenwood Memorial Park, Fort Worth, 1960

6.　　　　　　　　Care

↑ Figure 6.12
Harwell Hamilton Harris and Charles Adams, Mausoleum at Greenwood Memorial Park, Fort Worth, 1960

(Fig. 6.13). It stands several blocks from the Texas School Book Depository building overlooking Dealey Plaza, where the president was shot on November 22, 1963. The structure is an open-air, 50' by 50' by 30' cubic volume formed by a pair of U-shaped precast concrete walls. Supported on small footings, the walls do not quite meet. At the center, recessed in the ground, is a black granite slab inscribed with Kennedy's name. Narrative and sentimentality are eschewed in favor of an abstract monumentality and open-endedness, achieved through the juxtaposition of giant hovering masses, the slices of space that define them, and the austerity of the plaza where the memorial stands. Tomblike, it is a space of "empty presence," in the architect's words, a place for questions, not answers.[10] It includes neither heroic nor comforting phrases. Johnson's is a tough monument not so much to Kennedy as for the traumatized people of the city where he died.[11]

↑ Figure 6.13
Philip Johnson and Associates, John F. Kennedy Memorial,
Dallas, 1970

The local civic leaders who helped organize the president's visit that fall strongly considered recommending to the White House that he not come, because they feared for his safety in a city racked by partisan divisions and virulent conservatism. In the months before Kennedy was killed, right-wing extremism had grown to such an extent that when Adlai Stevenson, the US ambassador to the United Nations, visited the city in October of 1963, he was struck and spat upon by people in an enraged mob. At the same time, leaflets bearing mug-shot-like photos of Kennedy, declaring that the president was "wanted for treason" and listing his supposed crimes, circulated widely.[12]

As reporters and investigators descended on Dallas, and the city was thrust into world headlines, Dallasites turned inward in a special grief, horror, and self-examination. The events of that November led longtime resident and journalist Warren Leslie to observe, "There are many things about Dallas to like and respect. But it is a disturbed city in a disturbed nation, and the reasons for this will not vanish overnight."[13]

PART III   R&R AND R&D

7.	**Sports & Leisure**	213
8.	**On the Road**	243
9.	**Knowledge & Power**	269

7. Sports & Leisure

Previous Spread: Lloyd and Morgan, with
Milton McGinty, Rice Football Stadium,
Houston, 1950

7. Sports & Leisure

In Texas, sports and leisure are not just bound intimately; for many, they are a double lens through which the rest of life is refracted. Mountains, forests, beaches, deserts, cliffs, caves, rivers, and ten ecoregions make the state a veritable paradise for outdoor enthusiasts. Whether as park pavilions or main houses on ranches, architecture mediates relationships with nature, even for the heartiest. For those who prefer indoor recreation, theaters and private clubs dedicated to everything from aerobics to dancing to guns abound. Annexed to the pleasures of looking and buying, miles are walked in vast shopping palaces and strips. And Texans' exceptional fascination with football has made the state a world capital of stadia. In the postwar period, relatively widespread economic prosperity and high rates of waged employment for men, combined with the expansion of a consumer culture that celebrated recreation and leisure, often with the aid of an automobile and any number of new labor-saving machines in the home, undergirded all manner of nonwork activities and buildings that housed them. Built on the pillars of the unwaged labor of women and low-wage labor of nonwhites, the architecture and economy of sports and leisure both obscured and revealed the ways recreation structured social relationships.

On Stage, Screen, and Field

The roots of open-air theater are ancient. In Big Spring, they date to the late 1930s, when the Works Progress Administration (WPA) began building the limestone Comanche Trail Amphitheater in Comanche Trail Park (1939; Fig. 7.1). Banked, semicircular bench seating for 6,800 people sweeps around a concrete stage. A limestone pavilion at the back of the stage provides scale for the real backdrop—the vast open sky and landscape of West Texas. In its form, materials, and even climate, the Comanche Trail Amphitheater is an impressive descendant of the great theaters of ancient Greece. Its association with a major civic tradition in an ancient democracy is heightened by its status as a federally financed project created in the midst of New Deal efforts to define, consolidate, and sustain national culture—often imagined in relation to land and landscape—in art, literature, and infrastructure. In the 1920s, open-air theater was revived in many places, valued alternately for its associations with classicism and for its potential to support experimental works. The Big Spring amphitheater belongs to this context and was like other important amphitheaters in being located in a park.

↓ Figure 7.1
Works Progress Administration, Comanche Trail Amphitheater, Big Spring, 1939. Photograph by the Texas Works Progress Administration.

South and east, and related to the Comanche Trail Amphitheater typologically, formally, and materially, was Alamo Stadium in San Antonio (1940). Built of limestone and concrete, and funded by the WPA, this 23,000-seat building was designed by Phelps, Dewees and Simmons chiefly to host high school football games, a purpose it continues to serve. From its exceptional site atop a rise at the edge of Brackenridge Park, spectators could see both downtown and touchdowns. Glazed tile mosaics above the entry depict the history of sports in the city, ranging from rooster fights to football. These were created by artists in the Mexican Arts and Crafts Studio run by Ethel Wilson Harris, one of the city's major promoters of figurative ceramics.[1]

The WPA sponsored park facilities throughout the state in the late 1930s, especially in Central and West Texas. Many were built of stone and concrete and are recognizable by their distinctive genteel rusticity. In the pre-air-conditioning decades, and before suburbanization and television reorganized life and leisure, park pavilions played important roles in making the public realm a place for individual and shared recreation. The Austin Chapter of the National Women in Construction recognized the value of park pavilions well into the 1960s, when, inspired by Lady Bird Johnson's work to conserve and enhance the nation's landscapes, its members commissioned J. Sterry Nill to design the Fannie Davis Town Lake Gazebo on the south shore of Town Lake. The gazebo was the first structure to accommodate leisure on the new lake, which had been created in 1960 with the completion of the Longhorn Dam on the Colorado River. With large tapered limestone piers, the octagonal gazebo acknowledges the geology of the Hill Country and the tradition of WPA park architecture. Its folded steel plate hyperbolic paraboloid roof, however, is indebted to the designs of Félix Candela and playfully acknowledges the late work of Frank Lloyd Wright.[2] The pavilion's eclecticism and vitality were ideally suited to its program as an informal place for a diverse public to recreate. Austin's beloved Zilker Park is rich in architecture and park furniture as well as nature. Among the architectural standouts are the 1934 Civilian Conservation Corps–constructed limestone and wood clubhouse built for the Boy Scouts (its open-air cousin, the Joske Pavilion in San Antonio's Brackenridge Park, is grander in scale), as well as the Barton Springs Bathhouse of 1946 by Chester Nagel and Dan J. Driscoll, and Hugo Franz Kuehne's 1964 Zilker Park Garden Center.

↑ Figure 7.2
Fitch and Holcomb,
Strawberry Park Pavilion,
Pasadena, 1966

Strawberry Park in Pasadena was also the site of an exuberant 1960s pavilion (1966; Fig. 7.2). For parkgoers in a town best known for its close ties to the petrochemical industry, the architects created a building that channeled the forms of nature and the elemental shelters sometimes used to enjoy it. The roof of Fitch and Holcomb's large cast concrete structure reads as a cross between a low-slung tent and a giant flower. Its "petals" rest on gently curving supports in an arrangement that calls to mind those in Eero Saarinen's TWA Terminal at Idlewild (JFK) Airport in New York (1962), an icon from the age when airline travel itself could be experienced as a form of leisure.

Between 1930 and 1945, Hollywood studios released more than 7,500 films, and roughly eighty million people in the United States went to the movies at least once a week.[3] For young and old, air-conditioned movie theaters provided both entertainment and respite from the sweltering summer sun. As their location in downtowns suggests, they were important parts of the urban fabric, standing alongside banks, shops, offices, and government buildings. Today, an impressive number of theaters from this period survive in smaller cities, including the Crim Theater in Kilgore (1939) by Stone and Pitts, the Lynn Theatre in Gonzales (1948) by Jack Corgan of Dallas, the Edna Theatre in Edna (1950) by Ernest L. Schult of Houston, and the Ector Theater in Odessa (1951) by Wyatt C. Hedrick of Fort Worth (Figs. 7.3, 7.4, 7.5). Distinguished by their streamlined designs and vertical blade signs, which were usually illuminated in neon, the theaters have survived as local landmarks, and some still show films. Other striking examples are the Art Deco Plaza Theatre in Laredo (1946) by Harwood K. Smith of Dallas (Fig. 7.6) and the Border Theatre in Mission (1942) by William J. Moore of Dallas, which is one of the very few remaining Pueblo Revival style theaters in the United States and includes murals depicting colonization and Anglo settlement. Along with Art Deco, revival styles (particularly highly ornamental ones) were very popular for theaters throughout the country in the 1930s. As architectural languages, Art Deco was valued for its capacity to convey glamour, and revival styles, for their obvious theatricality and capacity to awaken fantasy.

↓ Figure 7.3
Stone and Pitts, Crim Theater, Kilgore, 1939

↘ Figure 7.4
Jack Corgan, Lynn Theatre, Gonzalez, 1948

7. Sports & Leisure

↑ Figure 7.5
Ernest L. Schult, Edna Theatre, Edna, 1950

← Figure 7.6
Harwood K. Smith, Plaza Theatre, Laredo, 1946

↑ Figure 7.7
N. Straus Nayfach, Alameda Theater, San Antonio, 1949

San Antonio was home to two magnificent revival-style atmospheric theaters, the Majestic (1929) and the Aztec (1926), as well as to the late–Art Deco Alameda Theater (1949) by N. Straus Nayfach. Because they were locuses of segregation in Texas, surviving pre-1960s theaters are among the buildings that today most pointedly recall the Jim Crow era. African American, and frequently Mexican American, Texans were forced to sit in balconies and sometimes to use separate entrances. The Alameda was built in part as a response to segregation and the suppression of Mexican culture in Texas, and in turn became a major center of Mexican and Mexican American arts (Fig. 7.7). It was one of the largest theaters in the United States to screen Spanish-language films, and it hosted live performances by María Félix, Pedro Infante, and Cantinflas, among other major Mexican actors and performers. Inside, murals painted in black phosphorescent paint (which glows in the dark) depict the histories of Texas and Mexico. The adjacent four-story Casa de México International Building provided office space for Mexican American professionals.

See and Be Seen

Three urban nightclubs built in the 1940s embody that decade's characteristic restrained streamlined modernism and the ways that segregation helped give rise to culturally distinctive places that nurtured talent and communities. The formal similarities among the buildings—they are all one or two stories and have rounded corners, small windows, and very little applied ornament—make them an exceptionally vivid architectural threesome. Houston's Eldorado Building (1939) by Lenard Gabert housed one of the premier upscale dance and music halls for African Americans in the state (Fig. 7.8). Founded in Third Ward by Anna Dupree and her husband, Clarence, the Eldorado hosted nationally renowned performers and a clientele that loved to dance in the upstairs Eldorado Ballroom, and provided spaces for Black-owned businesses on the ground level.[4] Jazz, blues, R&B, zydeco, and even gospel music were at home at the Eldorado, which was built in part by money Clarence saved from his work as a porter and locker room manager at the River Oaks Country Club, the city's most exclusive social club for whites. Gabert's career spanned from the 1920s to the 1970s, and he designed many commercial and residential buildings in Houston, as well as the Congregation K'Nesseth Israel Synagogue in Baytown, among other religious buildings.

← Figure 7.8
Lenard Gabart, Eldorado Building, Houston, 1939. Rehabilitation by Stern and Bucek Architects, 2023.

↓ Figure 7.9
Architect unidentified, Lerma's Nite Club, San Antonio, 1948. Rehabilitation by Richard Mogas and Alex Gonzales, 2023.

The Galván Ballroom in Corpus Christi (1950) by Everett Elijah Hamon and Lerma's Nite Club in San Antonio, which opened in 1951 in a commercial building constructed in 1948, were among the premier nighttime social spots for Mexican Americans in those cities. Lerma's was in San Antonio's West Side Mexican American neighborhood (Fig. 7.9). At street level, the building included the entrance to the club, originally called El Sombrero, along with commercial establishments, among them a dry cleaners, a bakery and donut shop, and a variety store. From 1948 to 2010, Lerma's was a center of conjunto music in Texas and hosted such conjunto titans as Lydia Mendoza, Eva Ybarra, and Santiago Jiménez.

By contrast, the Galván Ballroom primarily hosted big bands and jazz performances and catered to a somewhat more ethnically diverse audience. Its upper-level ballroom was the site of wedding receptions, *quinceaña* celebrations, school dances, and any number of other kinds of parties. The building is strongly associated with the Galván family, who owned it and ran the Galván Music Company store on the ground floor. Rafael Galván, businessman and civic leader, whose sons formed the Galván Orchestra, helped start the League of United Latin American Citizens in 1929. It is the oldest Latino/a civil rights organization in the United States, and its first convention took place in Corpus Christi. While segregation targeting Latino and Latina Texans was perhaps not always as visible and virulent as that directed at Black Texans, it was nevertheless rampant in the state. The Galván Ballroom was one of the places where some racial and cultural boundaries could be crossed, in music and in life, as happened at the building's grand opening, headlined by the Tommy Dorsey Orchestra. However, prior to integration, even as it welcomed Duke Ellington to play, the Galván admitted Black audience members only to segregated performances.

Farther east on the Gulf Coast, in Galveston, stood a club for whites. The origins of the Galveston Artillery Club date to 1840, when it was founded by members of volunteer militia groups dedicated to fighting Mexicans. Many members later fought for the Confederacy. In its resemblance to suburban houses of the period, the Galveston Artillery Club (1959) by Thomas M. Price continued a long tradition of adopting residential typologies for private clubs and supported casual sociability for a carefully controlled clientele. With its broad triangular gable, expressed structure, and floor-to-ceiling

Part III: R&R and R&D

↓ Figure 7.10
Thomas M. Price, Galveston Artillery Club, Galveston, 1959

Figure 7.11
Lucian T. Hood Jr., Berthea and Earl Carpenter House, Houston, 1959

windows, the club typified the architectural language of affluent white leisure in the 1950s that members would have recognized from new suburbs (Fig. 7.10). It resembled the luxuriously sprawling, steep-gabled one-story houses (many with double doors on the front façades) then being constructed in Houston's new affluent suburbs. Price, the city's leading modern architect at midcentury, designed houses in other Gulf Coast cities, and had a central role in shaping Galveston's tourist infrastructure as the architect for multiple extensions to the famous Jack Tar Court Hotel (1949–1961) and the Seahorse Motel (1956), both of which have been demolished. Like the Artillery Club, the houses Lucian T. Hood Jr. designed between the 1950s and 1980s in Houston were shaped for clients who prized relaxed sociability and leisure in spaces that could convey tastefulness through the careful orchestration of the languages of tradition and modernism. Although it was built closer to downtown, in Cherokee Place, rather than in the

Tanglewood neighborhood—Houston's locus of sprawling swanky ranch houses—Hood's Berthea and Earl Carpenter House (1959) is an excellent and lovingly cared for example of the type, and of the architect's prolific, agile, client-pleasing modern mannerism (Fig. 7.11).[5] It is an exact contemporary of the Artillery Club.

To outfit themselves for their coastal sojourns, or nights on the town, or perhaps just a lunch date, white shoppers in Houston might have visited the Lamar–River Oaks Shopping Center (1950) by the William G. Farrington Company, whose interior retains the detailing and decoration typical of midcentury upscale retail spaces (Fig. 7.12). Long, low, and built with plenty of close parking, this shopping center was like so many constructed then and since, designed for a society in which consumption was at once a pastime and the vital national economic engine. As symbolic and literal suburban centers, such suburban shopping centers helped speed the demise of the spatial and social patterns that sustained the urban nightclubs of earlier decades that had been worth getting dressed up for.[6]

↓ Figure 7.12
William G. Farrington Company, Raymond Brogniez, designer, Lamar–River Oaks Shopping Center, Houston, 1950

7. Sports & Leisure

Eating and Drinking

Whether paired with a cheeseburger, taken to soothe a stomachache, served as a bath for vanilla ice cream, or drunk alone on a hot day, Coca-Cola is *the* iconic brand-named beverage of the twentieth century. First mixed in 1886, in the twentieth century, Coke became virtually synonymous with US culture at home and abroad. While the universally recognizable typeface in which the soda's name is rendered was the company's most important contribution to modern design, Coca-Cola bottling plants were themselves landmarks in big cities and small towns. Two of the most interesting, those in Waco and Beeville, typify the development of modernism in the early part of midcentury. The Waco bottling plant (1939), by Robert V. Derrah of Los Angeles with T. Brooks Pearson, is a splendidly composed, stylistically almost-but-not-quite building that integrates the two chief Art Deco idioms, the streamline moderne and the stripped classical (Fig. 7.13). Axial symmetry in the upper two registers is relieved by formal variety in the fenestration and the judicious deployment of decoration in keeping with the style's 1930s tendencies. The entrance, however, with its self-conscious classicism is a throw-back to 1920s Art Deco. With its urns, decorative dentils and fluting, neobaroque cornice, and fluted half-pilasters, it contributed to the development of the genre that Los Angeles's real estate industry would term "Hollywood regency," and, even more tantalizingly, augurs the pastiche neoclassicism of postmodernism, which began to appear in the decade in which historian Bevis Hillier invented the term "Art Deco."[7] The Beeville bottling plant (1950) by W. C. Stephenson behaves itself a bit better, at least according to the conventions of high modernist design. Its asymmetrical massing, compelling play of brick, concrete, plate glass, and glass block, and its second-floor corner window qualify it as the "real thing," and mark it as one of the state's more interesting small-scale industrial buildings (Fig. 7.14).

If European classicism, broadly defined, undergirded the Waco Coca-Cola plant, a compilation of equally generic architectural elements coded as Chinese was the inspiration for the Ding How Restaurant in Amarillo (1957) by Bliss and Vaughan (Fig. 7.15). Here, in an almost Beaux-Arts manner, while using red and yellow pronouncedly, Arthur Vaughan assembled a low-sprung horseshoe arch, two prominent parapets that terminate in upward-pointing curves in the manner of pagoda rooflines, and a corrugated metal

↑ Figure 7.13
Robert V. Derrah, Coca-Cola Bottling Company, Waco, 1939

7. Sports & Leisure

↑ Figure 7.14
W. C. Stephenson, Coca-Cola Bottling Company, Beeville, 1950

Figure 7.15
Bliss and Vaughan, Ding How Chinese Restaurant, Amarillo, 1957

awning that reads as Texan even as it evokes the pattern of wooden roof beams in Chinese temples. Appropriately, the restaurant faced south, toward Route 66, in keeping with the conventions of geomancy and of commercial highway architecture. Regrettably, the restaurant's marvelous sign, which looked even more like a pagoda, has been defaced.

Built for the automobile age, the Ding How Restaurant is both a playful and serious reminder of the complexities of acknowledging cultural difference in architecture from the vantage of Western European or US Anglo norms. Although such questions were probably unimportant to the restaurant's patrons, in the middle decades of the century they were of great significance to leading modern architects, including Erich Mendelsohn, Louis I. Kahn, Frank Lloyd Wright, and Le Corbusier. Retrospectively, although their designs sometimes look rather bumbling, these architects wrestled genuinely with how to express distinct

7. Sports & Leisure

↓ Figure 7.16
Architect unidentified, The Tap Restaurant, El Paso, 1956

231

traditions as they began to look beyond the rules of high modernism and toward a more pluralistic future. The Ding How is one reminder of the fine line in architecture between stereotype and sensitive study.

No such worries appear to have troubled whoever designed The Tap, a bar and restaurant in El Paso. The building is a case study in the power of neon and an awning to transform a small, forgettable commercial storefront into a beloved dive bar (Fig. 7.16). The building is a reminder of Texas's characteristic informality and insatiable appetite for commercial neon, which coexist alongside the upscale stylishness prevalent in parts of some of the state's cities. Since 1956, the beer and nachos at The Tap have delighted El Pasoans and visitors alike. After all, it's more fun to eat in a bar than to drink in a restaurant.

Finally, if we could squeeze smokers and picnic tables into "architecture," we'd discuss barbeque, but being unable to make that leap, this brief discussion of food in twentieth-century Texas concludes with Whataburger. Founded in Corpus Christi in 1950, the iconic hamburger chain entered the annals of architectural history in

→ Figure 7.17
Harmon Dobson, former Whataburger, Abilene, 1964. Zion Lutheran Church is in the distance.

1961 with its 30-foot-tall A-frame buildings, designed by Whataburger founder Harmon Dobson and inspired by his knowledge of military construction. The design brilliantly integrated principles of vernacular industrial architecture with those of modern advertising and the rapidly expanding culture of the automobile (Fig. 7.17). The kitchen and indoor seating were accommodated under the A, while a large diamond-shaped canopy shaded cars, where some patrons preferred to sit to eat. Harmon painted the huge corrugated metal panels in orange and white stripes in the manner of aviation color patterns, which made them distinctive and easily visible at high speeds and from a distance. The first A-frame Whataburger was built in Odessa. Others soon appeared throughout the state. Many have since been converted to other kinds of establishments, including a *frutería* in San Antonio and a taquería in Lubbock, and their stripes have been exchanged for more (or less) subdued colors. Mesquite is home to one of the few originals still intact, complete with a giant orange W attached to the point of the A.[8]

Fitness and Fandom

Between 1961 and 2006, the Rice University football team did not play in a bowl game. Their last bowl win, prior to 2008, was in 1953 (they beat Alabama). In ninety-six meetings, the Texas Longhorns have beaten the Owls seventy-four times.[9] But Rice Stadium (1950), by Lloyd and Morgan and Milton McGinty, is spectacular. Built for seventy thousand fans and seven thousand cars, the building was a marvel of delicate engineering on soggy ground, and one of the foremost architectural statements of confidence ever created in Texas. The vast stands soar high above the even vaster 30-acre parking lot (Fig. 7.18). With unintentional irony, this marvel of sculptural tectonics beckons fans to a campus that is far more famous for architecture and engineering than athletics. And with typically Houstonian faith in the efficacy of hydraulic engineering, the architects sank the field and lower seating decks into the Harris Gully, a small bayou. One of Texas's foremost construction companies, Brown and Root, built the stadium in just nine months, encouraged in the process, no doubt, by company founder George R. Brown, who was chair of the university's board of trustees. As an emblem of ingenuity and optimism in a state suspicious of expensive government programs, the stadium was the ideal setting for President Kennedy to proclaim in 1962:

↑ Figure 7.18
Lloyd and Morgan, with Milton McGinty, Rice Football Stadium, Houston, 1950

We meet at a college noted for knowledge, in a city noted for progress, in a state noted for strength, and we stand in need of all three, for we meet in an hour of change and challenge, in a decade of hope and fear, in an age of both knowledge and ignorance. The greater our knowledge increases, the greater our ignorance unfolds. . . .

[T]his city of Houston, this State of Texas, this country of the United States was not built by those who waited and rested and wished to look behind them. This country was conquered by those who moved forward—and so will space. . . .

But why, some say, the moon? . . . Why does Rice play Texas? . . .

We choose to go to the moon. We choose to go to the moon in this decade and do the other things, not because they are easy, but because they are hard, because that goal will serve to organize and measure the best of our energies and skills, because that challenge is one that we are willing to accept, one we are unwilling to postpone, and one which we intend to win, and the others, too.[10]

Kennedy's speech captured the ambition of the age, even as it acknowledged the perils of hubris that accompanied technological advances. Perfectly keyed to its time and place, his words matched the building and embodied the characteristic fusion of humanism and science in the thinking of many of the era's leading intellectuals.

Most Texans were introduced to sports in buildings considerably smaller and substantially less historically charged than Rice Stadium. Nevertheless, for many, memories of primary and secondary school physical education classes, and the spaces where they occurred, such as in the Gymnasium and Music Building at Flores Middle School in Uvalde (Noonan & Noonan, 1946), remain surprisingly vivid decades later (Fig. 7.19). Although they were a bit less high flying than the building at Rice, CRS's pair of gymnasia at Jefferson High School in Port Arthur (1959) demonstrated that public school athletic facilities could also be fit for the space age (Fig. 7.20). The relentlessly innovative firm created arcuated steel-framed roofs that arced gently up from massive corner footings. The curvature of the vaults contrasted elegantly with the horizontality of the site and adjoining classroom buildings. Formally, the buildings recall Eero Saarinen's Kresge

Part III: R&R and R&D

← Figure 7.19
Noonan and Noonan, Gymnasium and Music Building, Flores Middle School, Uvalde, 1946

↓ Figure 7.20
Caudill Rowlett Scott, Jefferson High School Gymnasium, Port Arthur, 1959

Sports & Leisure

Auditorium at MIT, of 1953–1955. The Jefferson gymnasia were completed just in time for Janis Joplin (Class of 1960) and Jimmy Johnson (Class of 1961) to exercise and play in them.

But without question, Texas's most important twentieth-century sports venue was the Astrodome (1965), by Lloyd, Morgan and Jones and Wilson, Morris, Crain & Anderson, for its place in the histories of sports venues and of civil rights in Houston (Figs. 7.21–7.23). Built to accommodate baseball and football, the Astrodome is a giant circular building set on a 260-acre paved parcel with parking for thirty thousand cars. The Astrodome was the world's first indoor, air-conditioned sports stadium and originally had seats for sixty-six thousand people and fifty-three skybox suites ringing the perimeter. Fans could follow the action from a four-story scoreboard beneath the dome that spans 642 feet and rises 218 feet and was the second largest in the world when it was built. The Astrodome (and Houston's climate indirectly)

↓ Figure 7.21
Lloyd, Morgan and Jones and Wilson, Morris, Crain & Anderson, Astrodome, Houston, 1965

↑ Figure 7.22
Lloyd, Morgan and Jones and Wilson, Morris, Crain & Anderson, Astrodome, Houston, 1965

↑ Figure 7.23
Lloyd, Morgan and Jones and Wilson, Morris, Crain & Anderson, Astrodome, Houston, 1965

also gave the world a new product, a special artificial turf invented because grass does not grow in the absence of sunlight. Astroturf debuted in 1966, on the floor of the Astrodome.

The Astrodome was the project of former Harris County Judge Roy Hofheinz, who sought to lure a major league baseball team to Houston, and who had helped advance integration in Houston when he was mayor from 1953 to 1955. To secure approval of the public bond monies that would be required to build the Astrodome, Hofheinz worked with African American civil rights leader Quentin Mease and Eldrewey Stearns, a law student at Texas Southern University, to build support for the project among African American voters. Mease insisted that any stadium built with his backing have integrated bathrooms, seating, and employment. From 1962 to 1964, as the Astrodome was being built, the Colt 45s, Houston's integrated baseball team, played in temporary quarters. Renamed the Astros in reference to the space program then rapidly expanding in Clear Lake, the team played their first game in the integrated Astrodome in April of 1965. As at other times during the integration process in Houston, the press did not report on the desegregationist aspects of the project, purposely not drawing attention to integration so that it might be realized peacefully.[11]

Between 1965 and 2002, games, contests, and spectacles of many kinds were held in the Astrodome. The building was the home field of the National Football League team the Houston Oilers until 1996. In 1973, Billie Jean King, then the top-ranked women's tennis player, beat Bobby Riggs, who had once been the top-ranked men's tennis player, in three straight sets in the Astrodome, and took home the $100,000 prize money. The Supremes, Elvis, Selena, and George Strait all sang there, and the Republican Party nominated George H. W. Bush to the presidency under the dome in 1992. In 2005, thousands of people who had fled New Orleans during Hurricane Katrina took shelter in the Astrodome, and Houstonians and New Orleanians began to forge the bond of mutual assistance in natural disasters that would be renewed when people from New Orleans returned to help Texans after Hurricane Harvey (2017).

Quasi-religious regimes of personal fitness took off only in later midcentury, unsurprisingly perhaps, as the suburbs and Whataburger grew in popularity. If one wanted to work out in Texas in 1970, she or he might frequent the Presidents-First Lady Health Spa Building in

→ Figure 7.24
Harold Oberg, Presidents-First Lady Health Spa Building, Houston, 1970

Houston (Fig. 7.24). Richard Minns opened his first spa in Houston in 1961 and imagined it as the Neiman-Marcus of the exercise world—a place designed for feeling rich, but not so exclusive as to alienate the middle class. He soon expanded his operations. Originally, men's and women's clubs were housed separately and built on the model of a hub and satellite system, with larger and more elegant facilities in downtowns and more modest ones in the suburbs. Alluding to the Greco-Roman tradition of athleticism, the clubs adopted the discus thrower and Venus as gendered symbols.[12] Modernized classicism also defined the spa Harold Oberg designed in Sharpstown in Houston in 1970. With its expressed trabeated frame, the building is rooted in the tradition of Italian rationalism and even somewhat resembles the Casa del Fascio, the Fascist Party headquarters that Giuseppe Terragni designed in Como, Italy, in 1932–1936. The similarities are likely unintentional. Yet understood in the context of a state where sports and marching bands readily fuse with expressions of local, state, and national sentiment, the spa building nevertheless calls to mind the long-standing, and sometimes troubling, historical links between athleticism, politics, and choreographed performances by fit bodies.[13] As the buildings in this chapter suggest, sports and leisure are sometimes, but not often, as politically and socially neutral as we often imagine.

8. On the Road

Previous Spread: A. E. "Amos" Wilemon,
Good Luck Oil Company (GLOCO) gas
station #5, Dallas, 1939

8. On the Road

Cadillac Ranch (1974) is neither a ranch nor a work of architecture in the strict sense. Now in its second location at the western edge of Amarillo, this line of ten decaying, graffiti-saturated Cadillacs, all positioned at 52-degree angles, hood-first, in a wheat field is the work of the art collective Antfarm (Fig. 8.1). Set against the long horizon of the High Plains, like ancient temples, the cars mediate between humans and nature and sharpen concentration on the landscape. While somewhat humorous, 120 years after the first Cadillac was manufactured, Cadillac Ranch reads as an incisive and unsettling commentary on car culture and the spaces it helped shape. At once a representation of a collective nosedive and an embodiment of decay, Cadillac Ranch almost painfully symbolizes the environmental ramifications of industrialization. Halfway between a billboard and a Neolithic ceremonial center, the work also evokes the entwining of ambition, disappointment, and tenuousness that characterize the experience of both travel and social status in the United States. The mythology of the open road in US culture needs no rehearsing. But as a capital of the oil industry, the state that gave the world "On the Road Again" and "Amarillo by Morning," and is (or was) home to American, Braniff, Continental, and Southwest Airlines, does have a special relationship to travel.

↓ Figure 8.1
Antfarm, *Cadillac Ranch*, Amarillo, 1974

Yet even as it reflected changing tastes and design innovations, a bit like buildings for sports and leisure, the architecture of travel in Texas, at least until the late 1960s, was closely bound with the dynamics of race, class, and gender. Segregation in transit, hotels, and restaurants complicated travel for people of color, and many readily embraced the automobile as a means to safely move through landscapes that were hostile to them. With the aid of *The Negro Motorist Green Book*, published from 1936 to 1967, Black Texans could find accommodations, eateries, garages, and entertainment venues that welcomed them.[1] While histories of segregation are often readily evident in the original plans of train stations with their separate waiting areas, they are often less evident in buildings designed for cars. At the same time, the architecture of lodging reveals the ways racialized romanticism sometimes intersected with tourism. As flying was popularized, architects and their clients strove to express the thrills of air travel with architectural language of popular glamour and luxury typified by Eero Saarinen's famous TWA terminal at Idlewild Airport in New York City (1962) and Broad & Nelson and Jack Corgan and Associates' terminal at Love Field in Dallas (1957).

Let's Get Rolling

The bus shelter that George L. Dahl designed outside of the Sears, Roebuck & Company store on North Shepherd in Houston is one of the few remaining examples of midcentury street furniture in Texas (Fig. 8.2). The pavilion's diagonal lines, rounded canopy, and stylized typeface link it to the fusion of jazzy and streamlined forms with advertising characteristic of commercial Art Deco architecture. Having overseen the design and planning of the 1936 Centennial Exposition, Dahl knew the language well. Less celebrated in his long and multifaceted career were the thirty-two Sears stores his office designed throughout the United States. The bus shelter recalls the pre–shopping mall era, when many people used public transit to go not only to downtown department stores but to destinations on significant commercial corridors outside of urban cores. The structure symbolically extended the realm of the store onto the sidewalk, helping shape a pedestrian corridor that was public even as it was enframed by the architecture of private capital. The bus shelter is a reminder of the ways that public and private interests sometimes worked in tandem in Texas cities to support urban living, and of a time before travel by bus became rigidly coded by class, as it is today nearly everywhere in the state.

8. On the Road

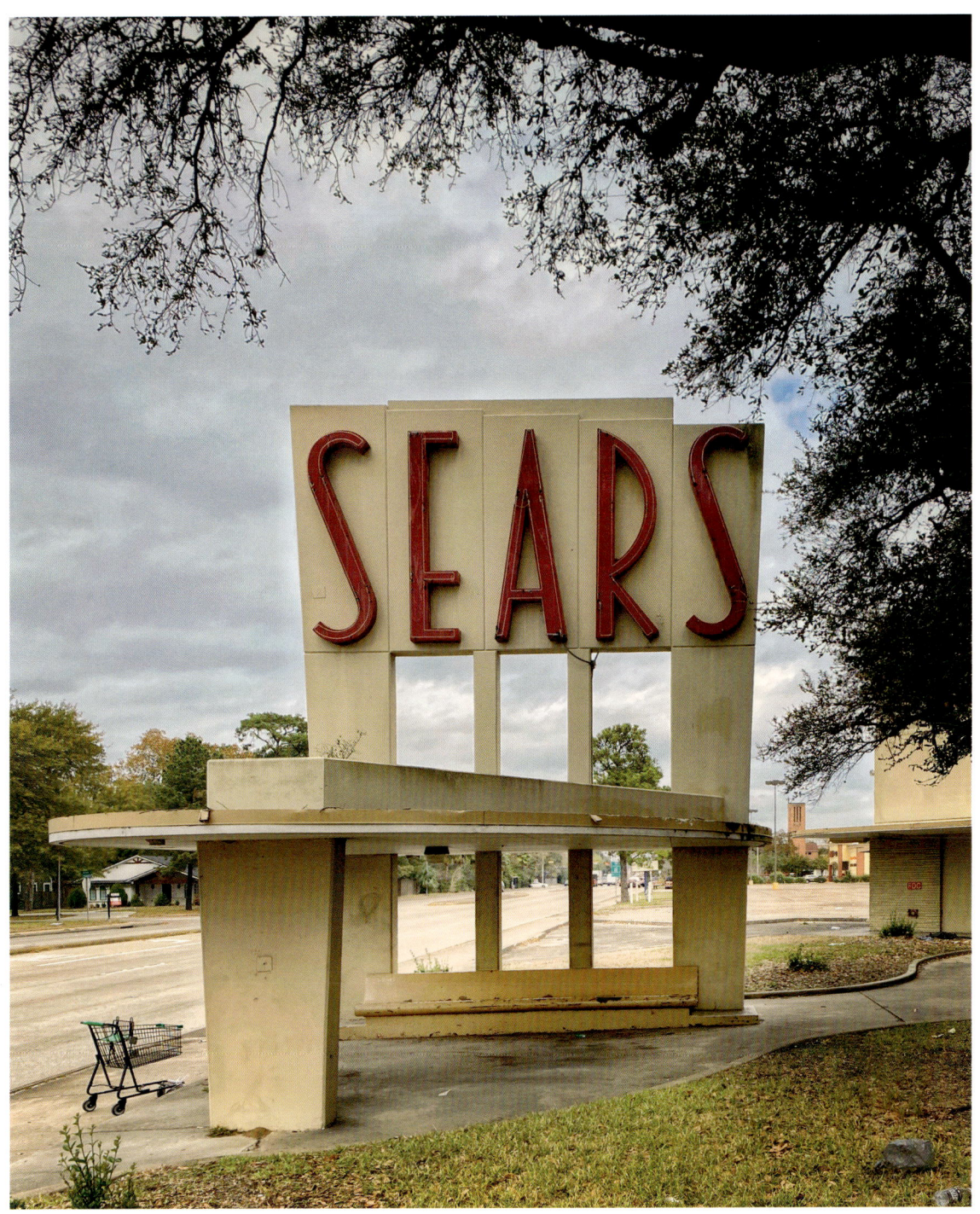

↑ Figure 8.2
George L. Dahl, Sears, Roebuck & Company Bus Shelter,
Houston, 1950

→ Figure 8.3
O'Neil Ford and Associates, Intercontinental Motors, San Antonio, 1963

In San Antonio, those who preferred to travel by car might have driven to Intercontinental Motors on Broadway (1963) by O'Neil Ford and Howard Wong to shop for a Volkswagen (Fig. 8.3). Set at the edge of Brackenridge Park amid live oaks in a landscape designed by Stewart King, the concrete-framed building has a transparent glass showroom and a solid brick service wing combined in a cruciform plan. Car dealerships and garages had crowded on and near Broadway closer to downtown since the 1920s. Many blocks north, Intercontinental Motors responded to the city's creeping northward growth at midcentury, sustained and motivated by the rise of the automobile. The glass pavilion that faces the street is a little prismatic folly, and in some respects was atypical of the work of its lead architect. The building's structural clarity and varied palette of materials and fixtures, including ceramic sconces designed by Beaumont and Martha Mood, were characteristic of Ford's work. But the expansive glazing, open plan, and small brick base of the showroom call to mind Ludwig Mies

Figure 8.4
Charles P. Donnelly and Morgan Spear, Lew Williams Chevrolet City Dealership, Corpus Christi, 1965

van der Rohe's buildings associated with industry, such as those at the Armour Institute (Illinois Institute of Technology) in Chicago and even Philip Johnson's Glass House in New Canaan (another jewel box set in nature), and reflected the requirements of an automobile dealership.

Texans who preferred Chevrolets to Volkswagens could have shopped at Lew Williams Chevrolet City dealership in Corpus Christi (1965) by Charles P. Donnelly and Morgan Spear. The showroom was but one part of a 13-acre campus that itself was an engineering marvel. Eight, 2-inch-thick concrete shell hyperbolic paraboloids formed the soaring roof of the main showroom, which was originally glazed and had a 185-foot clear span, one of the largest in the United States when it was built in 1965 (Fig. 8.4). A folded-plate-roofed service pavilion fanned out to the rear, and repair shops were housed in two long, low buildings similarly punctuated by the points of thin-shell plates. Other buildings included the offices where used car sales were handled, a gas pump shelter, and a car wash pavilion.

Part III: R&R and R&D

↑ Figure 8.5
Attributed to William R. Brown, Conoco Gas Station, Laredo, 1941

→ Figure 8.6
Attributed to William R. Brown, Conoco Gas Station, Corpus Christi, 1943. Canopy and sign added in 1954.

The dealership exuberantly embodied the vogue for thin-shelled concrete construction that swept North America in the late 1950s and early 1960s. Pioneered by Mexican architect Félix Candela in the early 1950s, thin-shelled concrete roof structures were embraced by a widely varied group of architects and clients for their technological prowess, visually daring qualities, and capacity to suggest excitement and futurity. Indeed, few architectural elements or techniques rivaled them in these decades in expressing the sense of dynamic optimism that characterized so many modern buildings in Texas. The form was ideally suited to a midcentury consumption-based economy that relied on enticement and efficiency simultaneously. The roofs at the Williams dealership were engineered by Wallace R. Wilkerson, who learned about Candela's methods while working in the office of Richard S. Colley. Colley and Ford had worked with Candela to create the roof at the Texas Instruments Semiconductor plant discussed in the next chapter.

Of course, until recently, all cars required gas. Texas has an impressive collection of early- and midcentury gas stations, many of which have been inventively transformed into barbeque joints, taquerías, bus stations, and, in at least one case, in San Antonio, a nationally recognized restaurant (Bliss, in the former Humble Oil & Refining Co. No. 48 service station on South Presa Street, its design based on a prototype by Houston architect John F. Staub). One of the most impressive is in Shamrock, east of Amarillo near the Oklahoma border. It is an outstanding 1936 Art Deco building originally leased by Conoco. Now known as the Tower Station and U-Drop Inn Café, it serves as a visitors' center, chamber of commerce, and community center all in one, and is a major landmark along Route 66. A bit less exuberant, but more accessible to much of the population is the old Good Luck Oil Company (GLOCO) gas station #5 in Dallas (1939; see page 242). Its rounded forms, pyramidal pylon, black tile, and sign make it a terrific example of the streamlined version of Art Deco that predominated in the United States in the 1930s and was so appropriate to the buildings and imagery of travel. The former Conoco gas stations in Laredo (1941; Fig. 8.5) and Corpus Christi (1943; Fig. 8.6), both attributed to William R. Brown, typify the company's 1940s buildings throughout the state, which stood in big cities and small towns, including Seguin, Beeville, Taylor, and Sulphur Springs.

Room at the Inn

Midcentury Texas had an impressive landscape of hotels and motels. Some of the most famous, such as the Shamrock Hotel in Houston or the Flagship Hotel in Galveston, have been destroyed, along with lesser-known works, including the Abilene Courts in Abilene (1930), but a few remain, either awaiting rehabilitation or still in use. Among these are the Stokes Motor Courts (subsequently the River Oaks Courts) in Medina (1939, Hough LeStourgeon, contractor) and the Admiral Auto Courts in Houston, designed by New Orleans-based architect H. T. Underwood in 1938 (Fig. 8.7). Among the most architecturally distinctive early lodgings where one can still find a bed are Indian Lodge in Davis Mountains State Park, near Fort Davis (1935), designed by William C. Caldwell and Arthur Fehr, and the El Capitan in Van Horn (1930; Fig. 8.8). The latter was the work of early twentieth-century El Paso's foremost architecture firm, Trost and Trost, and is a typological and stylistic cousin of Marfa's Hotel Paisano, also by the Trost firm. These 1930s buildings, like Indian Lodge, alluded broadly to the pueblo architecture of the US Southwest and reflected

↓ Figure 8.7
H. T. Underwood, Admiral Auto Courts, Houston, 1938

8. On the Road

↓ Figure 8.8
Trost and Trost, Hotel El Capitan, Van Horn, 1930

→ Figure 8.9
William C. Caldwell and Arthur Fehr, Indian Lodge, Fort Davis, 1935

their architects' distillation of Art Deco, as well as a characteristically 1930s impulse to create regionally distinctive buildings.

Indian Lodge is a particularly interesting case study (Fig. 8.9). Set in the Davis Mountains outside of Fort Davis, from a distance it almost calls to mind the famous Weissenhofsiedlung (Weissenhof Estate), the collection of modernist demonstration dwellings created by Europe's leading avant-garde artists in Stuttgart, Germany, in 1927. Somewhat like that project, which was built by the Deutsche Werkbund to propose new, economical approaches to mass housing during the era of the socially progressive Weimar government, Indian Lodge was built by the Civilian Conservation Corps, its site shaped by landscape architects at the National Park Service. Both projects were whitewashed, had flat roofs, and ran along hillsides. Unlike the

Weissenhofsiedlung, with its rounded corners and terraces, Indian Lodge was inspired by the Indigenous architecture of New Mexico. It belonged to a body of buildings and works created amid a surge of interest in the visual and architectural cultures of that state and typified (and advanced) by the restoration of the Palace of the Governors in Santa Fe in 1913. Originally constructed in 1610, that building is the oldest extant public building built for Europeans in what is now the United States. The 1913 renovation emphasized elements that came to be recognized as characteristic of Spanish colonial architecture in New Mexico, including wooden roof beams (*vigas*) and adobe walls.[2] The original wing of Indian Lodge, built from 1934 to 1935, was constructed of 40-pound adobe blocks formed onsite, as well as pine logs and river cane. Its formal abstraction, absence of historicist ornament, but strong association with place and history made Indian Lodge ideally suited to urban travelers with modernist sensibilities but eager (then as now) for the aura of authenticity.

To the twenty-first-century traveler, the lodge's name sounds anachronistic at best. The building is one of Texas's most significant New Deal–era works of architecture and a major West Texas landmark. But Indian Lodge embodies architecture's embedded historical prejudices, and the ways racist, exoticist, and sometimes sexist tropes were used to promote tourism and define regional identity during much of the twentieth century. Formally and rhetorically, Indian Lodge entwined leisure and colonialist adventure, as new roads and cars made travel in the West easier than ever. At the same time, a new and powerful national self-image centered on a white norm was coalescing through the combined works of artists, architects, and writers employed by the WPA to represent, imagine, and record US history and culture.[3]

The Tee Pee Motel in Wharton of 1947 typified romantic fascination with Indigenous culture on the part of white entrepreneurs, and was an example of the recovered, post–World War II market for roadside lodging (Fig. 8.10). The eleven reinforced concrete "tee pees" stood near Highway 59 and perhaps seemed particularly appropriate for those on road trips, given that real versions of the type were used in the North American Plains primarily by nomadic people, who valued them for their transportability. Actual teepees were built of buffalo skins draped over wooden supports. In a confusion of means, methods, and meanings characteristic of twentieth-century touristic

Figure 8.10
Designed by George and Toppie Belcher, Tee Pee Motel, Wharton, 1947

capitalism, the designer of the Tee Pee Motel used a material associated with Roman antiquity on the one hand and modern industry on the other to shape the structures. This choice enabled them to withstand hurricanes and disuse over decades. Wharton's Tee Pee Motel is a formal and conceptual cousin of the "Wigwam Villages" created in the 1930s and 1940s in Alabama, Arizona, California, Florida, Kentucky, and Louisiana, but was separate from that franchise.

By the 1950s, historicism and racially coded kitsch generally gave way to modernist forms, as hotels and motels expanded in size and increased the quantity of services they provided. One building that spanned the tendencies was the Fredonia Hotel in Nacogdoches (1955) by Dallas architect James N. McCammon and Miami architect Carlos B. Schoeppl (Fig. 8.11). Composed of a six-story slab, rotated

↑ Figure 8.11
James N. McCammon and Carlos B. Schoeppl, Fredonia Hotel, Nacogdoches, 1955

→ Figure 8.12
J. N. McCammon and Carlos B. Schoeppl with Merle A. Simpson, Echo Hotel, Edinburg, 1959

off the coordinates of the downtown street grid and extensively glazed on its long sides, set atop a one-story podium containing the lobby, which expands into a one-story "lanai" wing encircling a swimming pool, the Fredonia is unified visually by orange brick cladding. Delicate lacy iron grilles framing the slab's glass window walls locate the building in the trans-East Texas-Louisiana regional area by calling to mind the ironwork of nineteenth-century buildings in New Orleans. Such ornament became popular in residential buildings, particularly on porches, in Texas cities in the 1950s. Restrained neoclassical elements appear occasionally as exterior door frames, while more up-to-date abstract patterns appear in interior railings and grillwork.

McCammon and Schoeppl collaborated with Weslaco architect Merle A. Simpson on the design of Edinburg's Echo Hotel (1959), which was among the state's purpose-built convention hotels of the 1950s (Fig. 8.12). An acronym of the Edinburg Community Hotel Organization, the Echo was funded by a community-driven sale of shares in a locally organized stock corporation. Its more than one hundred rooms, along with 12,000 square feet of space for events and gatherings, including a large dining room and lounge, made it a major destination in the Lower Rio Grande Valley. With its angled porte-cochere projecting from the main slab; parking lot; swimming pool; and bold, eye-catching typeface (illuminated in green neon), the

→ Figure 8.13
Architect unidentified,
Siesta Motel, Laredo, 1960

Echo typified middle-market hotel design at midcentury. It remains an important modernist work in the region.

Farther upriver, travelers to Rio Grande City might have stayed at Bertha's Motel (1965), which captured the motorist's eye with its zig-zag awning and pair of signs—one vertical and the other horizontal—announcing the hotel and associated flower shop. Farther north still, in Laredo, was the Siesta Motel (1960), distinguished by its series of thin-shelled arcuated vaults, expressed upper-story beams, and brick sunscreens at ground level (Fig. 8.13). Even as they show the characteristic forms of hotel and motel architecture at midcentury, collectively, these borderlands lodgings recall the decades when travelers passed easily between Texas and Mexico, unencumbered by substantial bureaucratic and security burdens that define travel there today. Between these cities, in Port Aransas, was the Seahorse Inn (1956), designed by Jack Cobb, who was a protégé of O'Neil Ford. It was an informal, beachside, wood-and-brick building, with a dinner club called Club Miyako and a swimming pool. An only moderately well-kept secret, the Seahorse Inn was a beloved destination for fashionable nonconformists and was the site of legendary parties. Unusually for the time, it welcomed openly liberal and gay Texans.[4]

Three enormous Dallas hotels exemplify the growth of travel and the evolution of a national pattern in high-end hospitality architecture in which modernist forms came to be coded as luxurious and desirable. Dallas's Statler Hilton (1955) was impressive in all of the ways luxury hotels should be (Fig. 8.14). It was the first major hotel to open in the city in three decades and was built to host the largest conventions in the South. Originally, the hotel had one thousand rooms, distributed over eighteen floors on a Y-shaped plan. Helicopters could land on the roof, twenty-two hundred people could crowd into the ballroom, and every room had a 21-inch television, a novelty for the time. Its architect, William B. Tabler, created a vibrant composition that cleverly integrated the languages of glassy corporate international modernism with Wrightian ornament at the ground level, inset cruciform patterns in brick walls, and panels of glass and colored porcelain enamel-coated aluminum. Supported by thin cantilevered concrete slabs, the building had relatively few interior columns and thus expansive interior spaces. Rich finishes and fixtures continued the language of cool 1950s modernism on the inside and associatively extended the space of the hotel to an upper-level patio, where José de Rivera's sculpture *A Wishing Star*, an enormous abstract sculpture of stainless steel and gold plate whose form resembled the plan of the hotel, was installed. For better or worse, the Statler was the first hotel to use elevator music.

Less than a decade later, the ten-story Cabaña Motor Hotel (1963), by Miami architect Melvin Grossman, opened in Dallas. It had one of the state's finest concrete solar screens, which stretched across the entirety of the V-shaped main block. Built facing the

8. On the Road

→ Figure 8.14
William B. Tabler, Statler
Hilton Hotel, Dallas, 1955

Part III: R&R and R&D

↑ Figure 8.15
Welton Becket and Associates, Hyatt Regency Hotel and
Reunion Tower, Dallas, 1978

Stemmons Freeway, the Cabaña was approached via a divided driveway studded with fountains and reproduction classical statuary, including the Nike of Samothrace. Dramatic lighting further set a mood like that associated with palaces of popular glamour in Las Vegas and Miami Beach. Indeed, the Cabaña was part of the chain of hotels created by Las Vegas developer Jay Sarno, with investment financing supplied by actress Doris Day; her husband, Marty Melcher; and the Teamsters Union. Cabaña architect Melvin Grossman had trained under Morris Lapidus, who created some of South Florida's most astounding hotels. Shortly after he designed the Cabaña, Grossman reworked many of its signature elements in his even more famous hotel, Caesar's Palace, in Las Vegas (1966).[5]

Although their massing and languages differed significantly, the Hyatt Regency Dallas and Reunion Tower (1978), by Welton Becket and Associates (another firm known for shaping spaces of popular luxury, based in Los Angeles), shared with the Cabaña an almost obsessive emphasis on the building envelope (Fig. 8.15). Becket's office designed a composition of sheer planes, prisms, and semicircular towers for Ray Hunt, head of Woodbine Development Corporation. Surfaced in blue reflective glass, the building was a dazzling addition to the Dallas skyline and another shimmering mirrored jewel in the era-defining collection that ultimately included the Campbell Center and Fountain Place. The adjacent, late Space-Age concrete tower, with its tophouse enveloped in a wiry spherical web, energized the composition, as if having landed on the city like a great inverted exclamation point.

Friendly Skies

Between 1940 and 1954, people traveling to and from Houston by air passed through Joseph Finger's Houston Municipal Airport Terminal Building, which still stands within the grounds of Hobby Airport (Fig. 8.16). In that period, passenger numbers increased ten times as the city grew and travel boomed worldwide. Today, the building is a museum, and it remains one of the gems of Texas's collection of Art Deco buildings, with a tower-topped octagonal lobby flanked by setback wings. On the exterior, artist Dwight C. Holmes of San Angelo installed a series of small relief panels commemorating the history of flight. Figural art inspired by a building's program or institutional aims was typical in Art Deco architecture. Holmes's panels include an early airplane reminiscent of that of the Wright brothers, a modern

↓ Figure 8.16
Joseph Finger, Houston Municipal Airport Terminal Building, Houston, 1940

plane for carrying the mail, and a proto-helicopter. Mercury, the Roman god of flight, appears repeatedly, wearing a leather helmet, his loins covered by a propeller plane (rather than a fig leaf). The integration of works of art in important spaces in airports continued with the construction of Houston's new terminal at the site. For the entrance to this building, Elizabeth Drane Haynsworth, the head designer in Wyatt C. Hedrick's office, created mosaics; the US Air Force later adopted her color scheme for use on a large number of bases. In Dallas, Love Field was approached through a restrained Art Deco building, and in Galveston, the Gulf, Colorado, and Santa Fe Railway passenger station faces the Strand in a monumental Art Deco building (1932) by Chicago architect E. A. Harrison that skillfully incorporates an earlier building. As an architectural language that conveyed stylishness and modernity, Art Deco was ideally suited to buildings for travel.

By the 1960s, air travel was big business, not only predicated on speedy access to distant places but grounded in glamour and an experience of hospitality. To ensure that passengers received first-class service, wherever they sat, Dallas-based Braniff Airlines created a highly developed training program for flight attendants. While they learned to walk down the narrow aisle, pass magazines, and serve drinks, trainees lived together in the Braniff International Hostess College (1968) by the Pierce Lacey Partnership, a mid-rise, located 3 miles from Love Field (Fig. 8.17). In many respects, the building's exterior is an unremarkable example of International Style modernism. Inside, midcentury glamour reigned, from the interior decoration and furniture, especially in the lounge, with its central, sunken circular fireplace surrounded by couches, to the uniforms worn by trainees designed by Emilio Pucci, the celebrated Italian couturier famous for his bold colors and geometries. The building exemplified the association of stylish interior design, commercial air travel, and gender norms. It also reinforced the links between public (or semipublic) space and the narrow rules of appearance and demeanor expected of young middle-class women in the 1960s and required of Braniff's flight attendants. Modernist furniture, including chairs based on the designs of Eero Saarinen, and other decorative elements recalled other sexually coded interior spaces popularized as many as fifteen years earlier, such as the penthouse apartment *Playboy* magazine illustrated in 1953.[6] Both the cottage

↑ Figure 8.17
Pierce Lacey Partnership, Braniff International Hostess Cottage, Dallas, 1968

and the apartment used the forms, fixtures, and palette of popularized architectural modernism to support the norms of implicitly sexualized and subtly concealed consumerism. In the 1970s, women flight attendants unionized and began a long effort to fight gender discrimination within the industry.

Although women did not fly Braniff's planes, they did pilot aircraft for the US Air Force during World War II. Hangar 2, a 1929 industrial building at Avenger Field in Sweetwater, sheltered the planes in which over one thousand women trained as pilots. They went on to fly in noncombat missions throughout the United States and became known as Women Airforce Service Pilots, or WASPs, and were the first women military aviators in the nation's history. The hanger in Sweetwater is among the many buildings associated with the military in Texas. These range from industrial sheds to major works of architecture, such as the Administration Building at Randolph Field in San Antonio, a spectacular modern classical building of 1931 by Atlee B. Ayres and Robert M. Ayres. The city has been central to US air military training since the inception of the branch, originally within the army, in the 1910s.

Whether it was undertaken for business, pleasure, or the government, travel taught Texans about their state, its architecture, and each other. Buildings dedicated to discovery and knowledge similarly nurtured the spread of ideas, insights, and possibilities.

9. Knowledge & Power

Previous Spread: Shirley Simmons and Page Southerland Page, *Austin Daily Tribune* Building, Austin, 1941

9. Knowledge & Power

Power took many forms in twentieth-century Texas, and it was expressed in many building types, including some of the lavish private houses, gleaming skyscrapers, city halls, and houses of worship discussed in this book. But power is most interesting and productive when it emerges from and aims to extend discovery and knowledge. The buildings in this chapter are united by the ways they embody the entwining of knowledge and power for broad, collective aims. They are notable for their explicit and implicit formal and conceptual connections to nature and landscape. Modern architecture's characteristic optimism and forward-lookingness was particularly well suited to such projects. Collectively, these buildings embody the confidence that defined modern Texas, even as some of them subtly communicated apprehension about the explosive growth of science, industry, and technology, especially when these things were conjoined with Cold War policies and politics.

Temples of Industry

Semiconductors are essential components in many electronic machines used in everyday life and in high-powered military and scientific endeavors. In the 1950s, one of the world centers of semiconductor production was on the northeast edge of Dallas, in a building designed for Texas Instruments by O'Neil Ford, Richard Colley, Arch Swank, and Sam Zisman (1958; Fig. 9.1). At the time, TI's chief product was transistors, and the corporation was rapidly becoming a top defense-industry supplier of electronics and radar systems. It was also developing the world's first handheld calculator.[1] Composed of three floors, the Semiconductor Building accommodated busy engineers in offices and laboratories on the first floor, manufacturing activity on the third, and on a dramatic interstitial level between them, a dense network of 9-foot precast concrete tetrapods that formed a giant truss. This interstitial floor contained all of the building's systems, including air-conditioning and a complex network of pipes and ducts that could deliver, through fifteen hundred access points in the manufacturing floor above, natural gas, water, electricity, pressurized air, and rare gases used in manufacturing. The organization of the building, and particularly the interstitial floor, prioritized flexibility and was designed to accommodate spatial reconfigurations on relatively short notice as new technologies with new spatial requirements were invented.

    The roof of the building is constituted by thirty-seven thin-shelled concrete hyperbolic paraboloids, each of which spans 63 feet,

→ Figure 9.1
O'Neil Ford, Richard Colley, Arch Swank, and Sam Zisman, Texas Instruments Semiconductor Building, Dallas, 1958

designed by Félix Candela. From the outside, and particularly from a distance, the Semiconductor Building's hyperbolic parabaloids read less like cutting-edge works of engineering and more as low-pitched open gabled roofs arranged like an exceptionally dense new residential ranch house subdivision, or even the barracks of a military installation. With its widely spaced, ground-level concrete columns supporting solidly walled bays, the west façade conveys a sense of the building's underlying structural logic. The clearly articulated bays of the upper floor suggest the building's interior organization, as repeated forms evoke the idea of parts, assembly lines, and the repetition of industrial production. The upper portions of the bays are clad with panels of pearl-gray Georgia marble attached to the backup wall with X-shaped bronze clamps. These clamps formally reiterate the profile of the gabled bays and diagonal chords of the interior tetrapods, while clearly articulating the function of the marble as cladding. The marble provides chromatic and textural contrast with the narrow, vertically scored panels of stainless steel that face the rest of the upper-floor zone. While the tripartite disposition of the façade, the pediment-like form of the roof, and the application of marble make an appellation like "temple of industry" a tempting descriptor, the Semiconductor Building's intellectual and formal ancestors were not only Peter Behrens's temple-like AEG Turbine factory in Berlin (1910)—and any number of nineteenth-century factories with spindly cast-iron columns—but also Otto Wagner's Post Office Savings Bank in Vienna (1904–1906). Wagner's tempered classicism and bolted-on cladding similarly expressed simultaneous admiration for and reservations about modern industry, and a like impulse to civilize it with art. Candela's hyperbolic paraboloid roof structure and tetrapod space frame, like Wagner's great banking hall, proclaim faith in a high-tech future, while Ford, Colley, Swank and Zisman's materially layered façade, mosaics in the courtyards of the building by Tom Stell, and the landscape designed by Marie and Arthur Berger assert the enduring importance of nature and humanism in the face of rapid change.

The comingling of commerce, industry, and innovative architecture that the Semiconductor Building embodied was manifest in a smaller building for a very different purpose hundreds of miles south of Dallas in Rancho Viejo in the Lower Rio Grande Valley, one of the nation's capitals of citrus production. Here Harlingen architects Alan Y. Taniguchi and Charles B. Croft designed the House of Mo-Rose packing shed for the processing, packaging, and distribution of Ruby Red grapefruit (1962; Fig. 9.2). The architects arranged ten hyperbolic paraboloid umbrellas in two rows of five each. Light entered the plant through a gabled skylight that spanned the space between the umbrella edges, whose exterior edges soared far beyond the enclosure below.

Taniguchi was one of South Texas's leading architects in the 1950s and, after 1961, one of the state's most important architectural academics, serving as dean of architecture at the University of Texas from 1968 to 1972 and director of Rice University's architecture school from 1972 until 1974. As a partner in the Austin-based practice of Taniguchi Shefelman Vackar Minter, he helped shape projects throughout the state, including the master plan for Town Lake in Austin, with landscape architect Stewart King and planner Sam Zisman. Yet, as a Japanese American, in his life and career he confronted the warped dynamics of race and power that defined life for many in the twentieth century. The federal government

↑ Figure 9.2
Alan Y. Taniguchi and Charles B. Croft, House of Mo-Rose packing shed, Rancho Viejo, 1962

interned Taniguchi and his parents in camps in Crystal City, Texas, and in Arizona. After his parents were released, they settled south of Harlingen to farm, a decision that paved the way for their son's eventual move to Texas. Among Taniguchi's buildings were houses in Harlingen's elite Laurel Park subdivision, where deed restrictions prohibited sales to "any person or any descendant of any person of the following nationalities or races, to wit: Negro, Mexican, Chinese, Japanese."

The Fourth Estate Democracy depends on checking power, and in the United States no entity performs this duty more consistently and forcefully than the press. In the decades during which the Vietnam War and the Watergate scandal fundamentally reconfigured the relationships of people to government, the importance of journalism, with its special power to uncover facts and spread knowledge, came into sharp relief. Two Texas buildings exemplify the dramatic changes to both architecture and the delivery of news over the course of the twentieth century.

The eleven-story office building designed by Tyler architect Shirley Simmons with Page Southerland Page (1941) to house the *Austin Daily Tribune*, published from 1939 to 1942, is an assured statement of late Art Deco façade composition and siting (Fig. 9.3). The building stands on the corner opposite the Governor's Mansion, as if in permanent confrontation (or collusion) with the state's executive branch. Soaring rhetoric, inscribed in granite on the east façade of the building's base, further sets the stage for high-flying journalism:

> *A free press is the protagonist and preserve of all rights ... The foe and destroyer of all tyrannies. It insures every good cause a hearing and every false doctrine a challenge. It is the servant of religion, philosophy, science, and art ... The agent of truth, justice and civilization, possessing it no people can be held in intellectual or political bondage ... Without it none can be secure against any form of enslavement. ... The Austin Daily Tribune is independent dedicated to the service of a free people.*

→ Figure 9.3
Shirley Simmons and Page Southerland Page, Austin Daily Tribune Building, Austin, 1941

The design is marked by a vigorous but disciplined rhythm carried in the differing window patterns, Simmons's use of shallow planar setbacks and curvature, and his distribution of cladding materials: polished Morton gneiss, smooth cream and textured and fossilized limestone, and buff brick. Like the Texas Instruments Semiconductor Building and the House of Mo-Rose, the Tribune building was intended for production and marked by innovation: the printing presses were seated on a separate foundation so that they would not cause offices in the building to vibrate as they rolled out newspapers. Whatever the paper's claims to independence, and as if anticipating the twenty-first-century convergence of media and politics, the *Austin Daily Tribune* was tightly bound to the political aims and fortunes of its publisher, Houston lumberman, cattle rancher, oilman, and landowner James M. West. West opposed the New Deal and was a vocal supporter of populist governor W. Lee "Pappy" O'Daniel, whose own political career was based on his celebrity as a folksy radio host.

→ Figure 9.4
Paul Rudolph, with Frank Reese Associates; Alice O'Brien, interior design, One Broadcast Center, Amarillo, 1984

O'Daniel narrowly defeated Lyndon Johnson in a highly controversial special election for the US Senate in 1941. The *Austin Daily Tribune* ceased publication after West's death in 1941. Acquired by the state of Texas, the building is now named for one of O'Daniel's adversaries, longtime Texas Railroad Commission chair Ernest O. Thompson.

Four decades later, and 500 miles away in the Panhandle, late in his career Paul Rudolph designed One Broadcast Center (1984) with Frank Reese and Associates and with interior design by Alice O'Brien for Amarillo's ABC affiliate KVII-TV and its owner, Stanley Marsh 3 (Fig. 9.4). As at the Mo-Rose and Texas Instruments buildings, the dynamism of this design is a consequence of its roof structure, in this case a huge steel-framed, broad pyramid surfaced with glass that extends well beyond the perimeter of the building's enclosed space. The roof is a clever work of symbolism that exists on the knife's edge of high modernist technophilism and pithy postmodernist irony. Gleaming in the intense High Plains sun, with its web of wires and steel, it absorbs the sun's energy even as it beams its own in the form of television signals to audiences in New Mexico, Texas, and Oklahoma.

Marble and Monoliths

The presidential library is a curious building type. At once an archive, museum, and memorial, it is inherently political, even as it monumentalizes its subject's passage into history and the president's admission to the usually bipartisan and inevitably tiny club of former chief executives. The type was codified by an act of Congress, the Presidential Libraries Act of 1955, which empowered the National Archives and Records Administration to accept gifts of presidential records and make them accessible to researchers.

In keeping with so much that defined Lyndon Baines Johnson and his public life, the Lyndon Baines Johnson Presidential Library and Museum on the campus of the University of Texas at Austin (1971), designed by the New York office of Skidmore, Owings and Merrill and Brooks, Barr, Graeber and White, is vast in size and scale (Fig. 9.5). Numbers help convey its enormity. The complex stands on a 30-acre site that includes Sid Richardson Hall, a three-story, 900-foot-long slab housing the Lyndon B. Johnson School of Public Affairs, the Dolph Briscoe Center for American History, the Nettie Lee Benson Latin American Collection, and the Teresa Lozano Long Institute of Latin American Studies. Richardson Hall and the LBJ Library are set atop an immense podium elevated above the undulating (and completely engineered) landscape. The library is, as Skidmore, Owings and Merrill's designer Gordon Bunshaft intended, monumental. Its long, tapered east and west walls, clad in creamy travertine, are 100 feet tall. The principal interior volume of the library is 65 feet tall and 90 feet wide. Concealed in the podium are a one-thousand-seat auditorium, a lecture hall, and galleries.

→ Figure 9.5
Skidmore, Owings and Merrill and Brooks, Barr, Graeber and White, Lyndon Baines Johnson Presidential Library and Museum, Austin, 1971

The most important interior space is the Great Hall, which rises 55 feet and is capped by paired concrete girders that span the width of the hall. Visitors ascending the grand staircase come face-to-face with President Johnson repeatedly in Naomi Savage's photoengraved magnesium mural, *The Wall of Portraits* (1971), which depicts the president at various stages of his career, alongside presidents Franklin Roosevelt, Truman, Kennedy, and Eisenhower. They then look up to see a five-story wall, in which thirty-six rectangular openings reveal shelves containing 4,200 red buckram boxes, each with a gold presidential seal, that contain a small fraction of the 31 million presidential papers housed at the library. Incised on the opposite wall, and rising about four stories, is perhaps the largest presidential seal in the country. The LBJ Library recalls Bunshaft's Beinecke Rare Book Library at Yale University (1963), but his arrangement of red boxes behind a window wall that echoes the pattern of the roof structure is a brilliant piece of modernist showmanship. Here, ornament, structure, and purpose fuse spectacularly, addressing simultaneously the client's obsession with his place in history, visitors' desire for awesome and even sensuous contact with it, and modern architectural theory's long-standing love-hate relationship with historicity and decoration. The LBJ Library is surely the world's most glamorous archive.

As an amalgamation of formal associations with corporate office buildings, mausoleums, and palaces, the building was caught in a tangle of contemporary contradictions as it enshrined history. Bunshaft's attempts at modern monumentality laid bare fundamental tensions between concealment and revelation; public and private; death and life. As if to materialize the conceptual riddle of "confidential" and "classified" "public" documents in a democracy against the hard barriers of glass walls and concrete frames, the textural little red boxes tantalize as containers of secret information. Construction of this monument to one person was funded almost entirely by the people. The complex stands on property that the University of Texas acquired by exercising its right of eminent domain as part of the City of Austin's East University Urban Renewal slum clearance program in 1968, displacing impoverished families that Johnson's Great Society policies were meant to help. The library contains a 7/8-scale version of the Oval Office, open to visitors except when the former president declared it closed and went to work in it as if he were still in power. Observers compared this architecture for a larger-than-life personality to ancient funerary structures, with *New York Times* critic Ada Louise Huxtable noting that "even the descent to the men's room is like entering an Egyptian tomb."[2] The original exhibitions, the most significant of which were curated by Arthur Drexler of the Museum of Modern Art in New York, hardly mentioned the Vietnam War, but from 1964 through 1971, the years between Lyndon Johnson's taking of office and the opening of the library, 57,123 US soldiers were killed in that war, and many more Vietnamese.[3]

The building's somber crown contains librarians' offices, a reading room, Lady Bird Johnson's office, and the Oval Office replica, and serves as a landing pad for helicopters. Cantilevered rather ponderously, it joined the Austin skyline's other monuments where knowledge and power entwined, often discomfitingly: the dome of the capitol; the newly enlarged stands of the now 100,119-seat Darrell K. Royal-Texas Memorial Stadium; and the tower—the site of the nation's first mass shooting in 1966—that rises from the university's Main Building, which is inscribed with the biblical words "Ye shall know the truth, and the truth shall make you free."

Before Lyndon Johnson was elected to public office, he taught school to adolescents in Cotulla. Fifteen years before the presidential library opened, and less than 2 miles to the south, the Delta Kappa Gamma Society, a professional society for women teachers, moved into its new international headquarters building, designed by Kuehne, Brooks and Barr, in 1956 (Fig. 9.6). The organization was founded in 1929 by Annie Webb Blanton, a professor of rural education at the University of Texas, to support white women educators through advocacy, networking opportunities, and scholarships and prizes that helped mitigate the discrepancies in their salaries relative to those of men. Their new building, in the design of which Society members took active roles, was an understated and elegant interpretation of the 1920s architecture of Ludwig Mies van der Rohe, whose principles Bunshaft and his colleagues at Skidmore, Owings and Merrill propagated widely at midcentury.

With its flat, overhanging roof, intersecting planes, projecting canopy, floor-to-ceiling glazed entrance bay, and rich and varied palette of materials, the Delta Kappa Gamma building recalled aspects of Mies's famous German Pavilion at the Barcelona International Exhibition of 1929. The Austin building's pronouncedly veined, vibrant orangey-pink polished Rojo Coralito marble particularly evoked the luxurious green Moroccan onyx partition in the Barcelona Pavilion, while

↑ Figure 9.6
Kuehne, Brooks and Barr,
Delta Kappa Gamma
Society, Austin, 1956

its brick screen walls recall Mies's designs for brick country houses. The partners in Kuehne, Brooks and Barr represented different professional generations, and the Delta Kappa Gamma building typified their modernist work, which included the Department of Public Safety Building in Austin and the J. J. Pickle Federal Building. Such buildings helped reorient Texas architecture away from Beaux-Arts principles and toward those of international modernism. The firm's founder, Hugo F. Kuehne, began the architecture program at the University of Texas in 1910 and was an accomplished, eclectic architect.

The original furnishings and decoration in the Delta Kappa Gamma building were more Eisenhowerian than avant-garde, but having researched comparable buildings and anticipating future change, Society members embraced a flexible interior scheme that followed the ideals of the modernist free plan and supported adaptation. In this respect, the building fit well with the forward-looking ambitions of the group. Blanton was only the third woman promoted to full professor at UT (in 1933), and she was the first woman elected to state office (as State Superintendent of Public Instruction in 1918).[4] Between 1929 and 1960, Delta Kappa Gamma opened chapters in every state, and several in Canada, and became the nation's foremost professional society for women educators. Although it had been founded as a whites-only institution, the Society began to integrate in 1946. As little baby boomers filled new schools, the women of Delta Kappa Gamma, having organized themselves to combat sexism in the workplace a generation earlier, relied on one another to navigate rapidly changing conditions.

Concerning Totality

In the West, at least since the Enlightenment, knowledge of the natural world—from the microscopic to the telescopic—has been bound intimately to the impulse to control. The first steps in transforming nature into power are collecting, recording, and categorizing, concerns that shaped several of the buildings in this chapter and link them to others in the book's next section. This final section of Part III begins and ends with buildings dedicated to studying the world beyond earth, and includes one of the most architecturally astounding buildings built to collect and display what grows on it. All three are notable for the ways that research and information gathering comingle with aims to educate and inspire a wide public.

Any claims modern architects and their apologists made regarding the universality of abstract forms and functional requirements read as historically particular hyperbole when viewed against the timeless human instinct to look at the stars. Astronomy does not require architecture, but even in Texas, big, bright stars are more impressive when they are seen through telescopes. Far from the lights of big cities, Mount Locke, rising 6,780 feet in the Davis Mountains near Fort Davis, provides a superb location for stargazing. It was here that the University of Texas built the McDonald Observatory in 1939 (Fig. 9.7). Funded by a bequest from the Paris, Texas, banker William Johnson McDonald, the observatory housed an 82-inch telescope, which was built on site and was the second largest in the world until 1948. In an instance of patronage and architecture leading curriculum development, because UT did not have an astronomy department at the time of the gift, the university entered into a cooperative agreement with the University of Chicago to operate the observatory for the first thirty years.

9. Knowledge & Power

↓ Figure 9.7
Warner & Swasey Company, McDonald Observatory,
Fort Davis, 1939

283

→ Figure 9.8
Emilio Ambasz and Jones and Kell; James E. Keeter and George G. Cook, landscape architects, Lucille Halsell Conservatory, San Antonio Botanical Garden, San Antonio, 1988

The chief purpose of an observatory is to house a telescope. The first observatories that were visibly like modern ones were built in Maragheh (1259) and Samarkand (1424) and supported the research of the Islamic astronomers who built on the discoveries of their Greek and Roman predecessors and paved the way for further work by Europeans starting in the Renaissance. The building at the McDonald Observatory that houses the Otto Struve telescope has a formal simplicity and elegance that link it to the history of observatory architecture and place it firmly in the 1930s. Designed and built by the Warner & Swasey Company of Cleveland, a machine tool and instrument maker that specialized in astronomical observatories, the McDonald Observatory is circular in plan and consists of a three-story cylindrical drum that supports a faceted dome 73 feet in diameter that can be rotated to enable astronomers to point the telescope in any direction. Restrained stringcourses and an observation deck encircle the drum, accentuating its curvature. In plan, the Texas building resembles those at Maragheh and Samarkand, and belongs firmly among other twentieth-century observatories, which collectively reinstated the circle as the dominant form in observatory design.[5]

Like the observatory, the botanical garden is an ancient type that was reinvigorated during the Renaissance. Patrons and landscape gardeners reimagined it repeatedly to satisfy the demands of inquiry and the desire for awe, in the process freighting it with metaphor and romanticism. The Lucille Halsell Conservatory (1988), by New York architect Emilio Ambasz and Jones & Kell, is the centerpiece of the San Antonio Botanical Garden. It is dedicated to collecting, nurturing, and identifying plants, and to educating people about them (Fig. 9.8). Visitors come both to concentrate and to stop concentrating: to study and discover and to reset cognitive and emotional rhythms by surrounding themselves with horticulture. The Halsell Conservatory was the first major work realized by Argentina-born architect Emilio Ambasz, who went on to become known internationally for extremely high-budget, highly architectonic projects that, like the Texas building, meld architecture and landscape intensely. Six years before he began to design the conservatory, Ambasz curated an exhibition at the Museum of Modern Art in New York on Mexican architect Luis Barragán that helped catapult Barragán to international fame. Like his younger apologist, Barragán was as concerned with gardens as he was with the spectacular effects that could be achieved by playing with the dynamics of revelation and concealment.[6]

The Halsell Conservatory is animated by oppositions and tensions that intentionally or not evoke the dualisms inherent in the modern conservatory as a type that is at once precious and tendentious and that embodies the supreme elision of artifice and nature. Organized around a trapezoidal courtyard, in plan the conservatory is axial and asymmetrical. It is at once submerged and occluded by the grassy berms into which it is built, but then opens to the sky. The prismatic semiconical and pyramidal plant houses with their dramatic space frames link the Halsell Conservatory to famous glazed, iron-framed horticultural spaces, such as the Palm House at Kew Gardens in London (1848), and to the strand of early twentieth-century modernism informed by architects' obsessions with "pure form" and

→ Figure 9.9
Emilio Ambasz and Jones and Kell, Palm and Cycad Pavilion, Lucille Halsell Conservatory, San Antonio Botanical Garden, San Antonio, 1988

elemental geometric volumes typified by the work of Le Corbusier in the 1920s (Fig. 9.9). Depending on where viewers stand when they look at them, the roofs of the plant houses read as glass lawn sculptures or as the skylights of an underground building. They are counterbalanced by the massive forms of the great concrete colonnade that frames the courtyard and, aided by the visual presence of the giant palm house at the far end, reinforces the sense of spatial hierarchy and directionality of the plan.

Ambasz reinscribed mass (and complicated obvious circulation patterns and historical associations) with inclined concrete walls that frame stairs that meet the courtyard diagonally at one end. These evoke ancient Mesoamerican ceremonial spaces, an effect intensified by the short rise and broad tread of each step, which forces one to walk slowly. The conservatory's main entrance is through a massive concave wall of randomly coursed, dry-stacked limestone. The portal offers no clue about the sequence of spaces and forms beyond. It was originally approached by descending a short semicircular staircase; the absence of this element is an aesthetic loss, but one welcomed by those with limited mobility. As an embodiment of the conceptual underpinnings of the modern botanical garden—the ambition to transform botany into spectacle and blur the boundary between classification and connoisseurship—the Halsell Conservatory and the San Antonio Botanical Garden are among Texas's most engaging set pieces.

The National Aeronautics and Space Administration's Manned Space Center (MSC; now the Lyndon B. Johnson Space Center) was rapidly built beginning in 1962 to help realize President Kennedy's charge to land people on the moon by decade's end. It sprawls over a 1,600-acre campus near Clear Lake (Fig. 9.10). In the 1963 fiscal year, the US government dedicated $12.3 billion to research and development, more, *Architectural Record* noted, than it spent on those activities in all of the years between the American Revolution through World War II.[7] Although the MSC was included in this largesse, its formal austerity and uniformity, along with the identification of buildings by numbers rather than names, make it instantly legible in hindsight as a paradigmatic Cold War government project for science and defense.

As if organized to convey the immensity of the undertaking that it sheltered, the MSC campus was built on a huge scale and consists of twenty-eight rectangular, steel-framed box-like buildings of different heights and uses that are faced with precast concrete panels and aluminum-framed curtain walls. Many of these are set far apart and amid large lawns, and they are linked by roads that employees navigated on bicycles and cars, which could be parked in immense surface lots in a landscape designed by Robert F. White, who also advised Lady Bird Johnson on her beautification program and reshaped the landscape of Rice University (Fig. 9.11). As a collaboration between the US Army Corps of Engineers and a consortium of Texas architects working under the direction of Brown & Root, a Houston-based engineering firm, the campus adhered to strict design standards and a tight budget. The result was a complex of pronounced chromatic and formal uniformity. From the outside, the MSC reads as an archetypal

→ Figure 9.10
US Army Corps of Engineers; Brown and Root and Manned Spacecraft Center Architects Charles Luckman Associates, Brooks and Barr, MacKie and Kamrath, Harvin C. Moore, and Wirtz, Calhoun, Tungate and Jackson; Robert F. White, landscape architect, Johnson Space Center, Houston, 1962–1968. Campus plan, 1962. Drawing by Reanna Henson.

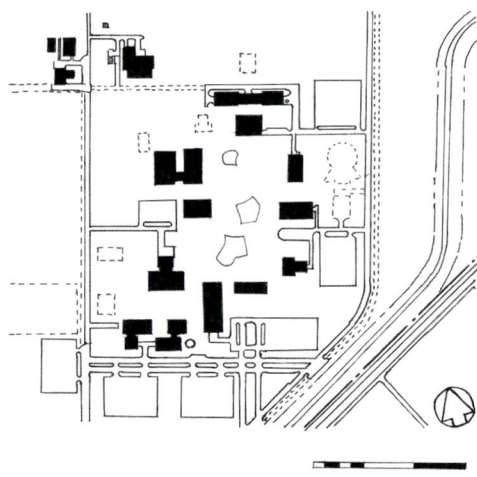

→ Figure 9.11
US Army Corps of Engineers; Brown and Root and Manned Spacecraft Center Architects Charles Luckman Associates, Brooks and Barr, MacKie and Kamrath, Harvin C. Moore, and Wirtz, Calhoun, Tungate and Jackson; Robert F. White, landscape architect, Building 1, Project Management, Johnson Space Center, Houston, 1964

9. Knowledge & Power

↑ Figure 9.12
US Army Corps of Engineers; Brown and Root and Manned Spacecraft Center Architects Charles Luckman Associates, Brooks and Barr, MacKie and Kamrath, Harvin C. Moore, and Wirtz, Calhoun, Tungate and Jackson; Robert F. White, landscape architect, Building 24, Central Plant, Johnson Space Center, Houston, 1964

→ Figure 9.13
US Army Corps of Engineers; Brown and Root and Manned Spacecraft Center Architects Charles Luckman Associates, Brooks and Barr, MacKie and Kamrath, Harvin C. Moore, and Wirtz, Calhoun, Tungate and Jackson, Building 13, Structure and Mechanics Laboratory, Johnson Space Center, Clear Lake, 1964

Part III: R&R and R&D

↓ Figure 9.14
US Army Corps of Engineers; Brown and Root and Manned Spacecraft Center Architects Charles Luckman Associates, Brooks and Barr, MacKie and Kamrath, Harvin C. Moore, and Wirtz, Calhoun, Tungate and Jackson, Building 1, Project Management, detail of doors, Johnson Space Center, Houston, 1964

work of the utilitarianist strand of modernism—built according to rationalist planning and design principles that express the economic limits and political urgency of its quintessentially twentieth-century program (Fig. 9.12). But even while working within their tight budgets, the architects sometimes managed to include details that enliven interiors and make the buildings engaging relics of a past era. In Building 13, the Structure and Mechanics Laboratory, for example, orange and turquoise panels frame the upper level of the lobby, with its floating, curving staircase (Fig. 9.13). Building 1, the Project Management Building, resembles an office building that could be almost anywhere in the world, but its circular door handles are imprinted with the NASA logo, an image that even today can conjure excitement, wonder, and nostalgia in those who remember the Space Age (Fig. 9.14).

Designed to accommodate many kinds of research, training, and testing, the MSC included buildings that were both adaptable and highly specialized. Within some, for example, tests were conducted that required that there be absolutely no vibrations, while in others, engineers studied the effects on people and instruments of vigorous jostling and gyrating. Some buildings functioned as monumental workshops; others housed research on the physiological and psychological effects of leaving Earth. Yet the buildings' gray-brown exteriors betrayed none of this variety, nor did they communicate the marvelously innovative character of the activities that went on inside.

That the Manned Space Center's buildings' exteriors are visually drab and rather uninspiring as architectural works is ironic given that there is surely nothing more thrilling and profound than seeing Earth from space. But there is poignancy in the complex's apparent ordinariness. Even as it was entwined with the mid-twentieth-century arms race and the explosive growth of the military-industrial complex, the MSC was also an unintentional monument to the power of human ingenuity and magisterial confidence and reward experienced within and by a society that educates widely and liberally. In the MSC's mundane-looking buildings, over the course of countless hours, ordinary men and women, consumed with all manner of minutia, solved problems their parents could not have imagined, as they figured out how to land people on the moon and bring them back safely. At the end of the day, many of these ordinary people drove in ordinary cars to ordinary houses in the Houston suburbs, from the lawns of which—Gulf Coast clouds permitting—it was still possible to see the stars.

PART IV ASSEMBLAGE

10.	Precious Objects	295
11.	Hearts & Minds	315
12.	Contact Zones	335

10. Precious Objects

Previous Spread: Renzo Piano and
Richard Fitzgerald, The Menil Collection,
Houston, 1987

10. Precious Objects

Amid the visual cacophony that defines so many landscapes in Texas, it is sometimes possible to discern patterns and occasionally a semblance of planning. Intentional architectural coordination is most legible in campuses such as the Manned Spacecraft Center and in purpose-built schemes for universities and civic institutions. It is also evident in many intact suburban real estate developments. Attempts to assemble, order, and unify distinct objects have defined Western modernity since the emergence of modern science in the seventeenth century, efforts that reflect Enlightenment impulses to understand and control.

The architecture of assemblage encompasses planned groups of buildings, campuses, and museums—characteristically modern forms and institutions upon which patrons have traditionally lavished substantial resources and used as highly visible symbols of personal, state, or institutional authority. The emergence of modern architectural assemblages in Texas increased in the postwar period. At roughly the same time, the designation of historic districts grew; efforts to rehabilitate swaths of deteriorating urban fabric began (as exemplified by Denise Scott Brown's *Action Plan for the Strand* in Galveston of 1975); and museum curators set about installing works that typified assemblage as a technique of art-making.

Since the 1820s, when Karl Friedrich Schinkel designed the Altes Museum in Berlin, the museum has been a typological locus for architectural innovation and bravado. Like well-designed districts and campuses, museums can help define neighborhoods and even cities, and in the best instances, they are rich in ideas as well as works. In the twentieth century, as the museum became perhaps the preeminent institutional type for architectural experimentation, architecture occasionally eclipsed the art inside, as at Frank Lloyd Wright's Solomon R. Guggenheim Museum in New York (1959) or Lina Bo Bardi's São Paulo Museum of Art in São Paulo, Brazil (1968), to name just two famous examples.

Texas is rich in museums. Among them are outstanding examples of adaptive reuse and conservation, as at San Antonio's McNay Museum of Art, which began life as a Spanish Colonial Revival–style country house built in 1929, and the San Antonio Museum of Art, housed since 1981 in the former Lone Star Brewing Company complex of 1904[1] (Fig. 10.1). Purpose-designed museums by major architects include the Art Museum of South Texas in Corpus Christi

Figure 10.1
Ford, Powell and Carson, McNay Museum of Art, Brown Sculpture Pavilion, San Antonio, 1972

(1972) by Johnson/Burgee, with an addition by Ricardo Legorreta (Fig. 10.2), the Amarillo Art Center (1972) by Edward Durell Stone & Associates, the Contemporary Arts Museum in Houston (1972) by Gunnar Birkerts & Associates, and the Dallas Museum of Art (1984, 1993) by Edward Larrabee Barnes. Museums appear in several parts of this book as examples of some of the themes that course through the state's architecture, as cornerstones of districts, and as objects that are themselves, like the works they contain, precious, in multiple senses of that word.

This chapter focuses on three museums, each designed by a world-famous architect: the Museum of Fine Arts, Houston, with additions by Ludwig Mies van der Rohe; the Amon Carter Museum of Western Art in Fort Worth, Philip Johnson's museum-as-memorial for Amon Carter; and the Kimbell Art Museum, by Louis I. Kahn, also in Fort Worth. These museums placed their cities on a national cultural map during the decades in which fine art still had broad appeal and

→ Figure 10.2
Johnson/Burgee, with an addition by Ricardo Legorreta 2006, Art Museum of South Texas, Corpus Christi, 1972

carried major currency in philanthropic circles. Yoked by their shared ambitions to be regarded among the nationally important centers and people in art, museums and patrons leveraged architects' reputations and designs in response to perceived and real scorn for provincial presumption on the part of critics, curators, and collectors in distant art world capitals.[2]

In 1920, William Ward Watkin began to design the first purpose-built art museum in Texas. The site was a triangular block along the boulevard extension of Main Street in Houston, in close proximity to the city's first university, Rice Institute. The first phase of Watkin's neoclassical building opened in 1924, followed two years later by a second phase, a harbinger of the Museum of Fine Arts, Houston's many stages of growth. Shaped like a wide, splayed W in plan, Watkin's wings grew "backward" toward the rounded edge of the site that faced Bissonnet Street. The addition by Kenneth Franzheim in 1953 of the Blaffer Wing reinforced Watkin's plan diagram, which was to have concluded with a long gallery along Bissonnet Street that enclosed a central courtyard. It was into this incomplete courtyard that Mies van der Rohe placed Cullinan Hall of 1958–1960. Just months before Mies died in 1969, design documents were completed for yet another wing, the Brown Pavilion, which was built in 1972–1973. Cullinan Hall curved responsively to the geometry of Watkin's building and was anchored to it. The roof of Cullinan Hall was suspended from four giant plate girders of steel, painted white, that splayed out from columns in the Watkin building, and from these was suspended the roof of Cullinan Hall. Columns on the north face of the building divided Mies's addition into five bays, the inner three of which were expansively glazed, while the ones on the end were infilled with brick. Inside was 10,000 square feet of exhibition space and a main gallery that rose 30 feet.

Grafted onto the Cullinan wing, the fan-shaped Brown Pavilion increased not just usable space but also the sense of spaciousness and even space as the main subject of Mies's final addition (Fig. 10.3). The conjunction of Mies's additions is perceptible in the vertical gap between sectionally differentiated floor plates, where the original wall of Cullinan Hall stood (Fig. 10.4). These elements communicate the additive character of the plan and together shape the transitional zone into threshold and antechamber to the enormously tall and expansive gallery opposite the entrance. With the seam between the wings, several core problems in modernism and Mies's work crystallized: the relationship between old (even if young) and new buildings; the concern for the shaping of interior space; and Mies's long-standing preoccupation with creating an architecture of becoming, in which fuller subjectivity might be realized by means of viewers' heightened consciousness of evolution. Today, the Brown Pavilion, subsumed along with Cullinan Hall in the museum's hierarchy of nomenclatures (they are part of the Caroline Wiess Law Building of the Susan and Fayez S. Sarofim Campus), is the public front of the multibuilding complex of the MFAH.[3] The Brown Pavilion's immense, upper-level black steel-framed windows relay the curve of the now internalized Cullinan Hall and follow the sweep of Bissonnet Street, dramatizing a rare moment of curvature in the Houston streetscape.

Cullinan Hall and the Brown Pavilions also reflected Mies's long-standing engagements with space, form, technology, urban context, and exhibition space, and laid bare the fundamental classicism in

→ Figure 10.3
Office of Ludwig Mies van der Rohe, Brown Pavilion,
Museum of Fine Arts, Houston, 1974

↑ Figure 10.4
Office of Ludwig Mies van der Rohe, Museum of Fine Arts, Houston, where original Cullinan Hall and Brown Pavilion buildings meet, 1958, 1974.

his work.[4] The shape of the new wings was anticipated by Franzheim's unrealized proposal for expanding the museum (1953), but they were also prefigured in Mies's decades-long research into the relationship of form and context, as expressed in his 1921 and 1922 schemes for a skyscraper on a roughly triangular site on Friedrichstrasse in Berlin. In a Nazi-era scheme for the Verseidag Administration Building in Krefeld (1937), Mies experimented with gentle curvature and the organization of splayed wings of a W-shaped plan. The building most closely related to his Houston work is S. R. Crown Hall, on the campus of Illinois Institute of Technology in Chicago (1956), where the architect realized a monumentally scaled, clear-span space that had occupied much of his attention since the early 1940s.

As two of Mies's few purpose-built art galleries, Cullinan Hall and the Brown Pavilion are significant in the architect's decades-long research into exhibition design, spatial planning, and museums. Beginning with the collage he created while designing the (unbuilt) Resor House in Wyoming in 1939, the architect regularly used representations of modern art, especially abstract paintings, to help conceptualize and depict his vision of architectural space. In these collages, he worked out issues of scale and the relationship of interior and exterior as experienced when viewing the outside from within. In the designs for the MFAH projects, all of these questions were at play. Extensive glazing on both wings opened the galleries to views of the street and, symbolically at least, toward downtown. The shift in scale between the wings, coupled with the experience of moving between them and beholding the buildings' great planes, awakened consciousness of the viewer's physical and subject position in space and even in time. Cullinan Hall was designed in the same years that abstract expressionist painters created ever larger works that, like Mies's architecture, explored issues of scale, finitude, and new kinds of spatial relationships. They were marvelously at home in his restrained yet pregnant spaces, with their vast white walls, black steel railings, wooden stair treads, and the dazzlingly dizzying pattern on the terrazzo floors.

The place where Mies's work joins Watkin's reminds us of the enduring presence of classicism in twentieth-century architecture (see Fig. I.25). At first glance, the historicist gray-brown masonry of the older structure seems to have little in common with the austere black steel and sleek glass panes of the new one. Yet even as he rigidly distinguished his work, Mies acknowledged Watkin's by aligning the cornices, composing with axial symmetry, and organizing the vertical plane in three layers. Few people likely stop to contemplate this juncture in the building, but it is an ideal spot in which to understand multiple meanings of architectural classicism: as pictorial and evocative of Greek and Roman building traditions; as an impulse to order and to represent order; as an abstract language widely used to convey propositions about continuity and civic significance; and as an expression of millennia-long preoccupations with the formal principles and symbolic potentials of proportion and balance.

Mies's additions to the MFAH came as Houston was emerging as an important center for contemporary art and innovative design, even as it remained a deeply southern, segregated city. During the first half of the 1950s, the Contemporary Arts Association maintained a breakneck exhibition schedule showing major works of modern art in an asymmetrical, A-frame metal building designed by MacKie and Kamrath (1949, 1955, demolished). As significant as the paintings and photographs borrowed from major collections throughout the United States and abroad was the 1953 exhibition *Painting/Sculpture/Ceramics by the Students and Faculty of the Texas Southern University*. It was organized by Ava Jean McDaniels and Herb Mears in conjunction with John Biggers, who chaired the Art Department at Texas Southern University, Houston's public college for African American students. The show was unusual in Texas in foregrounding the work of Black artists in an elite white arts institution. The exhibition anticipated the show at the MFAH the following year of drawings and paintings by Biggers and his counterpart at the University of Houston, Jack Boynton, a white artist. Yet in 1950, the year Biggers won the museum's purchase prize for *The Cradle*, he had been prohibited from attending the whites-only reception at the MFAH given to mark his award and the acquisition of the work. In exchange for Biggers's agreement to attend a separate party on a Thursday evening—the one day of the week the museum was open to African Americans—MFAH director James Chillman Jr. promised to desegregate the museum, which he did in 1951. Biggers's bargain meant that Mies's building would house one of the few integrated civic or cultural institutions in Texas.[5] This aspect of its history makes it a notable and complicated coda in the history of a European avant-garde that had frequently cloaked itself in the rhetoric of universality and proclaimed the emancipatory potential of its art in the years that Mies was among its leaders.

The careers of Philip Johnson and Ludwig Mies van der Rohe entwined in many ways, not least in Texas. Johnson was instrumental in promoting Mies's work at the Museum of Modern Art in the 1930s and bringing him to the United States, where he would influence architectural education at Rice University, among other schools. For his part, Johnson's adoption of the language of Miesianism in the 1940s endeared him to Dominique and John de Menil, two of his major patrons and supporters of the Contemporary Arts Association. The two architects worked together to design the Seagram Building (1958), which indirectly helped define the modernist Houston idiom beloved of the city's social and corporate elite.[6] Johnson's contemporaneous Munson-Williams-Proctor Art Institute (1960) in Utica, New York, was strikingly similar in its structural design to Cullinan Hall, but because it was windowless, the Utica museum read as massive and ponderous. However, the museum Johnson completed in Fort Worth, just three years after the opening of Cullinan Hall, marked his departure from the Miesian path and proclaimed a new era in US architecture.

Amon G. Carter was Fort Worth's biggest promoter and an ardent champion of the city's essential difference from, and superiority to, Dallas, 36 miles to the east. Carter made his fortune in the news business, first as the publisher of the *Fort Worth Star-Telegram*, which once had the widest circulation of any paper in the South, and then through the radio and television stations created under its auspices. The Fort Worth museum that bears his name was originally conceived as a memorial to him. Its transformation, programmatically and architecturally, was due to Carter's daughter Ruth Carter Stevenson, who envisioned it as a home for her father's collection of paintings and sculptures depicting the US West (Fig. 10.5). But as the project evolved, its institutional program shifted—with the encouragement of Rene d'Harnoncourt, director of the Museum of Modern Art in New York, and the Carter's first director, Mitchell A. Wilder—to collecting Western art. The institutional purview has expanded since to include US art, and the museum now includes three main wings, all additions by Johnson to his original building.

As a relative of both the Lincoln Memorial by Henry Bacon (1922) and Johnson and Richard Foster's New York State Theater at Lincoln Center (1964), the Amon Carter Museum is at its core a glamorous

→ Figure 10.5
Philip Johnson and Associates, Amon Carter Museum, Fort Worth, 1961

mausoleum: elegant, stylish, and still safely within the bounds of good-taste classicism. Seen across the giant lawn before it, the long, rectangular, pediment-less building summons the memorial, which, with its magisterial lawn-facing portico, is the twentieth-century's foremost civic shrine. The museum's great east-facing portico of fossilized limestone is formed of five bays of segmental arches supported on attenuated piers with concave surfaces (Fig. 10.6). Floor-to-ceiling glazing, set back behind the piers, forms the front wall. In a steady-handed but clever play of materials and rhythms, Johnson clad the wall opposite in warm teak panels punctuated at the upper and lower levels with a series of rectangular openings. Channeling Otto Wagner's work at the Vienna Post Office Savings Bank (as the architects of the Texas Instruments Semiconductor Building had), Johnson attached the limestone panels, with their irregular, prehistoric indentations and texture, using expressed bronze bolts, thereby introducing a sophisticated dialogue between industry and nature, smooth and rough, refined and coarse. A monument that implicitly championed the public value of private wealth, the Amon Carter Museum was pitch perfect for rich Texans of the early 1960s: forward looking but temperamentally conservative.

From its hilltop site, the building commandingly faces downtown. It stands in what is today called Amon Carter Square, which contains four museums, two civic buildings, and the Will Rogers Memorial Auditorium, Coliseum, and Pioneer Tower (1936). Johnson, who relished deploying historical references for strategic and associative purposes, named the Loggia dei Lanzi as an influence on the design

→ Figure 10.6
Philip Johnson and Associates, Amon Carter Museum, Fort Worth, 1961

of the museum, thereby conjuring the merchant princes who built late medieval Florence into a world center of banking, politics, and the arts.[7] The Amon Carter expresses the social function of the modern museum in a capitalist society as not just a repository of objects but as a privileged site used in the perpetuation of the sacred rites, rituals, and beliefs at the core of art history, the art market, and cultural philanthropy. The Fort Worth building anticipated Johnson's design for the Sheldon Memorial Art Gallery at the University of Nebraska in Lincoln (1963), and the spectacular New York State Theater, one of the three performance buildings that frame the plaza at Lincoln Center.

Deferentially sited to preserve views from, and of, the Amon Carter Museum, the Kimbell Art Museum (1972) nonetheless overshadows it. The building is one of the foremost works of Louis I. Kahn, the Philadelphia-based architect whose supreme command of geometry, composition, and the deep humanism at the core of great architecture gave rise to some of the century's most affecting and poetic buildings. While Johnson, brilliantly attuned to taste, flitted between architectural languages over the course of his long career, and Mies bore down with scholarly tenacity on precisely honed theoretical problems in an equally delimited vocabulary over five decades, in his shorter set of working years, Kahn developed a distinctive oeuvre of works marked by profound responsiveness to program, site, and a long, deep history of architecture.

In collaboration with the Kimbell's founding director, Richard F. Brown, Kahn shaped the museum that would house the collection of Kay and Velma Kimbell, which consisted chiefly of French and British paintings from the eighteenth and nineteenth centuries, as well as new acquisitions. The building is organized into two main wings, each defined by a series of five vaulted bays created by pairs of concrete cycloid shells that work as beams, which are curved in section. The vault-like spaces they shape are 100 feet long, 23 feet wide, and 20 feet high, with a portico of the same dimensions. The wings are connected by four more such vault-like spaces and frame the entrance courtyard (Figs. 10.7, 10.8). The wings are connected by four more such vaults and frame the entrance courtyard. Tucked within the wings are small outdoor "green rooms," in Kahn's words.

Light is both a central problem in museum design and one of the elements that Kahn used repeatedly in his major buildings to create spaces for contemplation, research, and repose. It was at the

↑ Figure 10.7, → Figure 10.8
Louis I. Kahn, with Preston M. Geren and Associates; August E. Komendant, engineer, Kimbell Art Museum, Fort Worth, 1972. Landscape by George Patton and Harriet Pattison.

core of the Kimbell project and remains one of its signature elements. Continuous narrow light channels run the length of the ceiling between the curved beams. Kahn suspended wing-shaped pierced aluminum reflectors, designed by lighting consultant Richard Kelly, beneath the slots inside each vault to throw light onto the curved interior surfaces of the concrete (Fig. 10.9). At the ends of each vault, narrow clerestory windows follow the curvature of the vaults. As he was at work on the design, in language that was characteristically informal and esoteric, Kahn explained his vision of the lighting in the Kimbell:

> *I felt that the light in the rooms structured in concrete will have the luminosity of silver. I know that rooms for paintings and objects that fade should only modestly be given natural light. . . . This light will give a touch of silver to the room without touching the objects directly, yet give the comforting feeling of knowing the time of day.*[8]

Kahn's conception of the lighting scheme addressed the practical problems of conservation and the exhausting sensation of being cut off from contact with nature and the outside world common in so many museum spaces. His solution was altogether different from Mies's, who preferred to install floor-to-ceiling curtains rather than sacrifice glazing to painting.

While a sense of lightness and delicacy animates the Kimbell's interior, the viewer perceives the exterior as massive, solid, and almost austere. The formal power of the Kimbell's exterior resides in the repetition of cycloid forms, lined up as if in recollection of the long, vast plains that spread out west of Fort Worth. The great rounded masses that form the roof call to mind the barrel vaults of Romanesque churches or the arches of Roman aqueducts and read as reconfigurations of the cylindrical volumes of Texas's grain silos— sliced in half and laid on their sides (Fig. 10.10). The dual allusions to architectural history and industrial vernacular forms located the Kimbell firmly within the mainstream of architectural modernism and addressed the demands of the commission.

Implicit in the program was the need to strike a balance between the associations with the high culture of European masterpieces in oil, marble, or bronze and the reality of a public that was still learning to care about art. Brown, who held a PhD in art history from Harvard, specified that the museum be "a creative contribution to the history

10. Precious Objects

↓ Figure 10.9
Louis I. Kahn, with Preston M. Geren and Associates; August E. Komendant, engineer, Kimbell Art Museum, Fort Worth, 1972

Part IV: Assemblage

↑ Figure 10.10
Louis I. Kahn, with Preston M. Geren and Associates;
August E. Komendant, engineer, Kimbell Art Museum, Fort Worth, 1972

of architecture on the same high level and of the same aesthetic quality as the arts it might house," but also that the visitor experience a sense of "warmth" and "mellowness" rooted in "harmonious simplicity" and "proportion."[9] The building that resulted elegantly integrated concrete, travertine, white oak, and modulated sunlight in acknowledgment of its historical and phenomenological briefs. Over the course of the design process, Kahn scaled the museum down, not just to conserve costs but to make it accessible to North Texas audiences. Brown imagined the "average visitor" as "a little old lady from Abilene," someone quite different from the highly privileged students, alumni, and faculty who frequented the Yale University Art Gallery, Kahn's first major commission.[10]

The museums examined in this chapter played leading roles in Texas's turn toward a wider world at midcentury. Far more than places to view art, they expressed their patrons' desire that their cities be nationally recognized as serious cultural centers. All three museums received substantial attention in the national architectural press when they were built. That the MFAH, Stevenson, and Brown hired architects outside of Texas reflected the potential of high-caliber architecture to confer status and prestige on institutions, patrons, and places. But for these clients, who sought and got the best that money could buy, ambition was laced with doubt, or at least a clear-eyed pragmatism, about whether Texas architects could deliver buildings that would be respected or even noticed by the critics, curators, and other gatekeepers of metropolitan cultural power. The specter of cultural inferiority haunts Texas even today, even as its cities, Houston foremost among them, have become internationally renowned for their collections of art and support of world-class artists. That this book carves out a chapter for just three buildings, by Mies, Johnson, and Kahn, is perhaps a legacy of that anxiety.

11. Hearts & Minds

Previous Spread: O'Neil Ford and
Associates, in collaboration with Paul Baker
and Arthur Rogers, Ruth Taylor Theater,
Trinity University, San Antonio, 1965

Powered by the economic and baby booms of the post–World War II period, and motivated by the acceleration of Cold War anxiety and research, the creation and expansion of modern university and secondary campuses exploded in the middle decades of the twentieth century.[1] This was a global trend. Notable examples abroad include the University City of the National Autonomous University of Mexico, shepherded by Mario Pani, Enrique del Moral, and Carlos Lazo (1952); the Central University of Venezuela in Caracas (1954), by Carlos Raúl Villanueva; and the Indian Institute of Management in Ahmedabad, India (1974), by Louis I. Kahn and B. V. Doshi. In each case, the campuses expressed their patrons' ambitions to modernize their respective societies and enable them to participate in a rapidly shifting international order. In Texas, the campuses of the University of Texas at Austin, Rice University, Texas Tech, Texas A&M, and the University of Texas at El Paso, all begun before World War II, provided powerful examples of hierarchical site planning and the utility of historicism for the purposes of conveying academic authority and stimulating in students emotional engagements with their institutions and one another.

But beginning around 1950, architects in Texas began exploring new directions in campus scheme. Mies van der Rohe's design for the campus of the Armour Institute in Chicago of 1939 had introduced the possibility that colleges need not evoke the past as they prepared students for the future. The campuses of Trinity University in San Antonio, the University of St. Thomas in Houston, and the Presbyterian Pan American School in Kingsville were defined by exceptionally consistent architectural unity and are among the preeminent examples of modernist campus planning in Texas. Kenneth Bentsen Associates' master plan and eighteen buildings at the University of Texas-Pan American (now University of Texas Rio Grande Valley) in Edinburg, designed from 1967 to 1982, made it one of the state's more architecturally coherent and evocative ensembles. Bentsen's assimilation of the patterns and forms of Border Brick architecture of the Lower Rio Grande Valley was evident in his design for the Betty Bentsen and R. Dan Winn House in McAllen (1965), but most striking at the Pan American campus are the similarities of the Science Complex, the Fine Arts Complex, and the Health and Physical Education Building to the buildings designed by Kahn and Doshi in Ahmedabad (Fig. 11.1).[2] In the 1960s, growth of the Stephen F. Austin

State University in Nacogdoches was defined by a group of exuberant buildings by Kent, Marsellos, and Scott. Texas Southern University in Houston (TSU), while less stylistically uniform than some other institutions, is a locus of buildings by important Texas architects. TSU, like Presbyterian Pan American School, represented the gradual expansion of access to higher (and secondary) education to Texans who, because they had historically been discriminated against and underserved, were effectively excluded from it.

When prospective Trinity University students opened their mail in 1953, they were greeted by a thin blue pamphlet inviting them to visit "America's Most Modern College Campus." In the central panel was a drawing of Trinity's new Classroom-Administration Building by O'Neil Ford, Bartlett Cocke, and Harvey P. Smith, with its striking flat roof and the long concrete slabs that separated the two stories and shaded the deeply recessed window walls from the searing South Texas sun. In September of 1951, in its second article on the campus, *Architectural Forum* had declared that the classroom-administration building embodied a "new 'horizontal gothic,'" and marveled that it was "the first full-sized structure erected by the Youtz-Slick 'lift-slab'" method, a new technique of concrete construction. The lift-slab method saved time and money and, the journal claimed, was "spreading through southern Texas like a longhorn stampede."[3] The classroom-administration building, the men's dormitory, and the George Storch Memorial Library established the forms that would govern architecture at Trinity throughout the 1950s (Fig. 11.2). The buildings' long horizontals echoed the line of the landscape, while their large windows opened interiors to it visually. Balconies that ran the length of buildings broadly recalled the porches typical of Texas ranch houses and the vernacular of German settler colonialist houses in Central Texas. Grouped near the edge of a jagged limestone escarpment that runs roughly east–west through the middle of the site and had a drop as great as 70 feet in some places, the buildings also established the pattern of organizing the campus in relation to the rockface and toward downtown San Antonio to the south.

Buildings that served students primarily were placed nearest the cliff, with the men's dormitory just below it and the slightly later dorms to the west hovering above it. The main volume of the student union at the campus's east end jutted out to the very edge. Academic buildings, on the other hand, stood on the cliff and were set back

11.   Hearts & Minds

↓ Figure 11.1
Kenneth Bentsen Associates, University of Texas Pan American, Fine Arts Complex, Edinburg, 1970

↑ Figure 11.2
O'Neil Ford, Bartlett Cocke, and Harvey P. Smith,
William W. Wurster, consulting architect, George Storch
Memorial Library, Trinity University, San Antonio, 1952

from the precipice but carefully sited so that none blocked the view to downtown. Residential and athletic buildings occupied the area below the escarpment, while Storch Library, with its two perpendicularly positioned volumes and terracing, stepped down the site, as if to express its dual purpose in serving faculty and students. Located at the terminus of a neighborhood street, Bushnell Avenue, the library definitively closed the campus to vehicular traffic from the west and helped shape what would become a pedestrian-friendly, tightly arranged campus core.

In the 1950s, Trinity's aesthetic of uncompromising postwar industrial practicality and the raw beauty of its unforgiving terrain differentiated it dramatically from those campuses with lush lawns and revival-style buildings that dominated collegiate architecture in Texas. An early scheme had called for flattening the site and constructing historicist buildings on a hierarchical plan, but in 1948, on the advice of William Wurster, whom Trinity's board of trustees had hired as a consulting architect, the university embraced the idea of working with the steep precipice. Upon seeing the site and what Ford described as "an abandoned rock quarry strewn with many years' accumulation of battered battery boxes, broken glass, twisted wire, and chunks of asphalt, and spotted with cactus, catclaw, and piles of tree trimmings," Wurster declared, "'what a truly beautiful piece of land. How wise you are and how great the promise with such a piece of earth to shape our work.'"[4] Arthur and Marie Berger, who also worked with Howard Meyer in Dallas, joined Ford and Cocke as part of Trinity's design team. The Bergers embraced the vegetation, topography, and climate of South Texas, and by the midfifties, the campus landscape was as impressive as its architecture. Small formal lawns coexisted with rough rocks, prickly cactuses, and native trees, contrasting dramatically with the uncompromising straight lines of long, low buildings. By bringing out the rugged picturesqueness of the site, the Bergers provided Trinity with a comparably low-maintenance, low-cost, ecologically sensitive landscape design.

Throughout the campus, the architects made contact with nature central to students' experiences. Their daily traipsing to class became athletic events as they climbed long concrete staircases that brought them near the cliff face and provided an encounter with South Texas geology. By contrast, the dormitories were arranged around courtyards and connected to one another by open-air bridges. Rooms opened directly onto the buildings' long balconies out of necessity until the installation of central air-conditioning, and louvered wooden screens affixed to balcony rails passively provided shade.

Coincident with increased budgets and a growing student population, a significant linguistic shift occurred in Ford's Trinity work in the 1960s—away from the ranch-style rationalism of lift-slab toward a more historically evocative language. In this period, the upper campus began to take on the character of a medieval hill town, anchored by the campanile of the T. Frank Murchison Memorial Tower (1964) and the plaza in front of the vaguely Romanesque Margarite B. Parker Chapel (1966; Fig. 11.3). With its soaring parabolic arches, its exquisite doors, carved wooden screen, and light fixtures created by the architect's brother, Lynn Ford, and the windows he designed with Ruth B. Dunn, the chapel is a descendant of the much smaller Little Chapel in the Woods in Denton. Indeed, as the Trinity campus grew, it turned inward, to small courtyards and intimate spaces, but the symbolic connection of the university to the city, primarily through sight lines, was reinforced repeatedly throughout the day, as students' vertical circulation put them in visual contact with the San Antonio skyline. After 1964, the connection was reinforced in the visual dialogue between the Murchison Memorial Tower, Trinity's only really tall building, and downtown skyscrapers. In 1968, the symbolic relationship between campus and city intensified further with the completion of the Tower of the Americas, downtown's striking new landmark, designed by O'Neil Ford and his colleagues at Ford, Powell and Carson, for HemisFair '68.

In 1953, *Vogue* magazine proclaimed Ford "one of twenty-two Texans who help run the place," and described him as "a brilliant, fertile-minded, rangy-talking architect."[5] Having begun to build a career on the patronage of wealthy Texans, primarily those based in and near Dallas and San Antonio, Ford shared the magazine pages with Jesse Jones, Stanley Marcus, Ima Hogg, Tom and Earl Slick, and Hugh Roy Cullen. Despite the tony company and clientele, throughout his career, Ford was a passionate advocate of progressive social and political causes and particularly concerned with education at all levels. The Trinity commission was followed by major campus designs for the University of Dallas, in Irving, Texas (Fig. 11.4); Skidmore College in Saratoga Springs, New York; and the University of Texas at San Antonio, the latter two shaped chiefly by Ford's partner Boone

11. Hearts & Minds

↓ Figure 11.3
O'Neil Ford and Associates, Margarite B. Parker Chapel (Murchison Tower foreground), Trinity University, 1966. Sculpture by Charles Umlauf.

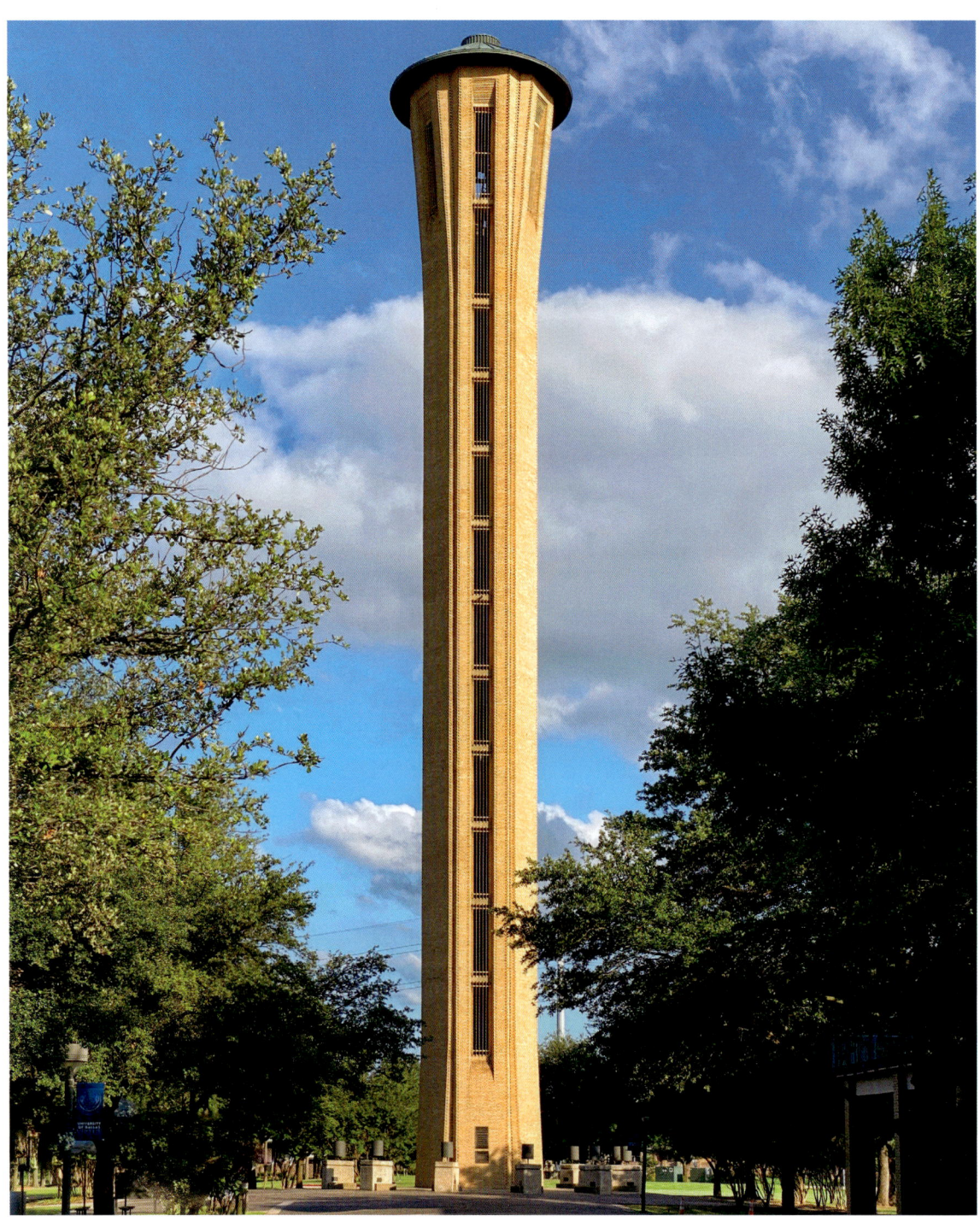

↑ Figure 11.4
Ford, Powell and Carson (Boone Powell, associate in charge), University of Dallas Memorial Tower, Irving, 1968

Powell. Ford's firm also designed secondary school campuses for St. Mary's Hall in San Antonio and the Selwyn School in Denton.

One of the most intact campuses Ford and his collaborators designed is Presbyterian Pan American School south of Kingsville. A boarding school for high school students, the institution was created in 1956 by merging the Texas-Mexican Industrial Institute for boys and the Presbyterian School for Mexican Girls in Taft. The schools were established in 1911 and 1923 by Anglo-Texan Presbyterians to instruct Mexican immigrant and Mexican American students in "American trades and crafts," including cultivating the Texas-Mexican Institute's agricultural fields and raising its livestock.[6] The effort to isolate, proselytize, and "Americanize" youth from the region's predominately Mexican-descended Catholic population reflected the racial and cultural anxieties of the local Anglo-American elites with respect to the people on whose labor they depended. The campus site was donated by Henrietta Chamberlain King, widow of the founder of the King Ranch, the largest ranch in Texas. An ardent Presbyterian, Henrietta King was the daughter of the Rev. Hiram Chamberlin, the first Presbyterian missionary to evangelize the lower Rio Grande border. Buttressed by support from Presbyterians throughout Texas, since its founding, the school has endeavored to forge connections across the Rio Grande. As a private, religiously oriented institution, it is a fascinating manifestation of the breadth of the conceptual and architectural aspects of the decades-long national project of Pan-Americanism.[7] Today, the school has an impressively diverse international student body, as well as an extraordinarily high rate of college acceptance.

Ford received the commission through one of the school's trustees, Garland Lasater, for whom the architect had designed a ranch house outside Falfurrias. On the South Texas coastal plain, Ford reprised many of the elements and materials used at Trinity. The architecture designed by Ford and his collaborators—first Alan Y. Taniguchi of Harlingen, then Richard Colley of Corpus Christi—evolved, just as it did at the San Antonio campus. Students were housed in two-story dormitories constructed with expressed concrete floor and roof plates, infilled with brick curtain walls, and served by exterior stairs and balcony corridors. Academic buildings are connected by walkways paved with Saltillo tile and protected by segmental vaults supported on concrete columns and arches

Part IV: Assemblage

↑ Figure 11.5
O'Neil Ford and Associates, Norcell Haywood, associate in charge; Isabel Thomas Miller Classroom Building walkway, Presbyterian Pan American School, Kingsville, 1965

↗ Figure 11.6
Ford, Powell and Carson, Norcell Haywood, associate in charge; Alice Kleberg Memorial Library, Presbyterian Pan American School, Kingsville, 1970

(Fig. 11.5). Like so many of Ford's buildings, the Presbyterian Pan American School campus buildings are enriched by ceramic fixtures designed by Martha and Beaumont Mood, which can be appreciated in the characteristically Fordian space of the Alice Kleberg Memorial Library (Fig. 11.6). The Morris Chapel, designed in Ford's office by Norcell Haywood, was inaugurated in 1959 (Fig. 11.7). Like the Parker Chapel, it is the gem of the campus. Rich in materials, textures, and patterns, the Morris Chapel is lighter and more delicate than the Trinity building. With its palette of materials and forms, the campus typifies its architect's particular facility in designing institutional complexes that read as unified without being monotonous or monumental. Ford's characteristic attention to craft, informality, and restraint—qualities so well suited to South Texas—are all present in the Presbyterian Pan American School.

Houston clients, however, tend to prefer shinier and edgier buildings than Ford's earthier ones. The buildings of black-painted steel infilled with panels of rose-colored brick or plate glass windows that Philip Johnson and his Houston associate architects, Howard Barnstone and Preston M. Bolton, designed for the University of St. Thomas in Houston (1956–1959) had a cosmopolitan severity so

→ Figure 11.7
O'Neil Ford and Associates, Morris Chapel, Presbyterian Pan American School, Kingsville, 1959

pronounced that it bordered on mannerism. Adapting the language, if not always the structural rigor, of his mentor, Ludwig Mies van der Rohe, Johnson created a complex of buildings that look strikingly like the slightly earlier Hunstanton School by Alison and Peter Smithson in Hunstanton, Norfolk, United Kingdom (Fig. 11.8). Like that work, the St. Thomas buildings formally descended from Erich Mendelsohn's Mosse House Power Station of 1926–1927 in Berlin. Johnson had been recommended to the university's trustees by John de Menil, and the campus was designed at the same time as the Cullinan Hall addition to the Museum of Fine Arts, Houston. Together, these projects helped

← Figure 11.8, ↓ Figure 11.9
Philip Johnson and
Associates, with Bolton and
Barnstone, Jones Hall and
Strake Hall, University of St.
Thomas, Houston, 1958, 1959

raise Houston's profile as a city serious about architecture and art.

While the St. Thomas buildings shared with those at Trinity from the 1950s flat roofs, avoidance of historical revivalism, emphasis on industrial materials, and prodigious use of covered walkways, the St. Thomas campus, with its axial plan and central lawn, had more in common with the hierarchical arrangements of Rice University and Southern Methodist University than with Trinity (Fig. 11.9). The antecedent of this manner of organizing university buildings was Thomas Jefferson's plan of the University of Virginia (1826), which Ford also admired. Johnson used the walkways much as Jefferson had: to define the edge of the central green of an "academical village." But in Houston, these elements performed an additional associational role insofar as they mimicked the organization of cloisters around central patios, an allusion that must have seemed particularly appropriate to an institution affiliated with the Catholic Church. Extending the play of substitutions and metaphors, the architect envisioned a chapel at the head of St. Thomas's mall, in the position where Jefferson's library stands.

Legibly rooted in tradition but cloaked in the dress of the avant-garde, the University of St. Thomas was a locus of the international reinvigoration of humanism and liberalism, undergirded by modern art and architecture, during the 1960s. Dominique de Menil, influenced by her contact with the French Dominican priest Father Marie-Alain Couturier, the champion of modern artists in France and the patron of Le Corbusier, embodied this cultural force in midcentury Houston.[8] From 1959 to 1964, the Art Department at St. Thomas was home to highly innovative exhibitions organized by Jermayne MacAgy, whom the Menils brought to St. Thomas from the Contemporary Arts Museum, where MacAgy had been director from 1955 to 1959.

Nacogdoches is more strongly associated with Texas history—including settlement by the Hasinai Confederacy, whose burial mounds, some dating from the thirteenth century, stood there until the nineteenth century; Spanish city planning; French trading; and revolutionary activity—than with modern architecture. But with the growth of Stephen F. Austin State University there at midcentury, the future became as important as the past. Today, students make up nearly half of Nacogdoches's population, and in the 1960s, using the designs of Kent, Marsellos, and Scott, the university built feverishly to accommodate their predecessors. The firm's work there was marked by a notable linguistic shift. Hall 14 (1964), a dormitory, embodies the architects' characteristically restrained Wrightian language, but slightly later works are impressive New Formalist set pieces rendered in red brick and concrete that reveal the architects' delight in the play of planarity and curvature in plan, elevation, and decorative detailing. Most striking among these buildings are the Martha T. Griffith Hall (1965; Fig. 11.10); the Gladys E. Steen Dormitories (1968; Fig. 11.11), a pair of giant cylindrical buildings; and the East College Cafeteria (1968; Fig. 11.12), a circular building ringed by an arcade that reads as a scaled-down inversion of Oscar Niemeyer's portico at the presidential palace in Brasilia (where the cathedral is circular in plan). Stephen F. Austin's new buildings could hardly have differed more from the monastic rationalism of the University of St. Thomas.

Two miles east of that institution, in Houston's Third Ward, another renaissance was underway on the campus of Texas Southern University. TSU grew out of Houston Colored Junior College and was founded by the Texas Legislature in 1947 to thwart the desegregation of other state universities. Like many campuses, TSU's expanded in a somewhat piecemeal fashion. It gained formal coherence over

↓ Figure 11.10
Kent, Marsellos, and Scott, Martha T. Griffith Hall, Stephen F. Austin State University, Nacogdoches, 1965

↘ Figure 11.11
Kent, Marsellos, and Scott, Gladys E. Steen Dormitories, Stephen F. Austin State University, Nacogdoches, 1968

↑ Figure 11.12
Kent, Marsellos, and Scott, East College Cafeteria, Stephen F. Austin State University, Nacogdoches, 1968

time, thanks to the closure of Wheeler Avenue to through traffic and the removal of the railroad track that divided the campus, which had been a Third Ward landmark and served as a powerful symbol of the history of segregation in the US landscape.[9] The campus includes notable buildings by Lamar Q. Cato and Clovis Heimsath Associates. The Science Building, designed in 1958 by Wyatt C. Hedrick, is an archetypal 1950s university building enriched by the relief sculpture *Man and the Universe* created by Carroll Simms, a founder of the Art Department. The incorporation of art on the exterior of the Science Building echoes practices of the 1930s, as at the 1936 Texas Centennial Exposition in Dallas. But it is also like the strategies used by artists and architects at UNAM's Ciudad Universitaria in Mexico City, where major buildings were clad in mosaics based on themes related to the buildings' uses.

Inside the Science Building, John Biggers painted the mural *Web*

Figure 11.13
John S. Chase, Martin Luther King Jr. Humanities Center, Texas Southern University, Houston, 1969. Carroll Simms, *African Queen Mother*, 1968.

of Life (1958). Dealing with concepts of fertility, nature, and regeneration in Africa and the Americas, the work has formal and thematic parallels to 1950s murals by David Alfaro Siqueiros and Diego Rivera. In May of 1964, Biggers was among those *Texas Architect* profiled in a series on artists in the state. He was by then known in art circles and universities throughout the United States, and along with Simms, was shaping TSU's extraordinary art program and collection. The legacy of the artists' work is readily evident today at TSU, which has more than 125 murals, many of them created by students.

TSU's Martin Luther King Jr. Humanities Center, designed by John S. Chase, is the campus's premier building (Fig. 11.13). Its three-story semicircular portico, flanked by a pair of glazed wings, opens expansively to the plaza before it, as if to materialize the highest aspirations of the humanities, and of Dr. King, to help bring into being a new world. The building is especially impressive when it is illuminated at night, when its sweeping curve recalls the monumental curvature of Mendelsohn's expressionist works of the 1920s, buildings similarly rooted in aspirations toward universal reform. In the fountain in the plaza stands one of four of Simms's works on campus: a large abstract bronze, *African Queen Mother* (1968), whose curvature, colors, and rhythms powerfully complement Chase's building and bring a sense of scale gradation to the large expanse of paving in front of it.

The King Humanities Center was followed by several more buildings by Chase: the Thurgood Marshall School of Law Building and the Ernest S. Sterling Student Center, both of 1976; and the School of Education Building of 1981. The law building is also defined by curvature, this time a rounded volume originally clad in bronze anodized aluminum and bronze solar glass adjacent to an orthogonal wing clad in white precast concrete panels. The tectonic student center, with its striated concrete panels, typifies the play of volumetricity and visual mass characteristic of a significant strand of 1970s modernism, and anticipates Chase's collaboration with Paul Rudolph one year later on a design for the Kresge administration building at Tuskegee Institute in Alabama.

Campuses, like all landscapes, change, and of necessity are caught between the needs of the present, hopes for the future, and legacies of the past. In this way, they present distinctive challenges to preservationists, architects, and university administrators. Whatever their age or style, campuses are special precincts within larger realms, sacred sites of growth, research, and teaching, as well as the backdrops against which important lifelong relationships are forged. Campuses are also exclusive, and in Texas, bound tightly to histories of discrimination. But they have also cradled the shaping of conscience and raising of consciousness when it was most urgently needed, something O'Neil Ford recognized when he linked the spatial and architectural evolution of the Trinity campus to the institution's "spirit of positive, progressive protest," in his commencement address to the class of 1967.[10]

12. Contact Zones

Previous Spread: Harwell Hamilton Harris
and Harold A. Berry, Stemmons Towers,
Dallas, 1962

Instances of architectural unity in Texas are rare, but they do exist. Although coherence may be easily identified in university campuses, or in unimaginatively designed suburban residential subdivisions, with a bit of effort, it is possible to discern the influence of architects in groups of buildings at urban scale and in urban contexts. Because they frequently blur the boundaries between public and private spaces (and wealth), such districts form a fascinating typological subset of Texas architecture. They can act as "contact zones," where architects, governments, real estate developers, and citizens converge in literal and metaphorical interactions laced with a subtle play of class, status, and power.[1] Like museums and campuses, such zones sometimes anchor and define substantial parts of cities, but they can also exist in suburban or even rural contexts. Occasionally, they are noncontiguous and comprise buildings linked less by propinquity and similarity than by patron or purpose. In a state that has often been distrustful of urban planning, these districts have usually resulted from private patronage on the part of a person or corporation acting as a developer or as an investor. Yet notable examples of public patronage remain. Whoever the client, architects and landscape architects bring to the design process their abilities to envision and orchestrate spatial and perceptual unity, which patrons value as means of representing and advancing their ideological, civic, or commercial agendas.

Public, Private, and Shared

Governmental sponsorship of purpose-built districts in Texas included the Texas Centennial Exposition in Dallas (1936) and, thirty-two-years later, HemisFair '68 in San Antonio, the only international exposition to date staged in the state. During the New Deal, the federal government's Farm Security Administration (FSA) built a district, the Lamesa Farm Workers Community (1942), designed by Hudson J. Elmo in what is now the town of Los Ybáñez, Texas (Fig. 12.1). One of nine labor camps that the FSA constructed in Texas, and one of ninety-five that it built from Texas to California, the Lamesa camp (essentially a small subdivision located in open farm country) housed seasonal migrant Mexican field workers (*braceros*) and their families, recruited annually by South Plains farmers to harvest their cotton crop. The camp contains a mix of wood-frame single-family and multifamily housing, the manager's house, a gatehouse, and the community center. From 1942 until 1980, when the camp was closed, the

↑ Figure 12.1
Hudson J. Elmo for the Farm Security Administration, Lamesa Farm Workers Community, Los Ybáñez, 1942. Photograph by Kathryn E. O'Rourke.

center housed provisions for childcare and healthcare, as well as medical, educational, and religious uses. In 1993, the camp was listed in the National Register of Historic Places as a historic district in recognition of its status as the best-preserved FSA farm labor camp in Texas.[2]

Federal funds also supported experimentation in community design, prefabrication, and alternatives to conventional ownership structures. Avion Village in Grand Prairie, designed by David R. Williams, Roscoe P. DeWitt, Arch B. Swank Jr. and Richard Neutra (1942; Fig. 12.2), was built to house workers and pilots training at nearby Hensley Field, where the US Army was building and testing the model T-6 "Texan" airplane. Adapting principles of Garden City planning and drawing on a variety of circular utopian and reformist schemes, the architects organized three hundred houses in rows around a central park. Vehicular traffic was limited to a ring road that looped around the rows of houses.[3] Buildings by Williams and Neutra bear the architects' distinctive vocabularies: those by Williams are two stories, have balconies, and masonry walls, reflecting his research on the architecture of rural nineteenth-century vernacular houses built by European colonists in Central and South Texas; Neutra's pronouncedly orthogonal buildings have flat roofs and ribbon windows. Before construction, contractors were invited to compete to see who could build the fastest using prefabricated parts. The winner succeeded in doing so in just under one hour. After 1948, when the Avion Village Mutual Housing Corporation purchased the property from the federal government, Avion Village was governed by a cooperative ownership scheme, in which residents owned shares in a mutual housing corporation and held "perpetual" occupancy rights to their dwelling, rather than a title. They participated in the management of the property through a board. Conceived by Lawrence Westbrook (born in Belton), who led the Mutual Ownership Defense Housing Division, under the auspices of the Federal Works Agency, the ownership structure was intended to be a more affordable alternative to traditional financing mechanisms for the middle-class because it did not require a large down payment.[4]

↑ Figure 12.2
David R. Williams, Roscoe DeWitt, Arch B. Swank Jr., and Richard Neutra, Avion Village, Grand Prairie, 1942

For a site 120 miles east of Grand Prairie, on the shore of Lake Palestine in Flint, Bruce Plunkett, a developer and contractor based in nearby Tyler, hired architect Bruce Goff to design eleven buildings, a pool bath house, and the signboards at the north entrance to Lake Village (later, The Villages), a 600-acre residential district (1970–1974). Goff moved his practice from Kansas City to Tyler to work on the Lake Village buildings, along with three others in the East Texas city. The most notable of Goff's buildings for Plunkett was the first house he designed for him, a two-story building with a wide, overhanging hip roof (Fig. 12.3). The cantilevered upper floor is distinguished by three large semicircular panels made of shingles, set in front of a glazed wall. The ground floor is faced in brick and has four semicircular windows that open toward the upper story. The building reflects the influence of Frank Lloyd Wright's Prairie houses and typifies Goff's characteristic manipulation of overscale geometries and varied materials. Composed of two wings that form an L, the first Plunkett house opens toward the lake and includes a spiral staircase and semicircular living area. Goff's other buildings in Lake Village were comparably sedate, owing to limited funds. With its

↑ Figure 12.3
Bruce Goff, Bruce Plunkett First House, Lake Village, Flint, 1970

large lots and winding streets and cul-de-sacs, the development as a whole resembles countless suburban residential real estate projects throughout the state.

Public patronage of government centers ballooned nationwide at midcentury. One of the most notable examples in Texas was in Denton, where in the mid-1960s, the city commissioned O'Neil Ford and Roland Laney to design a new civic center containing a community center, city hall and police station, and an expansion to the existing public library. In his characteristic language, with his usual keen attention to detail, and in concert with his craftsman brother, Lynn, and ceramists Beau and Martha Mood, Ford defined the city's governmental heart as a restrained, humanely scaled precinct altogether different from the monumental spaces that became increasingly commonplace in government centers in the 1970s (Fig. 12.4).[5] Nearby, Ford later designed an addition to the Emily Fowler Central Library, which was itself later sensitively enlarged by Duane Landry. Yet, the sensitivity to site and scale that Ford's Denton Civic Center exemplifies occludes the history of its 22-acre site, most of which is now a landscaped park. In the late nineteenth and early twentieth centuries, these 22 acres were the site of Quakertown, Denton's major African American neighborhood. In 1922, Denton's city government bought out Quakertown property owners in order to transform the neighborhood into City Park, demolishing existing buildings or moving them to a new neighborhood that did not lie between downtown Denton and what is now Texas Woman's University, which in 1922 was the state's major institution of higher education for (white) women.[6]

Denton itself constitutes a noncontiguous precinct of Ford buildings—several of which have already appeared in this book—reinforced by collections of architecturally sympathetic works by Howard Meyer of Dallas, local architects Roland Laney and Mount-Miller, and Jane and Duane Landry. At an even larger scale, it is possible to imagine a north-south axis of Ford's work that runs from Denton, through San Antonio, to the towns and ranches of South Texas, and out to San José Island in the Gulf of Mexico. The architectural and constructional similarities between the Denton Community Building and Ford's La Villita Assembly Building in San Antonio (1959), both of which are circular in plan and incorporate a "bicycle wheel" steel-tension-ring-and-cable roof system, vividly illustrate the regional district corridor notion (Fig. 12.5).

Part IV: Assemblage

← Figure 12.4
O'Neil Ford and Associates, with Roland Laney, City Hall, Denton, 1966

↓ Figure 12.5
O'Neil Ford and Associates, with Roland Laney, Denton County Civic Center, Denton, 1966

Spend Money, Make Money

In Dallas, which despite its proximity to Denton could hardly differ from it more, an entire district might be assembled based not on the work of a single architect but on that of a developer. Trammell Crow grew rich by building warehouses and other facilities to accommodate Dallas's economic development as the wholesale marketing and distribution center of the Southwest. From time to time, he patronized high-quality design.[7] In partnership with John M. Stemmons, Crow helped define the commercial corridor that runs along Interstate 35 in Dallas, known as the Stemmons Freeway, for which Stemmons donated the right of way. He and Crow took advantage of this publicly funded infrastructure improvement to develop Stemmons's adjacent real estate with the multibuilding Dallas Market Center, built between the mid-1950s and the mid-1980s. Between 1958 and 1960, Crow commissioned several projects from Harwell Hamilton Harris. The first was the spectacular four-story, air-conditioned, and skylit court of the Dallas Trade Mart (1959), spanned by cable-slung bridges that invite visitors to experience the 65-foot-tall court midair (Fig. 12.6). The court's foremost antecedent was the interior of Joseph Paxton's Crystal Palace (1851), built for the first world's fair, London's Great Exhibition. Notable for the delicacy and refinement of Harris's detailing, the Trade Mart Court anticipated the new generation of air-conditioned shopping malls just being introduced in Texan suburbs in the early 1960s.

The Stemmons Towers office complex (1962–1967) was the other Crow project designed by Harris, although it would be built under the supervision of Dallas architects Harold A. Berry and Associates (Fig. 12.7). The Stemmons Towers typify an emerging approach to suburban commercial office building organization and design that developer Kenneth Schnitzer would expand on in Houston at the end of the 1960s. The complex consists of four twelve-story towers set in a surface parking lot heavily planted with trees. Although the dimensions of the buildings' floor plates vary, their architectural design and detailing are identical: the towers' glass curtain wall is recessed 5 feet from the front face of their exposed structural frames. With their accentuated trabeation and pronounced parapets, the towers evoke the rationalist expression of Chicago's late nineteenth-century skyscrapers. Yet as disengaged abstract objects set in a park-like precinct alongside an elevated freeway, the Stemmons Towers also call to mind Le Corbusier's urban planning schemes of the 1920s and 1930s.

↑ Figure 12.6
Harwell Hamilton Harris and Harold A. Berry, Dallas Trade Mart, Dallas, 1959

12. Contact Zones

↑ Figure 12.7
Harwell Hamilton Harris and Harold A. Berry, Stemmons
Towers, Dallas, 1962

Houston's antipathy to zoning is legendary. Chiefly of benefit to real estate developers, the city's hands-off approach to land-use regulation helped create the conditions for urban revitalization and spatial creativity in the twenty-first century, as mixed-use zones became conduits of urban vitality. But in the absence of enormous amounts of capital and a minimum density, the results are more likely to be haphazard, and even hazardous, rather than hip. As Houston spread west in later midcentury, along Richmond Avenue, between Wakeforest Street and Buffalo Speedway, the city's two most important developers of the second half of the century, Kenneth L. Schnitzer, chair of Century Development Corporation, and Gerald D. Hines, created "Office Park," an office-building corridor that is a virtual museum of modish modernism by major Houston firms.[8] The entire zone, encompassing the Richmond buildings and Greenway Plaza to the west, is scaled to the automobile and includes several notable designs for parking.

→ Figure 12.8
Neuhaus and Taylor, 3323 Richmond Ave., Erwin, Wasey, Ruthrauff & Ryan, Inc. Building, Houston, 1961

Within the Richmond Office Park is a minidistrict of buildings by Neuhaus and Taylor. Among these are a pair of two-story white buildings at 3121 Richmond and 3323 Richmond, both of 1961, that could serve as case studies for formally differentiating similar buildings using mannered rooflines (Fig. 12.8). In place of the overhanging roof slab at 3121, 3323 was outfitted with arched eyebrows that billowed outward from perimeter structural columns. As one of Houston's many drive-thru buildings, 3323 accommodated cars beneath the main floor and in spaces denoted by a zig-zagging line aligned with the building's columns.

No less mannered, but possessing more gravitas owing to their scale and size, are the Neuhaus and Taylor–designed buildings at 3336 Richmond (1965) for Schnitzer and 2990 Richmond (1966) for Hines (Figs. 12.9, 12.10). The building at 3336 is a superb neoformalist temple set amid a plaza and atop a parking garage. With its rounded arches and ultrathin columns that terminate in repeating plaster ceiling vaults, this building is classical and Gothic at once. But its attic-level wrap-around balcony, recessed curtain wall of dark glass, and overhanging roof slab situate it firmly in the 1960s. The architectural inverse of 3336 Richmond is 2990 Richmond, located four blocks east. It is sheathed in mixed brown brick and, with its would-be solemnity and faux seriousness, just skirts being confused with industrial-era mortuary architecture. Rounded corners and convex brick bays separating vertical slot windows read like columns turned inside out, seeking to architecturally enliven the box-like building. It is perhaps the world's last expressionist building, or the first of the idiosyncratic neo-Romanesque revival, a style as yet undetected by historians. Next to the 2990 building, Wilson, Morris, Crain & Anderson's Addressograph-Multigraph Corporation Building at 2900 (1965) for Hines exhibited its architectural kinship with 2990, until it was "updated" in 2022.

Caudill Rowlett Scott designed the two-story Ketchum MacLeod & Grove Building at 3334 Richmond Avenue (1964) for Century, located between 3121 and 3336, formally and chronologically (Fig. 12.11). Low-rise, but with a huge white slab roof that appears to rest on a dark glazed prism and very thin columns, this Richmond building, despite the difference in the treatment of the columns, suggests that its architects were familiar with Ludwig Mies van der Rohe's unrealized design for the headquarters of the Bacardi Rum corporation in Santiago de Cuba.[9]

Part IV: Assemblage

← Figure 12.9
Neuhaus and Taylor, 3336 Richmond Ave., Jefferson Chemical Co. Building, Houston, 1965

↓ Figure 12.10
Neuhaus and Taylor, 2990 Richmond Ave., Houston, 1966

12. Contact Zones

↓ Figure 12.11
Caudill Rowlett Scott, Ketchum MacLeod & Grove Building,
3334 Richmond, Houston, 1964

The stretch of Richmond Avenue where these buildings stand functions almost as an architectural allée leading west to Schnizter's multiphased, multidecade mixed-use district, Greenway Plaza. Begun in 1967 on a 41-acre site assembled by Century Corporation, Greenway Plaza is a collection of modernist buildings laced together by driveways, plazas, terraces, ramps, an underground concourse, and a 5,900-car garage. The first five buildings that Century built were designed by Lloyd, Morgan and Jones between 1967 and 1975: the paired eleven-story Eastern Airlines and Union Carbide Buildings (both 1969), the twenty-one-story Kellogg Building (1971), the thirty-one-story Conoco Building (1973), and the eleven-story Traveler's Insurance Building (1975; Fig. 12.12). The buildings are unified by the insistent grids of their off-white concrete frames, which articulate each window. With their subtly classicizing proportions at ground level and attic levels, and their straightforward tectonics and clean proportions, the buildings manage to be elegant and completely ordinary seeming at once. They are entirely at home in Houston.

Greenway Plaza has an impressive infrastructure of its own, much of it invisible from the street. A basement-level concourse, once known as the Underground, contained movie theaters and shops. Now primarily a food court, it still provides air-conditioned pedestrian access to some of the buildings in Greenway Plaza. Fully enclosed skybridges connect buildings on either side of Richmond, making Greenway Plaza a case study in how architecture helps Houstonians avoid going outside. (There is a similar scheme downtown, where buildings are connected via a tunnel system and, in some cases, air-conditioned street-spanning bridges.) The concourse links phase one to a hotel (1976) and to the Summit (1976, by Kenneth Bentsen Associates and Lloyd Jones Associates). The Summit was once a sleekly understated freeway-oriented sports and entertainment arena, home to the Houston Rockets. Now, rather than accommodating professional basketball games, it houses spectacles of a different sort, having undergone an architectural conversion in 2005 to become Lakewood Church, one of the largest Evangelical churches in the world.

Part of Century's success was due to its skill in hiring architects who had a keen sense of restrained up-to-dateness. Phase three of Greenway Plaza includes two sets of twinned office buildings, Summit Tower East (1978) and Summit Tower West (1980), and the Summit Towers North (1981), by Lloyd Jones Brewer and Associates, all sheathed in gridded reflective glass. Set pieces of the late 1970s and early 1980s, they are the

12. Contact Zones

↓ Figure 12.12
Lloyd, Morgan and Jones, twenty-one-story Kellogg Building, 1971, thirty-one-story Conoco Building, 1973, eleven-story Travelers Insurance Building, 1975

Figure 12.13
Lloyd Jones Brewer and Associates, Greenway Plaza, Summit Towers North (left, curved wall, 1981), Summit Tower East (1978), and Summit Tower West (1980) on right

suburban counterparts of Dallas's Fountain Place and, with it, constitute a giant-scaled lesson in the manipulation of primary forms. Two are shimmery thirty-one-story light blue boxes; the other pair are long fifteen-story rectangles, whose short ends are rounded on one side and chamfered on the other (Fig. 12.13). The twin thirty-story Greenway Condominiums (1980, 1981), by Lloyd Jones Brewer and Associates, stand nearby.

Art and the City

Houston's other major modernist district is noncontiguous and is identified not with an architecture or use but by patronage. Although the Menil District encompasses the University of St. Thomas, a more circumscribed version would focus on the Rothko Chapel (1971) by Philip Johnson, Howard Barnstone, and Eugene Aubry, the Menil Collection museum (1987) by Renzo Piano and Richard Fitzgerald, and the gray-and-white-painted 1920s bungalows framing these institutional buildings (Figs. 12.14–12.15).[10] The museum takes its cues from the houses' forms, scale, and materials, and together the buildings are a compelling reminder of the influence vernacular forms have long exerted on modern architects. De Menil began buying the bungalows in the 1960s, in part to house artists, and with the completion of the Rothko Chapel and later the museum, knit a patch of an urbanistically discordant city into an internationally renowned arts precinct. The zone illustrates the value of preservation and understatement, while Piano and Fitzgerald's building masterfully illustrates that resolutely modernist buildings can live sympathetically alongside historic ones. The ferro-cement leaves, designed with engineer Peter Rice of Ove Arup, evoke the verdant courtyards of the Menil houses in Caracas and Houston. The pristine, subtly technophilic museum is enriched by its dialogue with the bungalows, just as the neighborhood benefits immeasurably from its proximity to the Menil Collection.

In the world of Menil architecture, Renzo Piano was preceded by Philip Johnson and Howard Barnstone. Barnstone admired Johnson tremendously. During the course of his long association with the Menils, Barnstone was called on to add to, adapt, and carry out Johnson's designs. With his partner, Eugene Aubry, Barnstone reworked the section of Johnson's design for the Rothko Chapel after Mark Rothko's strident rejection of Johnson's skylight proposal led Johnson to resign the commission. Johnson's first Houston building was a house for Dominique and John de Menil (1951), built 1.75 miles west of the museum on San Felipe Road (Fig. 12.16). Miesian in its flat-roofed austerity, length, and white, cornice-like fascia panel, the house comes from the moment in Johnson's career when he was working out his intensely complicated relationship to transparency and opacity in his own house in New Canaan, Connecticut (1949). The Menil House conceals a differentiated floor plan behind a long, planar front elevation penetrated by a glazed entry portal and a pair of narrow ribbon windows.

It calls to mind not so much Johnson's Glass House as the Guest House, which is windowless on three sides. Within the house is a

↓ Figure 12.14
Renzo Piano and Richard Fitzgerald, The Menil Collection, Houston, 1987

→ Figure 12.15 Architects unidentified, Menil Bungalows, Houston, 1920s. Rehabilitated and painted gray by Howard Barnstone et al., mid-1970s.

↑ Figure 12.16
Philip Johnson and Associates, Howard Barnstone; Charles James, Dominique and John de Menil House, Houston, 1951

garden court, opened to the main public spaces of the house by floor-to-ceiling glass, and which Barnstone later covered with a canopy. Dominique and John de Menil retained the couturier Charles James to install furniture and interior finishes that were considerably less restrained than the house's exterior.[11]

The artist Donald Judd (1928–1994), like Dominique and John de Menil, demonstrated the power of linking modern art to historic preservation in the noncontiguous district (really, more of a metadistrict) Judd conceptualized in the isolated Trans-Pecos town of Marfa, Texas.

With the acquisition, beginning in 1973, of a series of properties in the center of town and at its edge, Judd transformed the tiny West Texas town into a modern art mecca. The consequences of his undertaking are somewhat disconcerting. Marfa belongs to what might be called the Alpine–Fort Davis metro region, but the closest big city, El Paso, is nearly 200 miles away. Trains regularly thunder through the middle of the dusty, sunbaked town. Yet when it is filled with affluent art aficionados eager for the atmospheric thrill that Marfa delivers without being deprived of global, luxury consumption opportunities, Marfa's swanky brand of austerity can feel contrived and alienating. Judd could not have foreseen this result, but as a consequence of the town's status as one of the two poles of the Donald Judd Foundation—the other is in New York City—and its attraction for Texan urbanites in search of vacation houses, Marfa is an almost exaggerated case study in the double-edged sword of gentrification.

Financially and administratively separate from the Judd Foundation is the Chinati Foundation. Donald Judd controlled both foundations but assigned different assets and responsibilities to each. Between them, the two foundations own fifteen buildings in Marfa and are the biggest industry in town.[12] Judd began to create The Block, or La Mansana de Chinati, in 1973, when he bought the first of the three original buildings of what today is a nine-building complex just south of the railroad tracks and on Highway 90, and which includes several buildings Judd designed. The artist and his family moved into the compound in 1979. Maintained by the Chinati Foundation is the former Marfa Wool and Mohair Building. In the 1980s, Judd adapted this building with the artist John Chamberlain and installed twenty-five of Chamberlain's large chromium-plated steel sculptures. Some of these, including *Chili Terlingua*, *Glasscock-Notrees*, and *Panna Normanna*, had once stood on an Amarillo-area ranch and have names inspired by Texas places (Fig. 12.17).

The Marfa National Bank and the adjoining Brite Building on Marfa's main street, Highland Avenue, were designed by an obscure architect, Leighton G. Knipe, and constructed in 1931. In 1988, Judd bought the vacant but spritely bank building and reimagined it as the Architecture Studio (Fig. 12.18). The artist completed renovations only partially, making it a particularly interesting example of preservation as a process. The main banking hall remains in an in-between state, while entering the upstairs is a bit like taking a trip to Europe in the 1920s. Here one can see Judd's collection of modernist furniture, including works by Alvar Aalto and Gerrit Rietveld, along with the artist's own designs.

At the edge of town, the Chinati Foundation buildings stand on land that was part of Fort D. A. Russell, which Judd acquired for the purpose of housing his work and that of John Chamberlain and Dan Flavin. (The artist roster has grown since.) The centerpiece of the site consists of two aligned concrete and brick truck garages (renamed the Artillery Sheds) with vaulted Quonset roofs added by the artist. These house one hundred of Judd's aluminum boxes in dramatic fashion. Outside, seen against the landscape, are a series of his large concrete boxes. Nearby is the Arena, which was built as an airplane hangar and later used as a gymnasium for the fort (Fig. 12.19). The ensemble is affecting in the way it invites viewers to consider the relationships between industry, militarism, and modern art, some of the core issues

→ Figure 12.17
Architect unidentified, Marfa Wool and Mohair Building, Marfa; renovated by Donald Judd, 1980s. Sculptures by John Chamberlain, 1972–1975.

↓ Figure 12.18
Leighton G. Knipe, Marfa National Bank and Brite Building, Marfa, 1931

Part IV: Assemblage

↓ Figure 12.19
Architect unidentified, The Arena, Fort D. A. Russell, Marfa, 1930s; renovated by Donald Judd, 1980s.

in the history of the twentieth century. Understanding the multilayered history of the site adds to its complexity. The base was established during the Mexican Revolution to forestall raids and violence that might spill north; in 1924, it served as the base of a patrol created to keep Mexicans from crossing the border. During World War II, it continued to be used to deter immigration, was a base for the Women's Army Corps and a training center for chemical mortar battalions, and housed a German POW camp, where two inmates, Hans Jürgen Press and Robert Humpel, painted murals in 1945, in Building 98.

The Judd buildings in Marfa, particularly at Fort D. A. Russell, with the artist's sculptures constitute an important district in the state and represent a significant episode in the history of modern art. They help bring the town's buildings, the Texas landscape, and fraught histories into view. Yet, like all very successful projects, they can also obscure other buildings and histories. Less than a mile from Fort D. A. Russell is the single remaining building of the Blackwell School campus, which served Mexican American children in Marfa before de facto segregation ended in 1965, when the Marfa Independent School District integrated (Fig. 12.20). Here students were taught not to speak Spanish and, in 1954, made to write "I will not speak Spanish" on pieces of paper that were put into a box and buried during a "funeral" led by a Blackwell teacher on the school grounds. The children were told that they were burying "Mr. Spanish," and thereby marking the death of the language they and their families spoke.

↑ Figure 12.20
Architect unidentified, Blackwell School, Marfa, 1909–1965. Courtesy of the Blackwell School Alliance.

This episode is burned into the memories of Blackwell alumni, some of whom returned to the campus in 2007 to participate in a symbolic unearthing and reclamation of their language.[13] Even as it is a site associated with cultural suppression, the Blackwell School was an important locus in the development of a vibrant Mexican American community in West Texas. Today, the school is a small but powerful rejoinder to the Lamar High School map, 600 miles east. Together the two buildings invite Texans to reflect on whether their state is in fact big enough to redress the spatial, social, and historic erasures, omissions, and drawing of boundaries that have served to exclude, and to embrace instead, in the words of architect Robert Venturi, "the difficult unity of inclusion, rather than the easy unity of exclusion."[14] In 2021, the United States Congress designated the Blackwell School a National Historic Site.

CODA

What We Save and Why

Previous Spread: Page Southerland Page, Rio House Apartments, Austin, 1959. Gothic Revival elements of the original building, St. David's Hospital, by Giesecke & Harris (1928), are visible beneath the slipcover at lower right.

As fashionable as the modernisms of midcentury have become for some people, particularly those who are affluent and highly educated, for others, buildings like those in this book are objects to be treated with indifference at best and often with scorn. Lacking the obvious markers of historicity, seemingly abundant and overly familiar, often decontextualized in their landscapes, sometimes neglected, and as the formal predecessors of so many (often less well designed and built) buildings of our own time, such works are not infrequently disparaged as "ugly" and compared to "prisons," or even to the schools that were loci of apparently less-than-happy memories. Preservation in any era is an uphill struggle, but attitudes such as these present particular challenges to today's preservationists, especially because they are coupled with entrenched cultural obsessions with newness and economic conditions that often make demolition and new building cheaper—at least in the short term—than adaptive reuse and rehabilitation. But, using tax credit programs tied to the National Register of Historic Preservation, the governments of the United States and Texas have incentivized preservation, and fruitful and interesting results have followed. Whatever one's opinion about architecture, the value of preservation is unambiguous. Because buildings consume 40 percent of the energy used in the United States each year and emit (at some point in the building process) nearly half of all carbon dioxide, in the age of climate change, reuse is imperative. As every architect knows, but may be disinclined to say, the greenest building is the one that already exists. Many of the architects and patrons discussed here were fervent preservationists. In 1976, as energy prices soared and the environmental movement gained steam, *Texas Architect* devoted its entire March/April issue to architectural reuse. A building in the midst of demolition was pictured on the cover, along with the declaration "It could have been recycled."

    Architectural recycling can occur in a variety of ways and at many scales—through the reuse of materials and elements, for example, as Richard S. Colley did at the Dos Cruces Gallery in Corpus Christi (1967; Fig. C.1); or in the repurposing of entire blocks or swaths of a city, as Rick Lowe, Deborah Grotfeldt, and Michael Peranteau did twenty-five years later with Project Row Houses in Houston's Third Ward (1993; Fig. C.2); or by repurposing buildings, as Phillips/Ryburn Associates did in converting into office and studio spaces Frito-Lay's 1945 grain elevators, where some of the state's most beloved chips

Coda

↑ Figure C.1
Richard S. Colley, Dos Cruces Gallery, Corpus Christi, 1967

→ Figure C.2
Architect unidentified, Frank Cash Row, Houston, 1939–1941; repurposed as Project Row Houses by Rick Lowe, Deborah Grotfeldt, and Michael Peranteau, 1993

were prepared, in Dallas's Deep Ellum district (1985; Fig. C.3). San Antonio's Riverwalk, which now extends north and south of the core most familiar to tourists, is perhaps Texas's longest-running example of the value of history and adaptation for new purposes. The reinvention of the Pearl Brewery in that city is a national model of the power of commingling preservation with the patronage of high-quality new architecture to add value in the private and public sectors alike in an urban core. Even if they are less atmospheric than nineteenth-century industrial buildings like those at the Pearl, twentieth-century office buildings can be repurposed as housing or hotels, and often converted for new commercial uses. In Houston, the Barbara Jordan Post Office, a superb work by Wilson, Morris, Crain & Anderson (1962) built on the site of the 1934 Grand Central Station, and which incorporated some of the station's walls, has recently been reinvented as Post, a shopping and commercial hub with an impressive rooftop park and farm.

From the vantage of the twenty-first century, the Air Conditioned Village stands out as a reminder that time-tested ideas in architecture, such as mitigating heat using devices like overhangs, shutters, and lattices, and organizing plans to maximize ventilation, need not disappear with the introduction of new technologies. By today's standards, the houses' 1,500-square-foot size appears modest but brings into relief the excessive largeness of many new suburban houses today. Air Conditioned Village reminds us that less is in fact often much more. The potential to reconfigure, rezone, and reimagine suburban blocks, whether to accommodate accessory dwelling units or reshape communities to prioritize people instead of cars, is vast, as Dolores Hayden and other scholars and architects have explained.[1]

As important as its prospective ecological value is, preservation also has the capacity to help us understand history, interrogate the present, and imagine new futures and new narratives. Being able to study extant buildings helps historians understand them. The architectural history of the twentieth century has only begun to be written, and the buildings in this book, which represent a small fraction of the architecture of twentieth-century Texas, only hint at how much more there is to learn. They raise questions for scholars and students interested in the global reach of architectural modernism and the modes and meanings of its diverse manifestations. How, for example, did the patronage of modern architecture by a Texas elite made wealthy

Coda

↓ Figure C.3
Eugene Davis; Phillips/Ryburn Associates, adaptive reuse,
3800 Main Street/Silos, Dallas 1945, 1989

by oil differ from that sponsored by Europe's industrial elite in the 1920s—that is, what did Greta and Fritz Tugendhat have in common with Anne and Sid Bass, if anything? Are there parallels to be found in the invention of modern Texas and the creation of modern Israel, when considered architecturally through the works at the Centennial Exposition orchestrated by George L. Dahl on behalf of the state, on the one hand, and the buildings Erich Mendelsohn designed on behalf of the British government in Mandatory Palestine in conjunction with his great patron and Zionist, Salman Schocken, on the other? How might O'Neil Ford's architecture be understood differently if it were considered as part of a hemispheric brick modernism that included the works of Eladio Dieste in Uruguay, Rogelio Salmona in Colombia, and the unfinished art schools in Havana by Ricardo Porro, Vittorio Garatti, and Roberto Gottardi?

Preservation also makes it easier to look within and discern episodes and transformations in national and local cultures. The restoration—down to the fabric on the chairs and the ashtrays on the tables—of Mission Control at the Manned Space Center to its 1960s guise reminds visitors of a heroic age of science and space travel (Fig. C.4), while Voertman's Bookstore in Denton (now a real estate office), of the same era, recalls the time when small, independent bookstores were more numerous than they are today and, often, anchors of communities.[2] In downtown Tyler, the Union Bus Station typifies architectural recycling (Fig. C.5). It began life in 1932 as the Campbell Building, a mixed-use commercial and residential building, with retail spaces on the ground level and five apartments above. In 1946, Dixie-Sunshine-Trailways bought the building, added a new wing designed by Tyler architect George Howard, and reopened it as a bus station, with racially segregated waiting rooms. Buses arrived and departed there as recently as 2019. In 2023, the building is being transformed once again, this time into a boutique hotel.

When buildings are thoughtfully and consistently maintained, they can serve as examples of historic design and community, and even family, histories. One outstanding example is the Childress Optometrists building in Longview (Fig. C.6). The single-story medical office building was designed by Wilson, Morris & Crain in 1951. With sloping ceilings that follow the roofline, brick walls, wooden panels, and expansive glazing, the building has elements and materials common to small and informal midcentury Texas structures.

Coda

↑ Figure C.4
US Army Corps of Engineers; Brown and Root and Manned Spacecraft Center Architects Charles Luckman Associates, Brooks and Barr, MacKie and Kamrath, Harvin C. Moore, and Wirtz, Calhoun, Tungate and Jackson, Building 30, Mission Control, Johnson Space Center, Clear Lake, 1962–1964. Restoration led by Stern and Bucek Architects, 2019.

→ Figure C.5
Union Bus Station, Tyler, 1932; 1946 addition by George Howard

↑ Figure C.6
Wilson, Morris & Crain, Childress Optometrists, Longview, 1951

But with its original cabinetry and countertops, period furniture, and even some historic tools—from chalk boards, to machines, to manuals—the interior is unusually intact. Today, the building houses the practice of Dr. Carl W. Childress. His parents, Drs. Raymond and Mary Childress, began practicing optometry in Longview in the late 1930s. Historic modern interiors such as those at Childress Optometrists are increasingly rare and valuable documents of earlier eras of design.

Losses, and the struggles to prevent them, help crystalize historically significant events and contemporary values for new generations. In 2013, the San Antonio building where the nation's first Spanish-language radio and television station, KCOR-TV, the predecessor of Univisión, began broadcasting in 1955 was demolished, over the objections of the Texas Historical Commission, the Conservation Society of San Antonio, and the Esperanza Peace and Justice Center (Fig. C.7). Designed by Cerf Ross-Edwin Nicholson Associates, the sleek, high-modernist gem was razed to make way for a 350-unit apartment complex built by an out-of-state developer. The loss was not only architectural. The demolition symbolically erased a major part of US cultural and journalism history and, to many, read as part of a long pattern in city governance of privileging the interests of mostly white real estate developers over Spanish-speaking Texans.

↑ Figure C.7
Cerf Ross-Edwin Nicholson Associates, KCOR Radio and Television Station, San Antonio, 1955 (demolished). UTSA Libraries Special Collections.

Other buildings, such as the Geraldine D. Humphreys Cultural Center in Liberty by William R. Jenkins (1970), a monumental structure built of reinforced concrete, with an exposed steel space-frame roof and faced in unfinished concrete block, serve as links to complicated histories (Fig. C.8). The Humphreys Center is named for Liberty benefactor Geraldine Davis Humphreys, who was a descendant of one of Texas's early Anglo settler colonists, Benjamin Franklin Hardin. Like some other white men who moved to Texas in the 1820s, Hardin seems to have come to escape being arrested in another state. He participated in the Texas Revolution in several capacities and managed the internment of Mexican soldiers on his brother's plantation. Hardin participated in battles against Indigenous Texans in 1836 and owned at least one enslaved person, whose name is recorded as Aunt Harriet. As a state legislator and a surveyor, Hardin worked to advance the rights of white landowners. Geraldine Humphries inherited Hardin's plantation,

↑ Figure C.8
William R. Jenkins, Geraldine D. Humphreys Cultural Center, Liberty, 1970

Seven Pines, which her foundation donated to the city of Liberty, and she was a significant donor to the Kalita Humphreys Theater in Dallas, one of the state's most important buildings by Frank Lloyd Wright.

As preservationists and architectural historians increasingly recognize, histories that prioritize form and style above all other issues are likely to leave out the stories of many people and groups. Formal preservation processes address this by including categories of significance beyond strictly architectural ones. The value of such an approach is not only that it makes it easier to include more buildings in official records but that it opens the door for historians and preservationists of the future to designate works that, in hindsight, are significant for reasons that may only become clear in the future. Whole Woman's Health Clinic in McAllen may be one such building (Fig. C.9). When the first draft of this book was written, Whole Woman's Health housed the only health care facility in South Texas where it was possible to get an abortion. Architecturally, there is little to distinguish the one-story, 1981 building other than the pilasters on the long exterior wall. But since abortion became almost entirely illegal in Texas in 2022, the Whole Woman's Health Clinic building has taken on new meaning. Its historical significance lies not in what it looks like or who designed it, but in the fact that it was a place that helped Texans exercise rights that the state now denies.[3] In 2015, on the building's façade, artist Carina Carmona painted a mural that in its use of figures rendered as types and set against landscapes recalls the WPA-era murals that appeared in courthouses, post offices, and other public buildings throughout the state. But rather than depicting battle, colonization, or resource extraction, the images are of care and cooperation, a point that Carmona emphasized by painting the words "dignity," "empowerment," "compassion," and "justice" above the bays.

↑ Figure C.9
Whole Woman's Health Clinic, McAllen, 1981. Mural by Carina Carmona, 2015. Photograph by Ángela García.

One of Texas's greatest and most beloved assets, and the focus of some of the most impressive design work being done today, is the state's landscape, particularly along rivers and waterways. For this reason, *Home, Heat, Money, God* concludes with the former headquarters of the Brazos River Authority in Waco (1960; Fig. C.10). The Brazos River watershed runs through Texas from New Mexico in the northwest to the Gulf of Mexico in the southeast, over roughly 1,050 miles, nearly all of them in the state. It crosses the High Plains, the

Blackland Prairie, the Edwards Plateau, and the Gulf Coast Prairies and Marshes. Among the cities in the river basin are Lubbock, Waco, Temple, Belton, Georgetown, Round Rock, Bryan-College Station, Freeport, and Galveston. The Dallas-Fort Worth, Austin, and Houston metropolitan areas are just outside the watershed. Indigenous Texans who spoke Caddoan languages called the river Tokonohono; the Spanish named it Los Brazos de Dios (The Arms of God).

Separated from the street by a large parking lot, in its spatial relationship to its context, the former River Authority headquarters fits into familiar Texas patterns, but its architect was one of midcentury Waco's leading designers. Robert S. Bennett's building has a thin slab roof and a hexagonal honeycomb solar screen that contrasts elegantly with courses of beige Roman brick. A long rear brick wall adds to the building's association with Mies's brick houses of the 1920s, even as the screen locates it firmly in the 1960s. The building belongs to Texas's body of well-designed and well-executed nonmonumental governmental works, and its formal restraint makes it easy to overlook, like much of what government does.

↓ Figure C.10
Robert S. Bennett,
Brazos River Authority
Headquarters, Waco, 1960

Coda

The Brazos River Authority was created in 1929 by the state of Texas and was the first such agency in the United States tasked with managing an entire river basin. When the agency moved into its new building, the sweeping environmental laws that helped restore and clean Texas waterways had not yet been passed. Today, as flooding and drought become more frequent and severe throughout Texas, the River Authority faces new challenges. But it does so from another building. The old Brazos River Authority Headquarters is now the offices of the Waco Housing Authority and Affiliates, which, in being dedicated to helping provide homes for low-income Texans, likewise endeavors to address one of the titanic challenges of our time.

Responsibly balancing human needs and care of the earth has long animated Texans' discussions of architecture. In June of 1968, Lady Bird Johnson delivered the B. Y. Morrison Lecture at the 100th annual meeting of the American Institute of Architects. She told the members of the AIA:

> *I speak to you today . . . only as a citizen deeply concerned about the relationship between the natural world and the world we are building. I am one of millions of Americans who are both troubled—and hopeful—about the physical setting of life in our country.*[4]

The First Lady contrasted Indigenous attitudes toward land with those that prevailed in her time, saying that the first Americans "were users and sharers of their environment—not exploiters of it." She decried the "sacrifice of human values to commercial values" and outlined the principles of the "New Conservation," which included banning advertising signage on highways, limiting vehicles in city centers, preserving historic structures, and building on a human scale to create places where "people's imagination and variety of choice can flourish." Mrs. Johnson concluded her remarks by imploring the architects, "So deep is the environmental crisis; so urgent is the demand for change, that architecture must become not only a profession—but a form of public service . . . I know that the nature we are concerned with, ultimately, is *human* nature. That is the point of the beautification movement—and that, finally, is the point of architecture."[5]

Acknowledgments

This book is built on the research of others, and especially that of Stephen Fox, whose knowledge of the architecture of Texas is unsurpassed. I am grateful to Stephen for creating through his work a monumental foundation for the continued study of Texas's architectural history; for relentlessly modeling meticulous research practice and incisive critique; and for the generosity he has shown to me for many years. The extraordinary attention and care he gave to this manuscript when it was in draft form improved it immeasurably. The errors in it are mine.

Always stimulating, the conversations Kathryn E. Holliday and I have had about Texas architecture have made me a more curious and better scholar and, especially since 2020, led me to think about architectural history writing in new ways. I thank her for these; for her many excellent suggestions for improving the manuscript; and for her leadership in architectural history writing, teaching, and preservation in this state.

For six years, I had the privilege of serving on the State Board of Review of the Texas Historical Commission reviewing nominations to the National Register of Historic Places. Much of what I learned then

Acknowledgments

about Texas architecture and saw of the state ripples through this book. The History Programs Division, through which nominations are processed, is a gem within the THC, and among its staff I especially thank Gregory Smith, Bonnie Tipton, Alyssa Gerszewski, and Judy George-Garza for their work and for letting me be part of the fun.

I am grateful to friends and family for encouraging me in this project, and especially to Susanna Morrow for helping me understand the Texas Panhandle by sharing her experiences of growing up there. Kenyon Weaver helped me recall the recent history of Lamar High School, and Mark Gunderson made it possible for me and Ben Koush to spend an astounding afternoon at the Bass House. Perky Beisel and Judy Kugle helped us to see, appreciate, and illustrate the architecture of East Texas. Enormous thanks go to our wonderful editor, Robert Devens, and to Robert Kimzey, Adrienne Gilg, Derek George, Nancy Warrington, and the team at the University of Texas Press. Ian Searcy's creative and insightful design work helped make this a beautiful book. Five Trinity University students organized captions, made drawings and a photograph, and let me bounce ideas off them. I thank them all heartily: Alia Ahmed, Olivia Bowness, Ángela García, Ryanna Henson, and Luke Leblanc.

As ever, I am grateful to Curtis Swope, Patrick Swope, and Miranda Swope for their patience, humor, and love, and for driving with me from San Antonio to Lubbock one Thanksgiving so that I could look at buildings.

—Kathryn E. O'Rourke

First I must thank my coauthor Kathryn O'Rourke for enthusiastically agreeing to collaborate on this project. In addition to many of the people named above, especially Stephen Fox, the THC staff, Ian Searcy, and the editors at the University of Texas Press, I would like to express my gratitude to and admiration for the Houston Mod board, who have organized a series of extraordinary architectural tours throughout Texas and Louisiana during the past decade. Special thanks must go to Marty Merritt, who has enthusiastically tracked down architects' names and dates for many projects. Finally, I would like to acknowledge Luis M. de las Cuevas, who patiently accompanied me on many trips to faraway places.

—Ben Koush

Notes

Introduction: History and Mythology in Texas Architecture

1. "Secondary Schools," *Architectural Forum* 70 (May 1939): 351–366.
2. Cheryl Caldwell Ferguson, *Highland Park and River Oaks: The Origins of Garden Suburban Community Planning in Texas* (Austin: University of Texas Press, 2014), esp. 269–271.
3. On the Rosenwald School program, see Mary S. Hoffschwelle, *The Rosenwald Schools of the American South* (Gainesville: University Press of Florida, 2006; reprinted 2014); Frank Lloyd Wright also designed schools for the Rosenwald program. On these, see Mabel O. Wilson, "Rosenwald School: Lessons in Progressive Education," in *Frank Lloyd Wright: Unpacking the Archive*, ed. Barry Bergdoll and Jennifer Gray (New York: Museum of Modern Art Books, 2017), 96–113.
4. On Rosenwald Schools in Texas and the ongoing effort to catalogue and preserve them, see https://www.thc.texas.gov/rosenwald.
5. On the Columbia Rosenwald School, see Ben Koush, "Neglected Legacy," *Texas Architect* (January–February 2003): 20.
6. For an overview of modern architecture in the United States, see Gwendolyn Wright, *USA* (London: Reaktion Books, 2008).
7. Texas architecture has been documented and interpreted chiefly by architects and critics. On this history, see Stephen Fox, "The Tradition of Architecture and Criticism in Texas," in *The Open-Ended City: David Dillon on Texas Architecture*, ed. Kathryn E. Holliday (Austin: University of Texas Press, 2019), 400–414.
8. *La patria y la arquitectura nacional: Resúmenes de las conferencias dadas en la casa de la Universidad Popular Mexicana del 21 de octubre de 1913 al 29 de julio de 1914*, ed. Federico Mariscal (Mexico City: Imprenta Stephan y Torres, 1914); Le Corbusier, *Vers une architecture* (Paris: Les Éditions G. Crès, 1923); Frank Lloyd Wright, "Architecture and Modern Life" (1937), in *The Essential Frank Lloyd Wright*, ed. Bruce Brooks Pfeiffer (Princeton: Princeton University Press, 2008), 276–291; Robert Venturi, *Complexity and Contradiction in Architecture* (New York: Museum of Modern Art, 1966).
9. On the International Style exhibition, see Mark Crinson, *Rebuilding Babel: Modern Architecture and Internationalism* (London: I. B. Tauris, 2017), 142–153.
10. Anthony Alofsin, *The Struggle for Modernism: Architecture, Landscape Architecture, and City Planning at Harvard* (New York: W. W. Norton, 2002); William J. R. Curtis, *Modern Architecture Since 1900*, 3rd ed. (London: Phaidon, 1996); Neil Levine, *Modern Architecture: Representation and Reality* (New Haven: Yale University Press, 2009); Thomas S. Hines, *Architecture and Design at the Museum of Modern Art: The Arthur Drexler Years, 1951–1986* (Los Angeles: Getty Research Institute, 2019); Charles L. Davis II, *Building Character: the Racial Politics of Modern Architectural Style* (Pittsburgh: University of Pittsburgh Press, 2021).
11. Irene Cheng, Charles L. Davis II, and Mabel O. Wilson, eds., *Race and Modern Architecture: A Critical History from the Enlightenment to the Present* (Pittsburgh: University of Pittsburgh Press, 2020).
12. For an example, see Gabriela Campagnol, "Hell-Hole of the Brazos into Model Company Town: Architecture and Urban Space in Texas's Sugar Land," *Arris: Journal of the Southeastern Chapter of the Society of Architectural Historians* 32 (2021): 22–39.
13. See, for example, proceedings of the seminar at the 25th annual Texas Society of Architects Convention, "Is There an Antidote for Ugliness?," *Texas Architect* (December 1964): 6–15.
14. Lyndon B. Johnson, "Quality of American Life," *Texas Architect* (August 1964): 3.
15. Arthur Fehr, "Cities Can Be Beautiful," *Texas Architect* (March 1963): 3.
16. On Cret, see Carol McMichael Reese and Drury Blakely Alexander, *Paul Cret at Texas: Architectural Drawing and the Image of the University in the 1930s*, exhib. cat. (Austin: Hart Graphics, 1983).
17. On Fair Park, see David Dillon, *Dallas Architecture, 1936–1986* (Austin: Texas Monthly Press, 1985), 10–30; Lawrence W. Speck, *Landmarks of Texas Architecture* (Austin: University of Texas Press, 1986), 71–75.
18. As part of the Texas Historical Commission's work to document the sites associated with the 1936 fair, Bonnie Tipton Wilson created a thorough history of the fair and its reach. See Wilson and Gregory Smith, "Monuments and Buildings Erected by the State of Texas to Commemorate the Texas Centennial, 1936–1939," National Register of Historic Places, Multiple Property Documentation Form (2018) and "Monuments and Buildings of the Texas Centennial," https://www.thc.texas.gov/TexasCentennial (accessed July 11, 2023).
19. Don Edward Legge, "The Plight of the San Jacinto Monument," *Texas Architect* (March 1963): 4–9.
20. Legge, "The Plight of the San Jacinto Monument," 4.
21. Louis I. Kahn, foreword to Clovis Heimsath, *Pioneer Texas Buildings: A Geometry Lesson* (Austin: University of Texas Press, 1968), no page number.
22. On Harris in Texas, see Lisa Germany, *Harwell Hamilton Harris* (Austin: University of Texas Press, 1991), 139–187.
23. Alexander Caragonne, *The Texas Rangers: Notes from an Architectural Underground* (Cambridge, MA, and London: MIT Press, 1995), xi.
24. On the College of Architecture at the University of Houston, see Drexel Turner, *Open Plan: the History of the*

College of Architecture, University of Houston, 1945–1995 (Houston: Atrium Press, College of Architecture, University of Houston, 1995); and Bruce C. Webb, "Barnstone and the University of Houston," in *Making Houston Modern: The Life and Architecture of Howard Barnstone*, ed. Barrie Scardino Bradley, Stephen Fox, and Michelangelo Sabatino (Austin: University of Texas Press, 2020), 240–263.

25. Avigail Sachs, "Marketing through Research: William Caudill and Caudill, Rowlett, Scott (CRS)," *Journal of Architecture* 21, no. 4 (2016): 524–529; Paulo Tombesi, "Capital Gains and Architectural Losses: The Transformative Journey of Caudill Rowlett Scott (1948–1994)," *Journal of Architecture* 21, no. 4 (2016): 540–563.

26. On the Kalita Humphreys Theater, see Joseph M. Siry, "Modern Architecture for Dramatic Art: Frank Lloyd Wright's 'New Theatre,' 1931–2009," *Art Bulletin* 96, no. 2 (2014): 211–237; On the Kraigher House: *Kraigher House by Richard Neutra, Brownsville, Texas* (Brownsville: University of Texas at Brownsville and Texas Southernmost College, 2005).

27. Frank D. Welch, *Philip Johnson & Texas* (Austin: University of Texas Press, 2000).

28. Alice T. Friedman, *American Glamour and the Evolution of Modern Architecture* (New Haven: Yale University Press, 2010).

29. Mark Lamster, *The Man in the Glass House: Philip Johnson, Architect of the Modern Century* (New York: Little, Brown, 2018).

30. The design for the New National Gallery evolved from a 1957 scheme for the Bacardi corporate headquarters in Santiago, Cuba.

31. See Mary Carolyn Hollers George, *O'Neil Ford, Architect* (College Station: Texas A&M University Press, 1992), 44–50.

32. After a thirty-year career at Skidmore, Owings & Merrill, Natalie de Blois worked at Neuhaus and Taylor (renamed 3-D International) in Houston (1975–1980) and taught in the School of Architecture at the University of Texas at Austin from 1980 to 1993, during which time she practiced at Graeber, Simmons & Cowan in Austin. On de Blois, see https://pioneeringwomen.bwaf.org/natalie-griffin-de-blois.

33. On the Texas Pool, see "Texas Pool," National Register of Historic Places Form (approved by the National Parks Service, 2019): https://atlas.thc.texas.gov/NR/pdfs/100003598/100003598.pdf.

34. Timothy M. Matovina, *The Alamo Remembered: Tejano Accounts and Perspectives* (Austin: University of Texas Press, 1995); Bryan Burrough, Chris Tomlinson, and Jason Stanford, *Forget the Alamo: the Rise and Fall of an American Myth* (New York: Penguin Random House, 2021); Mario Marcel Salas, *The Alamo: A Cradle of Lies, Slavery, and White Supremacy* (Lakeway, TX: Sentia, 2022).

35. Beatriz Colomina was among the first scholars to analyze architecture and photography together. See, for example, Colomina, "Le Corbusier and Photography," *Assemblage*, no. 4 (October 1987): 6–23. More recent discussions include Claire Zimmerman, "Reading the (Photographic) Evidence," *Journal of the Society of Architectural Historians* 76, no. 4 (December 2017): 446–448; Mike Christenson, "Critical Dimensions in Architectural Photography: Contributions to Architectural Knowledge," *Architecture, Media, Politics, Society* 11, no. 2 (January 2017): 1–17.

36. Paul Hester, *The Elusive City: Photographs of Houston* (Houston: The Menil Collection, October 16, 1998–January 3, 1999). See also Kathryn E. O'Rourke, "Houston Is Almost All Right: Postmodernism on the Texas Gulf Coast," *Journal of the Society of Architectural Historians* 79, no. 3 (September 2020): 308–330.

37. On Barnstone and *The Galveston That Was*, see Kathryn E. Holliday, "To Be Modern in Texas: Lone Star Avant-Garde," in *Making Houston Modern: The Life and Architecture of Howard Barnstone* (Austin: University of Texas Press, 2020), 94–117; and Kathryn E. O'Rourke, "Houston Is Almost All Right: Postmodernism on the Texas Gulf Coast," *Journal of the Society of Architectural Historians* 79, no. 3 (September 2020): 308–330.

38. Email, Ben Koush to Kathryn E. O'Rourke, June 2, 2021.

39. Email, Ben Koush to Kathryn E. O'Rourke, July 12, 2021.

40. Garnette Cadogan, "Black and Blue" (2015), published in *The Fire This Time: A New Generation Speaks about Race*, ed. Jesmyn Ward (New York: Scribner, 2016), 129–144.

41. Stephen Fox, "The Architecture of John S. Chase," in David Heymann and Stephen Fox, *John S. Chase—The Chase Residence* (Austin: University of Texas School of Architecture, 2020), 23–25.

42. On Welch's work, see Mabel C. Welch, *El Paso Architecture* (El Paso: Woman's Department, El Paso Chamber of Commerce, 1938).

43. I am grateful to Stephen Fox for calling my attention to the Sobrino-Cherry house and sharing his research on Ruth McGonigle and her clients with me. Stephen Fox, "Ruth Young McGonigle: Art, Architecture, and Ethnocultural Engagement on the South Texas Border," paper presented at the Thirteenth Annual CASETA Symposium, Center for the Advancement and Study of Early Texas Art, University of Houston, Houston, Texas, April 2015.

44. Alice T. Friedman, "Poker Faces: Seeing Behind the Mask of Convention," *Docomomo Journal* 51, no. 2 (2014): 69–73; *Women and the Making of the Modern House: A Social and Architectural History* (New York: Abrams, 1998).

45. Gwendolyn Wright, *Building the Dream: A Social History of Housing in America* (Cambridge, MA: MIT Press, 1981); Dolores Hayden, *Redesigning the American Dream: The Future of Housing, Work, and Family Life* (New York: W. W. Norton, 1984); Elaine Tyler May, *Homeward Bound: American Families in the Cold War Era* (Basic Books, 1988, 1999); Dianne Harris, *Little White Houses: How the Postwar Home Constructed Race in America* (Minneapolis: University of Minnesota Press, 2013).

46. On Rudolph and the homosexual "witch hunts" of the 1950s, and the damage to the careers of Bruce Goff and Charles Moore, both of whom worked in Texas, see Timothy M. Rohan, *The Architecture of Paul Rudolph* (New Haven and London: Yale University Press, 2014), 61–62.

47. Quoted in Rebecca Sherman, "Peace Prize!," *Dallas Modern Luxury* (November 2010), 64.

48. On recent and ongoing revisions to architectural

historical scholarship, see Fernando Luiz Lara et al., "What Frameworks Should We Use to Read the Spatial History of the Americas?," *Journal of the Society of Architectural Historians* 81, no. 2 (June 2022): 134–153.

49. The names of architecture firms are identified as they appear in the two Texas volumes of the Buildings of the United States series: Gerald Moorhead et al., *Buildings of Texas: Central, South, and Gulf Coast* (Charlottesville and London: University of Virginia Press; Society of Architectural Historians, 2013); Gerald Moorhead et al., *Buildings of Texas: East, North Central, Panhandle and South Plains, and West* (Charlottesville and London: University of Virginia Press; Society of Architectural Historians, 2019).

50. Houston Mod, founded in 2003, was the first organization in Texas dedicated to advocating for the preservation of modern architecture.

51. Wendy Grossman, "Strong Reservations," *Houston Press* (November 11, 1999).

Chapter 1. Home

1. Scholarship on the meanings of "home" in relation to US social, economic, and political structures abounds. For example, see Barbara Miller Lane, ed. *Housing and Dwelling: Perspectives on Modern Domestic Architecture* (New York: Routledge, 2006); Gwendolyn Wright, *Building the Dream: A Social History of Housing in America* (Cambridge, MA: MIT Press, 1981); Dolores Hayden, *Redesigning the American Dream: The Future of Housing, Work, and Family Life*, rev. ed. (New York: W. W. Norton, 2002, 1984); Bernard Friedman, ed., *The American Idea of Home: Conversations about Architecture and Design* (Austin: University of Texas Press, 2017).

2. Malcom Andrews, *Landscape and Western Art* (New York: Oxford University Press, 2000), 1–22, 164–165.

3. Stephen Fox, "Border Modern: Modern Architecture of the Texas-Mexican Border," Lower Rio Grande Valley Chapter, American Institute of Architects, Building Communities Conference, South Padre Island, September 28, 2013, 40, http://lrgvaia.org/wp-content/uploads/Border-Modern-Architecture.pdf.

4. Emily Post, *The Personality of a House* (New York and London: Funk & Wagnalls, 1930); Monica Penick, *Tastemaker: Elizabeth Gordon, House Beautiful, and the Postwar American Home* (New Haven: Yale University Press, 2017).

5. On public housing in Houston, San Antonio, and Dallas, see Robert B. Fairbanks, "Public Housing for the City as a Whole: The Texas Experience, 1934–1955," *Southwestern Historical Quarterly* 103, no. 4 (April 2000): 403–424.

6. "War Needs: Housing," *Architectural Record* 91 (April 1941): 47–62; "War Needs: Community Facilities," *Architectural Record* 91 (May 1942): 42–62; United States Department of the Interior, National Register of Historic Places Inventory—Nomination Form, San Felipe Courts Historic District, 1988; Curtis Lang, "A Depleted Legacy: Public Housing in Houston," *Cite* 33 (Fall/Winter 1995): 10–15; Willa Granger, "Order, Convenience, and Beauty": The Style, Space, and Multiple Narratives of San Felipe Courts," *Buildings and Landscapes: Journal of the Vernacular Architecture Forum* 26, no. 1 (Spring 2019): 32–47.

7. Stephen Fox, *Houston Architectural Guide*, 3rd ed. (Houston: AIA Houston, Minor Design, 2012), 104–105.

8. Other architects involved were Atlee B. and Robert M. Ayres (community center), and Gordon Smith. On the Courts, see Donald L. Zelman, "Alazan-Apache Courts: A New Deal Response to the Mexican American Housing Conditions in San Antonio," *Southwestern Historical Quarterly* 87, no. 2 (October 1983): 123–150. On housing in Mexico, see Esther Born, *The New Architecture in Mexico* (New York: The Architectural Record, William Morrow, 1937), 80–83.

9. United States Department of the Interior, National Register of Historic Places Registration Form, "Ray Sherman Place"; United States Department of the Interior, National Register of Historic Places Registration Form, "Tays Place."

10. "Apartments," *Architectural Record* 136 (August 1946): 103–128.

11. Sandy Eisenstadt, *The Modern American House: Spaciousness and Middle Class Identity* (Cambridge, UK: Cambridge University Press, 2006).

12. Martin Luther King Jr., *Where Do We Go From Here: Chaos or Community?* (Boston: Beacon Press, 1967).

13. The house was under renovation during the course of this project and could not be photographed. For images, see "House and Garden's Hallmark House for 1967," *House & Garden* (April 1967): 125–193.

14. Helen Delpar, *Enormous Vogue of Things Mexican: Cultural Relations between the United States and Mexico, 1920–1935* (Tuscaloosa: University of Alabama Press, 1992); Lisa Pinley Covert, *San Miguel de Allende: Mexicans, Foreigners, and the Making of a World Heritage Site* (Lincoln: University of Nebraska Press, 2017).

15. I am grateful to Stephen Fox for alerting me to Marshall Steves's family history.

16. As of 2023, the Bass House remains in the family and is in excellent condition, with its collections and grounds intact. We were unable to secure permission to photograph it. Images may be found in Lisa Germany, *Great Houses of Texas* (New York: Harry N. Abrams, 2008). Photographs, drawings, and models of the house are in Paul Rudolph's materials at the Library of Congress. On the Basses and Yale, see Tyler Hill, "Bass Money Funds Univ." *Yale News* (November 3, 2006), https://yaledailynews.com/blog/2006/11/03/bass-money-funds-univ.

17. We were unable to secure access to photograph these houses, but images of both are readily available in published sources and archival collections.

18. On staircases as decorative devices in modern interiors, see Alice T. Friedman, "Do Tread on Me: Disciplined Design and the Sensuous Staircase," *Thresholds*, no. 37 (2010): 34–41.

19. Clarence W. Dunham and Milton D. Thalberg, *Planning Your Home for Better Living* (New York: Whittlesey House, McGraw Hill, 1945). I am grateful to Stephen Fox for alerting me to this house and source.

20. "Mrs. Sanger Meets at Luncheon with El Paso Doctors," *El Paso Herald-Post*, December 8, 1934, 5.

21. Wright, *Building the Dream*; Elaine Tyler May, *Homeward Bound: American Families in the Cold War Era* (New York: Basic Books, 1988, 1999); Dianne Harris, *Little White Houses: How the Postwar Home Constructed Race in America* (Minneapolis: University of Minnesota Press, 2012); Alice T. Friedman, "Home on the Avocado-Green Range: Notes on Suburban Décor in the 1950s," *Interiors* (July 2010): 45–60.
22. Alice T. Friedman, *Women and the Making of the Modern House: A Social and Architectural History* (New York: Harry N. Abrams, 1998), 146–159.
23. "A Neat Town House for $20,000," *Architectural Record* (February 1963): 153.
24. Lyn Billingsley, "Not for the Nook and Cranny Conscious," *The Houston Post*, Oct 27, 1965, page 4, sec. 2.
25. "A House with a Built-In Landscape," *House & Garden* (May 1964): 171.
26. "Lesser Materials, More Labor," *Progressive Architecture* (June 1969): 118. On the house, see also Carlos Jimenez, "The Light Between Gardens: John Zemanek's House," *Harvard Design Magazine* (Summer 1997): 65–67, and "Architecture Is about Life," *Cite* (Summer 2008): 30–34.

Chapter 2. Heat

1. President's Science Advisory Committee, "Restoring the Quality of Our Environment" (Washington, DC: The White House, 1965), 127.
2. Richard P. Dober, *Campus Planning* (New York: Reinhold, 1964).
3. Philip L. Goodwin, *Brazil Builds: Architecture New and Old, 1652–1942* (New York: Museum of Modern Art; Simon and Schuster, 1943).
4. On sun mitigation in Houston's architecture, see Michelangelo Sabatino, "Heat and Light Thematised in the Modern Architecture of Houston," *Journal of Architecture* 21, no. 4 (2016): 500–523.
5. The Water Gardens were the site of tragedy as well: six people died there, in two separate accidents. This tragic history haunts the site. Sensitive design adjustments to improve safety were made in 2007. In 2008, the Water Gardens received the twenty-five-year award for design excellence from the Texas Society of Architects. Stephen Sharpe, "Water Gardens Picked for 25-Year Award," *Texas Architect* 58, no. 5 (September–October 2008): 12.

Chapter 3. Money

1. On Texas Commerce Tower, see John Bloom, "Three Gentlemen, One Ghost, and a Skyscraper," *Texas Monthly* (May 1980), 116–123; 242–263.
2. W. Mark Gunderson, "The Birthday," *Texas Architect* (September–October 2017); Mark Gunderson, "Obituary: Frank D. Welch, FAIA, 1927–2017," *Architectural Record* (June 28, 2017), https://www.architecturalrecord.com/articles/12835-obituary-frank-d-welch-faia-1927-2017.
3. Gerald Moorhead, ed., *Buildings of Texas: Central, South, and Gulf Coast* (Charlottesville and London: University of Virginia Press; Society of Architectural Historians, 2013), 234–235.
4. Daniel Paul, "Not Cool: Fleeting Moments and Telling Afterlives with Gold Mirror Architectural Glass," in *Saturated Space* (London: Architectural Association, School of Architecture), 1–28. Published online: https://en.calameo.com/read/00598992252f5d793b39c?page=1.

Chapter 4. God

1. For examples of new works and discussion, see Albert Christ-Janer and Mary Mix Foley, *Modern Church Architecture: A Guide to the Form and Spirit of Twentieth Century Religious Buildings* (New York: McGraw Hill, 1962); G. E. Kidder Smith, *The New Churches of Europe* (New York: Holt, Rinehart and Winston, 1964).
2. James Oles, "In Pursuit of Salamone," *Cabinet* 34 (Summer 2009), https://www.cabinetmagazine.org/issues/34/oles.php (accessed May 2, 2023).
3. On the theoretical and practical aspects of postwar religious architecture, see Jay M. Price, *Temples for a Modern God: Religious Architecture in Postwar America* (Oxford and New York: Oxford University Press, 2013).
4. Wilfried Wang, ed., *O'Neil Ford & Arch Swank: The Little Chapel in the Woods* (Berlin: Wasmuth & Zohlen, 2021).
5. Ada Louise Huxtable, "Deep in the Heart of Nowhere," *New York Times*, February 15, 1976, D1, D36.
6. Quoted in Rothko Chapel pamphlet, "Open Your Mind" (Houston: Rothko Chapel).
7. Susan Williamson, "Wives and Husbands," *Texas Architect* (May–June 1998): 29–32. Anna Wilgenbusch, "What You Might Not Know about the Church of the Incarnation," *The Cor Chronicle* (October 30, 2019), https://udallasnews.com/2019/10/30/what-you-might-not-know-about-the-church-of-the-incarnation.
8. Quoted in Mary Carolyn Hollers George, *O'Neil Ford, Architect* (College Station: Texas A&M University Press, 1992), 138.
9. On Haywood and Ford, see Mary Carolyn Hollers George, *O'Neil Ford, Architect* (College Station: Texas A&M University Press, 1992), 168–169.
10. On midcentury synagogues, see Samuel D. Gruber, Paul Rocheleau, and Scott J. Tilden, *American Synagogues* (New York: Rizzoli, 2003), 83–174.

Chapter 5. Government

1. Robinson & Associates, Inc., Judith H. Robinson, and Stephanie S. Foell, *Growth, Efficiency and Modernism: GSA Buildings of the 1950s, 60s, and 70s* (Washington, DC: US General Services Administration, Office of the Chief Architect, Center for Historic Buildings, 2005), 42–45.
2. Daniel M. Abramson, "Representing the American Welfare State," *Grey Room* 78 (Winter 2020): 96–123.

3. Emily Widra and Tiana Herring, "States of Incarceration: The Global Context 2021," *Prison Policy Initiative*, September. 2021, https://www.prisonpolicy.org/global/2021.html.
4. Matthew Griffis, "Colored Carnegie Library, Houston, Texas (1913–1961)," *Black Past* (November 17, 2019), https://www.blackpast.org/african-american-history/institutions-african-american-history/colored-carnegie-library-houston-texas-1913-1961.

Chapter 6. Care

1. Annmarie Adams, *Medicine by Design: The Architect and the Modern Hospital, 1893–1943* (Minneapolis: University of Minnesota Press, 2008); Margaret Campbell, "What Tuberculosis Did for Modernism: The Influence of a Curative Environment on Modernist Design and Architecture," *Medical History* 49, no. 4 (2005): 463–488; Beatriz Colomina, "X-ray Architecture: The Tuberculosis Effect," *Harvard Design Magazine* 40 (2015): 70–91; Sarah Williams Goldhagen, "Ultraviolet: Alvar Aalto's Embodied Rationalism," *Harvard Design Magazine* 27 (Fall–Winter, 2007–2008): 38–52.
2. Martin Herman Kuhlman, "The Civil Rights Movement in Texas: Desegregation of Public Accommodations, 1950–1964" (PhD diss, Texas Tech University, 1994).
3. "Advanced Center for the Retarded," *Architectural Forum*, vol. 127 (December 1967): 49.
4. "Advanced Center for the Retarded," *Architectural Forum*, 49.
5. "Advanced Center for the Retarded," *Architectural Forum*, 50.
6. Rohan, *The Architecture of Paul Rudolph*, 121–129; Mark Pasnik, "Concrete Therapy: Paul Rudolph's Architecture of Mental Health," *Harvard Design Magazine*, No. 40, http://www.harvarddesignmagazine.org/issues/40/concrete-therapy-paul-rudolphs-architecture-of-mental-health.
7. "Memorial Nurses' Home to be Dedicated Nov. 21," *Palacios Beacon* 47, no. 45 (November 11, 1954), 1.
8. Quoted in Edgar Velazquez Reynald, "Roseville Housing Trust and Alpha Tau Omega," ScoutSA blog, February 24, 2021, https://www.scoutsa.com/blog/roseville.
9. Jesse Henry Jr. "The Community Architect Concept," *San Antonio Express-News*, September 17, 1972, 10-G.
10. Quoted in Frank D. Welch, *Philip Johnson and Texas* (Austin: University of Texas Press, 2000), 124.
11. The memorial embodies the strand of "tough-minded humanism" in modern architecture that William H. Jordy admired ten years earlier: "Humanism in Contemporary Architecture: Tough- and Tender-Minded," *Journal of Architectural Education* 15, no. 2 (Summer 1960): 3–10. The monument has long been critiqued. Among its defenders was architecture critic David Dillon: "Let it be: Don't move it or redesign it. The JFK Memorial is what it is," reprinted in Kathryn E. Holliday, ed., *The Open-Ended City: David Dillon on Texas Architecture* (Austin: University of Texas Press, 2019), 396–399.
12. On Dallas just before and after the Kennedy assassination, see Warren Leslie, *Dallas Public and Private: Aspects of an American City* (New York: Grossman, 1964).
13. Leslie, *Dallas Public and Private*, 222.

Chapter 7. Sports & Leisure

1. Susan Toomey Frost, *Colors on Clay: The San José Tile Workshops of San Antonio* (San Antonio: Trinity University Press, 2009).
2. Fannie Davis Town Lake Gazebo, Austin, Texas, National Register Nomination, https://atlas.thc.texas.gov/NR/pdfs/100004970/100004970.pdf.
3. April Edlin, "The Golden Age of Hollywood: 1930s and 1940s," School of Information and Library Science, University of North Carolina at Chapel Hill, https://ils.unc.edu/dpr/path/goldenhollywood/index.htm.
4. Leigh Cutler, "Eldorado Ballroom," *Houston Review* 4, no.1 (Fall 2006): 45–49.
5. On Lucian T. Hood Jr., see Stephen James, "Attention to Detail: The Architecture of Lucian T. Hood, Jr.," *Houston History* 15, no. 1 (2017): 42–46; David Putz and Emily Ardoin, "Earl and Berthea Carpenter House," Protected Landmark Designation Report (City of Houston: Houston Archeological & Historical Commission Dept., 2022), https://www.houstontx.gov/planning/Commissions/hahc_2023/C-5330-MANDELL-PROTECTED-LANDMARK-NOMINATION-Final.pdf.
6. Meredith L. Clausen, "Northgate Regional Shopping Center-Paradigm from the Provinces," *Journal of the Society of Architectural Historians* 43, no. 2 (1984): 144–161; Richard Longstreth, *City Center to Regional Mall* (Cambridge, MA: MIT Press, 1997), and *The Drive-In, the Supermarket, and the Transformation of Commercial Space in Los Angeles, 1914–1941* (Cambridge, MA: MIT Press, 1999).
7. Bevis Hillier, *Art Deco of the 20s and 30s* (London: Studio Vista, 1968).
8. Brantley Hightower, "'Whatabuilding': The Evolution of Whataburger's Architecture," *San Antonio Report*, July 23, 2016, https://sanantonioreport.org/whatabuilding-the-evolution-of-whataburgers-architecture.
9. As of 2021.
10. "Text of President John Kennedy's Rice Stadium Moon Speech," September 12, 1962, https://www.jfklibrary.org/learn/about-jfk/historic-speeches/address-at-rice-university-on-the-nations-space-effort
11. Thomas R. Cole, *No Color Is My Kind: The Life of Eldrewey Stearns and the Integration of Houston* (Austin: University of Texas Press, 1997); Lauren Huckaby Glen, "The Astrodome and Desegregation," East Texas History, https://easttexashistory.org/items/show/361.
12. Marilyn Van Suan, "Presidents-First Lady Health Spas," *Tempo* 15, no. 3 (September 1969): 9–15.
13. Siegfried Kracauer, *The Mass Ornament: Weimar Essays*, trans. and ed. by Thomas Y. Levin (Cambridge, MA: Harvard University Press, 1995).

Chapter 8. On the Road

1. Gretchen Sorin, *Driving While Black: African American Travel and the Road to Civil Rights* (New York: Liveright, 2020).
2. Kenneth Hafertepe, "Restoration, Reconstruction, or Romance? The Case of the Spanish Governor's Palace in Hispanic-Era San Antonio, Texas," *Journal of the Society of Architectural Historians* 67, no. 3 (September 2008): 412–433.
3. See, for example, Philip Parisi, *The Texas Post Office Murals: Art for the People* (College Station: Texas A&M University Press, 2004).
4. Rob Linné, "Design for Liberation: Port A's Fabled Salon on the Dunes," *Texas Architect* (March/April 2023): 23–26.
5. Cindy Hamilton and Texas Historical Commission Staff, Cabana Motor Hotel National Register Nomination. On Lapidus, see Friedman, *American Glamour and the Evolution of Modern Architecture*, 149–186.
6. Kristina Wilson, *Mid-Century Modernism and the American Body: Race, Gender, and the Politics of Power in Design* (Princeton: Princeton University Press, 2021); "Playboy's Penthouse Apartment, a High, Handsome Haven for the Bachelor in Town," reprinted in *Stud: Architectures of Masculinity*, ed. Joel Sanders (New York: Princeton Architectural Press, 1998), no page numbers.

Chapter 9. Knowledge & Power

1. On the history of Texas Instruments, see Caleb Pirtle III, *Engineering the World: Stories from the First 75 Years of Texas Instruments* (Dallas: Southern Methodist University Press, 2005); for discussion of the building, see 94–97.
2. Ada Louise Huxtable, "A Success as Architecture and as Monument," *New York Times*, May 23, 1971, 39.
3. Statistics on US war deaths come from the National Archives, "Vietnam War US Military Fatal Casualty Statistics," https://www.archives.gov/research/military/vietnam-war/casualty-statistics.
4. Ann Fears Crawford and Crystal Sasse Ragsdale. *Women in Texas: Their Lives, Their Experiences, Their Accomplishments* (Austin, TX: State House Press, 1992), 182–193.
5. Miguel Ángel Castro Tirado and Alberto J. Castro-Tirado, "The Evolution of Astronomical Observatory Design," *Journal of the Korean Astronomical Society* 52 (August 2019): 99–108; see esp. 102.
6. Emilio Ambasz, *The Architecture of Luis Barragán* (New York: Museum of Art, New York, 1976).
7. "Buildings for the Space Program," *Architectural Record* 133 (January 1963): 147.

Chapter 10. Precious Objects

1. Larry Speck, "San Antonio Museum of Art," September 4, 1986; accessible at https://larryspeck.com/writing/san-antonio-museum-of-art.
2. On the social dynamics at work in the patronage and conceptualizations of the museums, see Stephen Fox, "Cullinan Hall: A Window on Modern Houston," *Journal of Architectural Education* 54, no. 3 (February 2001): 158–166; Welch, *Philip Johnson and Texas*, 93–103.
3. On the architectural changes to the MFAH through 1974, see Michael Grogan, "Texas Two Step: Ludwig Mies van der Rohe's Addition(s) to Houston's Museum of Fine Arts," *Arris* 31 (2020): 88–107.
4. Phyllis Lambert, "Clear Span," in *Mies in America*, ed. Phyllis Lambert (Montreal and New York: Canadian Centre for Architecture; Whitney Museum of American Art, Harry N. Abrams, 2001), 422–473.
5. Peter Gershon, *Collision: The Contemporary Art Scene in Houston, 1972–1985* (College Station: Texas A&M University Press, 2018), 396. Segregation was a matter of state law in Texas. Institutions that succeeded in integrating before laws were changed often did so because they did not publicize their decision to not comply with the law. On this topic in Houston, see Thomas R. Cole, *No Color Is My Kind: The Life of Eldrewey Stearns and the Integration of Houston* (Austin: University of Texas Press, 1997).
6. On Mies's influence in Houston, see Michelangelo Sabatino, "Translating Mies: Barnstone and Houston Modernism," in *Making Houston Modern: The Life and Architecture of Howard Barnstone*, 64–95.
7. Johnson's remarks on the Loggia dei Lanzi are quoted in Welch, *Philip Johnson and Texas*, 90.
8. Quoted in Patricia Cummings Loud, "Kimbell Art Museum," in Brownlee and De Long, *Louis I. Kahn: In the Realm of Architecture*, 397.
9. Quoted in Welch, *Philip Johnson and Texas*, 102.
10. Quoted in Patricia Cummings Loud, "Kimbell Art Museum," in Brownlee and De Long, *Louis I. Kahn: In the Realm of Architecture*, 396.

Chapter 11. Hearts & Minds

1. On modern campus architecture, see Stefan Muthesius, *The Postwar University: Utopianist Campus and College* (New Haven and London: Paul Mellon Centre for Studies in British Art and Yale University Press, 2000).
2. Stephen James, "Kenneth Bentsen's Pan American University: Regionalist Architecture and Identity in the Borderlands," *Arris: Journal of the Southeast Chapter of Architectural Historians* 28 (2017): 46–67.
3. "Trinity University Starts Off a Whole Series of Buildings Erected by the 'Youtz-Slick' Lift-Slab Concrete Method, Teaches Cost-cutting Industrialization of Building," *Architectural Forum* 95 (September 1951): 180.

4. Quoted in O'Neil Ford, "The End of a Beginning," reprinted in *O'Neil Ford on Architecture*, ed. Kathryn E. O'Rourke (Austin: University of Texas Press, 2019), 169.
5. Alene Talmey, "Power in Texas: 22 Who Help Run the Place," *Vogue* (January 1953), 140–144.
6. "Industrial School Trustees Plan Expenditures," *San Antonio Express*, November 30, 1911, 18. I am grateful to Stephen Fox for alerting me to this source and history. On the history of the school, see James S. Currie, *Planting Trees: A History of the Presbyterian Pan American School* (Waco, TX: Nortex Press, 2011).
7. Robert Alexander Gonzalez, *Designing Pan-America: U.S. Architectural Visions for the Western Hemisphere* (Austin: University of Texas Press, 2011).
8. William Middleton, *Double Vision: The Unerring Eye of Art World Avatars Dominique and John de Menil* (New York: Alfred A. Knopf, 2018), 247–254.
9. Alvia Wardlaw, "Heart of Third Ward: Texas Southern University," *Cite* 35 (Fall 1996): 20–21.
10. Ford, "End of a Beginning," quoted in O'Rourke, *O'Neil Ford on Architecture*, 166.

Chapter 12. Contact Zones

1. On "contact zones," see Mary Louise Pratt, "Arts of the Contact Zone," *Profession* (1991): 33–40.
2. Sally S. Abbe, Donald R. Abbe, and Yolanda Romero with assistance from Bruce Jensen, National Register of Historic Places nomination of Lamesa Farm Workers Community Historic District, Los Ybáñez, Texas, 1993.
3. On utopian planning in a US context, see Dolores Hayden, *Seven American Utopias: The Architecture of Communitarian Socialism, 1790–1975* (Cambridge, MA: MIT Press, 1979).
4. David Dillon, "Avion Village, Grand Prairie, Texas: Richard Neutra, David Williams, and Roscoe DeWitt," *Center* 5 (1989): 118–120; Kristin M. Szylvian, "Our Mutual Friend: A Progressive Housing Legacy from the 1940s," *Cite* 33 (1995): 19–27, 37.
5. On the architecture of modern government centers, see Daniel M. Abramson, "Representing the American Welfare State," *Grey Room* 78 (Winter 2020): 96–123.
6. Stephen Fox informed me of this history and its documentation: "Negro Moving Is Discussed," *Denton Record-Chronicle*, April 16, 1961, 4; "Coit Tells Rotary Club of Federated Activities' Work," *Denton Record-Chronicle*, May 19, 1922, 8; "New Negro Colony to Be Known as Solomon Hill," *Denton Record-Chronicle*, June 13, 1922, 5; "Purchase of Park Site Is Nearing Completion Now," *Denton Record-Chronicle*, July 23, 1922, 5.
7. On real estate development in Dallas, see David Dillon, "Why Is Dallas Architecture So Bad?" (1990), and "The Education of Harlan Crow" (1984), both reprinted in Kathryn E. Holliday, ed., *The Open-Ended City: David Dillon on Texas Architecture* (Austin: University of Texas Press, 2019); 22–33, 280–288.
8. On the Richmond buildings, see Barry Moore and Anna Mod, *City Houston, Style Modern: The Richmond Corridor: An Architectural Survey of Richmond Avenue from Kirby Drive West to the Railroad Tracks, Houston, Texas* (Houston: Intown, 2002).
9. On the Bacardí project and its descendants in Mies's oeuvre, see Phyllis Lambert, "Ron Bacardí y Compañía Administration Building, Santiago, Cuba (1957–1960); Georg Schaefer Museum, Schweinfurt (1960–1962); The New National Gallery, Berlin (1962–1968)," in *Mies in America*, ed. Phyllis Lambert (Montreal and New York: Canadian Centre for Architecture; Whitney Museum of American Art, Harry N. Abrams, 2001), 474–521.
10. On Menil architectural projects, see Stephen Fox, "John and Dominique de Menil as Patrons of Architecture, 1932–1997," in *Art and Activism: Projects of John and Dominique de Menil*, ed. Josef Helfenstein and Laureen Schipsi (New Haven and Houston: Yale University Press; the Menil Collection), 199–217.
11. On James's work in the house, see William Middleton, *Double Vision: The Unerring Eye of Art World Avatars Dominique and John de Menil* (New York: Alfred A. Knopf, 2018), 334–341.
12. Urs Peter Flückiger, *Donald Judd: Architecture in Marfa, Texas* (Basel: Birkhäuser Verlag AG, 2007).
13. Gretel Enck, Blackwell School, National Register of Historic Places Nomination, 2019; Mia Warren and Heidi Glenn, "The Day a Texas School Held a Funeral for the Spanish Language," broadcast on *Morning Edition*, National Public Radio, October 20, 2017, https://www.npr.org/2017/10/20/558739863/the-day-a-texas-school-held-a-funeral-for-the-spanish-language.
14. Robert Venturi, *Complexity and Contradiction in Architecture*, 2nd ed. (1977, reprinted, New York: Museum of Modern Art, 1996), 16.

Coda: What We Save and Why

1. Dolores Hayden, *Redesigning the American Dream: The Future of Housing, Work, and Family Life*, rev. ed. (New York: W. W. Norton, 2002; 1984), 79–190.
2. Stephanie Waldek, "How NASA Restored Mission Control for the 50th Anniversary of the Moon Landing," *Architectural Digest* (July 19, 2019), https://www.architecturaldigest.com/story/how-nasa-restored-mission-control-50th-anniversary-moon-landing.
3. Women make up 50.3 percent of the state population. 2020 US Census.
4. Lady Bird Johnson, "The Vital Balance . . . Nature . . . Architecture . . . and Man," B. Y. Morrison Memorial Lecture, delivered at the 100th Annual Meeting of the American Institute of Architects, Portland, Oregon (Washington, DC: US Department of Agriculture, 1968), no page numbers.
5. Johnson, "The Vital Balance," no page number; emphasis in original.

Further Reading

Constructing a history of modern architecture in Texas requires drawing on many kinds of sources. Below is a short list of volumes that provide information on buildings and architects included in this book and starting points for further exploration of some of the ideas and themes discussed in the text. Please consult the notes for additional references.

Many of the buildings that appear in this book have been listed on the National Register of Historic Places. Building nominations often contain outstanding research and detailed histories of architecture, places, people, and topics in Texas history. Final nominations are kept by the National Park Service and may be accessed through the electronic atlas of listed buildings maintained on the website of the Texas Historical Commission.

Excellent accounts of Texas buildings are to be found in *Texas Architect*, the magazine of the Texas Society of Architecture, and *Cite*, the magazine of the Rice Design Alliance, focused on Houston. Issues of *Texas Architect* dating to October of 1950 are accessible at https://magazine.texasarchitects.org/issues. The archives of *Cite*, dating to 1982, are accessible at https://www.ricedesignalliance.org/publications/cite-archive.

Guides

Beasley, Ellen, and Margaret Culbertson. *Waxahachie Architecture Guidebook*. College Station: Texas A&M University Press, 2021.

Beasley, Ellen, and Stephen Fox. *Galveston Architecture Guidebook*. Galveston: Galveston Historical Foundation, 1996.

Cleary, Richard, and Lawrence W. Speck. *The University of Texas at Austin*. New York: Princeton Architectural Press, 2010.

Fisher, Lewis F., and Maria Watson Pfeiffer. *San Antonio Architecture: Tradition and Visions*, ed. Julius M. Gribou, Robert G. Hanley, and Thomas E. Robey. San Antonio: San Antonio AIA, 2007.

Fox, Stephen. *The Campus Guide: Rice University*. New York: Princeton Architectural Press, 2001.

Fox, Stephen. *Houston Architectural Guide*. 3rd ed. Houston: American Institute of Architects, Houston Chapter; Minor Design, 2012.

Fuller, Larry Paul, ed. *The American Institute of Architects Guide to Dallas Architecture with Regional Highlights*. Dallas and New York: American Institute of Architects, Dallas Chapter, and McGraw Hill Construction Information Group, 1999.

Moorhead, Gerald et al. *Buildings of Texas: Central, South, and Gulf Coast*. Charlottesville and London: University of Virginia Press; Society of Architectural Historians, 2013.

Moorhead, Gerald et al. *Buildings of Texas: East, North Central, Panhandle and South Plains, and West*. Charlottesville and London: University of Virginia Press; Society of Architectural Historians, 2019.

Smith, Gary Wooten, and Sally Still Abbe. *A Guide to Lubbock's Architectural Heritage*. Lubbock: City of Lubbock, 1993.

Smith, Hank Todd, ed. *Austin, Its Architects and Architecture, 1836–1986*. Austin: American Institute of Architects, Austin Chapter, 1986.

State and City Surveys

Arreola, Daniel D. *Postcards from the Río Bravo Border: Picturing the Place, Placing the Picture, 1900s–1950s*. Austin: University of Texas Press, 2013.

Barna, Joel Warren. *The See-Through Years: Creation and Destruction in Texas Architecture and Real Estate, 1981–1991*. College Station: Texas A&M University Press, 1993.

Bradley, Barrie Scardino. *Improbable Metropolis: Houston's Architectural and Urban History*. Austin: University of Texas Press, 2020.

Cohen, Judith Singer. *Cowtown Moderne: Art Deco Architecture of Fort Worth, Texas*. College Station: Texas A&M University Press, 1988.

Dillon, David. *Dallas Architecture, 1936–1986*. Austin: Texas Monthly Press, 1985.

Ferguson, Cheryl Caldwell. *Highland Park and River Oaks: The Origins of Garden Suburban Community Planning in Texas*. Austin: University of Texas Press, 2014.

Henry, Jay C. *Architecture in Texas, 1895–1945*. Austin: University of Texas Press, 1993.

Merritt, Marty, Benjamin Hill, and Stephen Fox. *After Alden: Mid-Century Architecture in Brazosport, Texas*. Houston: Houston Mod, 2019.

Roark, Carol. *Fort Worth's Legendary Landmarks*. Fort Worth: Texas Christian University Press, 1995.

Robinson, Willard B. *Reflections of Faith: Houses of Worship in the Lone Star State*. Waco, TX: Baylor University Press, 1994.

Scardino, Barrie, William F. Stern, and Bruce C. Webb, eds. *Ephemeral City: Cite Looks at Houston*. Austin: University of Texas Press, 2003.

Shafer, Kathleen. *Marfa: The Transformation of a West Texas Town*. Austin: University of Texas Press, 2019.

Shopoff, Karen Anne. "Pathways of Art Deco into Texas." M.Arch. thesis, University of Texas at Austin, 1998.

Speck, Lawrence W. *Landmarks of Texas Architecture*. Austin: University of Texas Press, 2012.

Thurman, David Alan. "Towards a Unified Vision of Modern Architecture: The Texas Experiment, 1951–1956." M.Arch. thesis, University of Texas at Austin, 1988.

Williamson, Roxanne Kuter. *Austin, Texas: An American Architectural History*. San Antonio: Trinity University Press, 1973.

Architects, Firms, and Institutions

Adams, Nicholas. *Gordon Bunshaft and SOM: Building Corporate Modernism*. New Haven and London: Yale University Press, 2019.

Bradley, Barrie Scardino, Stephen Fox, and Michelangelo Sabatino, eds. *Making Houston Modern: The Life and Architecture of Howard Barnstone*. Austin: University of Texas Press, 2020.

Brownlee, David Bruce, and David Gilson De Long. *Louis I. Kahn: In the Realm of Architecture*. Los Angeles and New York: Museum of Contemporary Art Los Angeles and Rizzoli, 1991.

Caragonne, Alexander. *The Texas Rangers: Notes from an Architectural Underground*. Cambridge, MA: MIT Press, 1995.

Deutsch, Stephanie. *You Need a Schoolhouse: Booker T. Washington, Julius Rosenwald, and the Building of Schools for the Segregated South*. Evanston, IL: Northwestern University Press, 2011.

Dillon, David. *The Architecture of O'Neil Ford: Celebrating Place*. Austin: University of Texas Press, 1999.

Eisenshtat, Sidney. *Sidney Eisenshtat*. Ed. James Steele. Los Angeles: University of Southern California Architectural Guild Press, 2012.

Flückiger, Urs Peter. *Donald Judd: Architecture in Marfa, Texas*. Basel: Birkhauser Architecture, 2007.

Garlock, Maria E. Moreya, and David P. Billington. *Félix Candela: Engineer, Builder, Structural Artist*. New Haven and London: Yale University Press, 2008.

George, Mary Carolyn Hollers. *O'Neil Ford, Architect*. College Station: Texas A&M University Press, 1992.

Germany, Lisa. *Harwell Hamilton Harris*. Austin: University of Texas Press, 1991.

Goldhagen, Sarah Williams. *Louis Kahn's Situated Modernism*. New Haven: Yale University Press, 2001.

Griggs, Brian H. *Opus in Brick and Stone: The Architectural and Planning Heritage of Texas Tech University*. Lubbock: Texas Tech University Press, 2020.

Grove, Carol, and Cydney Millstein. *Hare & Hare, Landscape Architects and City Planners*. Amherst, MA: Library of American Landscape History and Athens: The University of Georgia Press, 2019.

Heymann, David, and Stephen Fox. *John S. Chase—The Chase Residence*. Austin: University of Texas at Austin School of Architecture; Tower Books, 2020.

Further Reading

King, Jonathan, and Philip Langdon, eds. *The CRS Team and the Business of Architecture*. College Station: Texas A&M University Press, 2002.

Koush, Ben. *Constructing Houston's Future: The Architecture of Arthur Evan Jones and Lloyd Morgan Jones*. Houston: Houston Mod, 2017.

Koush, Ben. *Hugo V. Neuhaus, Jr.: Residential Architecture, 1948–1966*. Houston: Houston Mod, 2007.

Laurence, Dianne Susan Duffner. "A Symbiotic Relationship Between Mid Century Modern Masters: The Collaborative Works of Arthur and Marie Berger, Landscape Architects, and O'Neil Ford, Architect." M.L.A. thesis, University of Texas at Arlington, 2007.

Mackey, Jann Patterson. "Howard Meyer: Architect." PhD diss., University of Texas at Dallas, 2010.

Mertins, Detlef. *Mies*. London and New York: Phaidon, 2014.

McCullar, Michael. *Restoring Texas: Raiford Stripling's Life and Architecture*. College Station: Texas A&M University Press, 1985.

Miller, Scott Reagan. "The Architecture of MacKie and Kamrath." Master's thesis, Rice University, 1993.

Palmore, William. *Modernism for the Borderland: The Mid-Century Houses of Robert Garland and David Hilles*. El Paso: Stanlee and Gerald Rubin Center for the Visual Arts, 2008.

Papademetriou, Peter C. *Transportation and Urban Development in Houston 1830–1980*. Houston: Metropolitan Transit Authority of Harris County, 1982.

Rohan, Timothy M. *The Architecture of Paul Rudolph*. New Haven and London: Yale University Press, 2014.

Smart, Pamela. *Sacred Modern: Faith Activism and Aesthetics in the Menil Collection*. Austin: University of Texas Press, 2010.

Welch, Frank D. *On Becoming an Architect*. Fort Worth: TCU Press, 2014.

Welch, Frank D. *Philip Johnson and Texas*. Austin: University of Texas Press, 2000.

Woo, Lillian C. *Preston Morgan Bolton, Texas Architect and Civic Leader*. College Station: Texas A&M University Press, 2022.

Zemanek, John. *Being, Becoming: An Acorn Is to Become an Oak*. Self-published, 2016.

Architectural Modernism in the United States: Surveys and Thematic Treatments

Anderson, Ross, and Maximilian Sternberg, eds. *Modern Architecture and the Sacred: Religious Legacies and Spiritual Renewal*. London and New York: Bloomsbury Visual Arts, 2020.

Cheng, Irene, Charles L. Davis II, and Mabel O. Wilson, eds. *Race and Modern Architecture: A Critical History from the Enlightenment to the Present*. Pittsburgh: University of Pittsburgh Press, 2020.

Friedman, Alice T. *American Glamour and the Evolution of Modern Architecture*. New Haven: Yale University Press, 2010.

Geva, Anat. *The Architecture of Modern American Synagogues, 1950s–1960s*. College Station: Texas A&M University Press, 2023.

Jackson, Kenneth T. *Crabgrass Frontier: The Suburbanization of the United States*. New York: Oxford University Press, 1985.

Lieber, Jeffrey. *Flintstone Modernism: or The Crisis in Postwar American Culture*. Cambridge, MA: MIT Press, 2018.

Penick, Monica. *Tastemaker: Elizabeth Gordon, House Beautiful, and the Postwar American Home*. New Haven: Yale University Press, 2017.

Price, Jay M. *Temples for a Modern God: Religious Architecture in Postwar America*. Oxford and New York: Oxford University Press, 2013.

Reitzes, Lisa B. "Moderately Modern: Interpreting the Architecture of the Public Works Administration." PhD diss., University of Delaware, 1989.

Siry, Joseph M. *Air-Conditioning in Modern American Architecture, 1890–1970*. University Park: Pennsylvania State University Press, 2021.

Upton, Dell. *Architecture in the United States*. Oxford and New York: Oxford University Press, 1998.

Wright, Gwendolyn. *USA: Modern Architectures in History*. London: Reaktion Books, 2008.

Yanni, Carla. *Living on Campus: An Architectural History of the American Dormitory*. Minneapolis: University of Minnesota Press, 2019.

Address List

ABILENE

Permian Building
317 North Willis St.

Former Whataburger
1041 North Mockingbird Ln.

Zion Lutheran Church
(now Galilee Baptist Church)
1011 Briarwood St.

AMARILLO

Amarillo Art Center
2200 South Van Buren St.

Cadillac Ranch
13651 I-40 Frontage Rd.

Ding How Restaurant
2415 East Amarillo Blvd.

Harrington Cancer Center
1500 Wallace Blvd.

KVII-TV Studio
1 Broadcast Center

Potter County Courthouse
501 S Fillmore St.

Taber House
2612 South Hayden St.

ANAHUAC

Chambers County Courthouse
404 Washington Ave.

AUSTIN

Air-Temp House
2502 Park View Dr.

Austin Daily Tribune Building
920 Colorado St.

Delta Kappa Gamma International
416 West 12th St.

Fannie Davis Town Lake Gazebo
9307 Ann and Roy Butler Hike and Bike Trail

J. J. Pickle Federal Building
300 E 8th St.

Lorine and Chester E. Nagel House
3215 Churchill St.

Lyndon Baines Johnson Presidential Library and Museum
2313 Red River St.

Rio House Apartments
606 West 17th St.

Texas Department of Public Safety Headquarters
5805 North Lamar Blvd.

BANDERA

First Baptist Church
1302 Pecan St.

BEAUMONT

First Security National Bank
501 Orleans St.

BEEVILLE

Coca-Cola Bottling Company Building
300 South Washington St.

BIG SPRING

Comanche Trail Amphitheater
100 Whipkey Dr.

St. Mary's Episcopal Church
1000 S Goliad St.

BROWNSVILLE

All Souls Unitarian Universalist Church
124 Paredes Line Rd.

George Kraigher House
525 Paredes Line Rd.

BRYAN

Earl C. Cunningham House
2111 Wayside Dr.

Holiday Inn
2300 South Texas Ave.

Searcy Medical Clinic
701 South Texas Ave.

CANYON

Panhandle-Plains Historical Museum
2401 4th Ave.

COLEMAN

Coleman County Courthouse
100 West Live Oak St.

Address List

CORPUS CHRISTI

Art Museum of South Texas
1902 North Shoreline Dr.

Dos Cruces Gallery
602 Furman Ave.

Galván Ballroom
1632 Agnes St.

Lew Williams Chevrolet City
2323 Leopard St.

Mercantile National Bank
4211 Ayers St.
(scheduled for demolition at time of publication)

Nueces County Courthouse
901 Leopard St.

Ross L. Allen House
240 Oleander St.

600 Building
600 Leopard St.

CORSICANA

First National Bank Building
100 North Main St.

DALLAS

Ben Lipshy House
5381 Nakoma Dr.

Cabaña Motor Hotel
899 Stemmons Freeway

Campbell Centre
8150 and 8350 North Central Expressway

Dallas City Hall
1500 Marilla St

— Fair Park, Dallas
  Centennial Building
  1001 Washington St.

— Hall of State
  3939 Grand Ave.

— Magnolia Oil Company Pavilion
  1121 First Ave. at Grand

— Tower Building
  3809 Grand Ave.

Fountain Place
1445 Ross Ave.

GLOCO Gas Station #5
903 Cadiz St.

Hyatt Regency and Reunion Tower
300 Reunion Blvd.

John F. Kennedy Memorial
600 block of Main St.

Josephine Herbert and Bruno Graf House
5423 Park Ln.

Kalita Humphreys Theater
3636 Turtle Creek Blvd.

Mayflower Investment Company House (R. Fisher)
6851 Gaston Ave.

Mayflower Investment Company House (L. Sadler)
5012 Pershing St.

Patricia Davis and John C. Beck House
9009 Capri Dr.

Statler Hilton Hotel
1914 Commerce St.

Temple Emanu-El
8500 Hillcrest Rd.

Texas Instruments Semiconductor Building
13500 North Central Expressway

3525 Turtle Creek Apartments
3525 Turtle Creek Blvd.

3800 Main Street Silos
3800 Main St.

DENTON

Denton City Hall
215 East McKinney St.

Denton Civic Center
321 East McKinney St.

First Christian Church
1203 Fulton St.

Fowler Library
502 Oakland St.

Little Chapel in the Woods
415 Chapel Dr.

Voertman's Bookstore
1320 West Hickory St.

EASTLAND

Eastland County Courthouse
100 W Main St.

EDINBURG

Echo Hotel
1903 South Closner Blvd.

University of Texas-Pan American
(University of Texas Rio Grande Valley)
1201 West University Dr.

EDNA

Edna Police and Fire Department
105 North Allen St.

Edna Theater
201–207 West Main St.

EL PASO

Federal Reserve Bank of Dallas, El Paso Branch
301 East Main Ave.

Max Grossman House
730 Kerbey Ave.

Norma Egg and Gladys Gregory House
900 Galloway Dr.

Ray Sherman Place
4528 Blanco Ave.

Tap Restaurant
408 San Antonio St.

Tays Place Apartments
2021 Cypress Ave.

Temple Mount Sinai
4408 N Stanton St.

FLINT

Bruce Plunkett First House (Lake Village)
17148 Fountain Circle

FORT DAVIS

McDonald Observatory
3640 Dark Sky Dr.

FORT WORTH

Amon Carter Museum
3501 Camp Bowie Blvd.

Cynthia Brants Studio
5102 Sealands Ln.

Fort Worth Masonic Temple
1100 Henderson St.

Address List

Fort Worth Water Gardens
1502 Commerce St.

Kimbell Art Museum
3333 Camp Bowie Blvd.

Sid Richardson and Anne Bass House
1801 Deepdale Dr.

FREDERICKSBURG

Victor Keidel Memorial Hospital
258 E Main St.

GALVESTON

Far-Mar-Co Export Grain Elevator
3100 Wharf Rd.

Galveston Artillery Club
3102 Avenue O

Galvestonian
1401 East Beach Dr.

Windsor Court Apartments
1705 35th St.

GLADEWATER

Gregg County Community Building
116 Pacific Ave.

T. W. Lee Apartments
800 East Broadway Ave.

GONZALES

Lynn Theater
510 Saint Paul St.

GRAND PRAIRIE

Avion Village
800 Skyline Rd.

HARLINGEN

Frank G. Parker House
1910 South Parkwood Dr.

HEMPSTEAD

Waller County Courthouse
836 Austin St.

HOUSTON

Addressograph-Multigraph Building
2900 Richmond Ave.

Admiral Auto Courts
4703 N Main St.

Anderson and Lucie Wray Todd House
9 Shadowlawn Circle

Astrodome
3 NRG Parkway

Bank of Houston
5115 Main St.

Berthea and Earl Carpenter House
5330 Mandell St.

Carnegie Branch, Houston Public Library
1050 Quitman St.

Cullinan Hall, Museum of Fine Arts, Houston
1001 Bissonnet St.

Dominque and John de Menil House
3363 San Felipe Rd.

Drucie Raye Rucker and John S. Chase House
3512 Oakdale Court

Eldorado Building
2310 Elgin St.

Greenway Plaza 3,4,5
3, 4, 5 Greenway Plaza

Greenway Plaza Summit Towers North and Coastal
8-12 Greenway Plaza

Harris County Center for the Retarded
3350 West Dallas St.

Harris County Family Law Center Building
1115 Congress Ave.

Houston City Hall
901 Bagby St.

Houston Port Public Export Elevator
8300 High Level Rd.

Humble Oil Building
800 Bell Ave.

Humble Oil Garage
1616 Milam St.

Inwood Manor
3711 San Felipe Rd.

Lamar High School
3325 Westheimer Rd.

Lamar–River Oaks Shopping Center
3256-3272 Westheimer Rd.

Manned Space Center (Johnson Space Center)
2101 NASA Rd. 1

Menil Collection
1533 Sul Ross St.

Pennzoil Place
711 Louisiana St.

Phillis Wheatley High School
4801 Providence St.

Project Row Houses
2521 Holman St.

Ralph A. Anderson Jr. House
1638 Banks St.

Rice University
6100 Main St.

Riverside National Bank
2602 Blodgett St.

Rothko Chapel
1409 Sul Ross St.

San Felipe Courts
1400 Allen Parkway

Sears Roebuck & Company Bus Shelter
4000 North Shepherd Dr.

Texas Southern University
3100 Cleburne St.

3344 Richmond Building
3344 Richmond Ave.

Tranquility Park
400 Rusk St.

2990 Richmond Building
2990 Richmond Ave.

University of St. Thomas
3800 Montrose Blvd.

US Post Office—Barbara Jordan/Post
401 Franklin St.

John Zemanek House
1723 Colquitt St

IRVING

University of Dallas Chapel of the Incarnation
1845 East Northgate Dr.

Address List

KILGORE

Crim Theater
110–114 S Kilgore St.

Replica oil derricks
Commerce and Main Streets

Tincy and Liggett N. Crim House
2023 S Henderson Blvd.

KINGSVILLE

Presbyterian Pan American School
223 FM 772

LA PORTE

San Jacinto Monument
1 Monument Circle

LAREDO

Blessed Sacrament School
1501 Bartlett Ave.

Cigarroa Medical Building
1502 Logan Ave.

Conoco Station
1099 Matamoros St.

Evelyn Motor Inn
2720 San Bernardo Ave.

Mercy Hospital
1500 Logan Ave.

LEVELLAND

Hockley County Jail
1310 Avenue H

LIBERTY

Geraldine D. Humphreys Cultural Center
1710 Sam Houston Ave.

LONGVIEW

Childress Optometrists
408 E Magrill St.

First Baptist Church
209 E South St.

LUBBOCK

First National Pioneer Building
1500 Broadway St.

Great Plains Life Insurance Company
1220 Broadway St.

Lubbock County Courthouse
Texas Ave. between Main and Broadway Streets

Lubbock County Sheriff's Dept. and Jail
712 Broadway St.

Texas Tech Library
2802 18th St.

LUFKIN

Angelina County Courthouse
215 East Lufkin Ave.

Lufkin Federal Savings and Loan Building
111 South 3rd St.

MARFA

Blackwell School
501 S Abbot St.

Block/Mansana de Chinati
400 W El Paso St.

Brite Building
103-11 North Highland Ave.

Chamberlain Building
106 Highland St.

Chinati Foundation
1 Cavalry Row

Hotel Paisano
207 Highland St.

Marfa National Bank Building
101 North Highland Ave.

MCALLEN

Ann Maddox Moore House
111 East Erie Ave.

Rafael Garza House
201 West Jackson Ave.

Whole Woman's Health Clinic
802 South Main St.

MIDLAND

Forest Oil Company
405 North Marienfeld St.

MINEOLA

Mary Bryan and Tom C. Reitch House
615 N Johnson St.

NACOGDOCHES

Hotel Freedonia
200 North Freedonia St.

Taylor & Allen Clinic
1301 Raguet St.

— Stephen F. Austin State University
 East College Cafeteria
 608 East College St.

— Gladys E. Steen Dormitories
 609 East College St.

— Hall 14
 514 East College St.

— Martha T. Griffith Hall
 118 Griffith Blvd.

ODESSA

American Bank
620 North Grant Ave.

Ector County Courthouse
300 North Grant Ave.

Ector County Public Library
622 North Lee Ave.

Ector Theater
500 North Texas Ave.

ORANGE

Park Avenue Medical Center
1301 West Park Ave.

PADUCAH

Cottle County Courthouse
815 9th St.

PASADENA

St. Pius V Catholic Church
924 South Main St.

Strawberry Park Pavilion
2900 Lafferty Rd.

PHARR

Rosemary June and Eugene B. Darby House
510 West Rosemary Ave.

Address List

PLAINVIEW

Harvest Queen Mill and Elevator
1208 North Columbia St.

PLANO

Texas Pool
901 Springbrook Dr.

PORT ARANSAS

Seahorse Inn (now Belles Sea Inn)
630 Banyan Beach Dr.

PORT ARTHUR

Phillis Wheatley Elementary
1100 Jefferson Dr.

Taft School
2500 Taft Ave.

RANCHO VIEJO

House of Mo-Rose packing shed
Eldorado Ave. and Hidalgo Ave.

RAYMONDVILLE

First Presbyterian Church
376 South 10th St.

REFUGIO

O'Connor Public Library
815 Commerce St.

RIO GRANDE CITY

Bertha's Motel
610 East 2nd St.

SAN ANGELO

St Luke's Methodist Church
2781 West Ave. N

SAN ANTONIO

Alameda Theater
318 West Houston St.

Alazán Apache Courts
1101 South Brazos St.

Antioch Baptist Church
1001 North Walters St.

Claude Black Community Center
2805 E Commerce St.

Hemisfair Theater, San Antonio
200 E Market St.

Lerma's Nite Club
1612 N Zarzamora St.

Lullwood Apartments
337 East Lullwood Ave.

Patsy Galt and Marshall Steves House
501 Grandview Place

Roseville Apartments
4139 E Houston St.

San Antonio Public Library, Carver Branch
3350 E Commerce St.

San Antonio Public Library, Main Branch
(now Briscoe Western Art Museum)
210 W Market St.

Trinity University
1 Trinity Place

USAA Building
9800 Fredericksburg Rd.

USAA Building
E Hildebrand Ave. and Broadway

SAN AUGUSTINE

US Post Office
117 West Main St.

SHAMROCK

Conoco Gas Station
(now Tower Station and U-Drop Inn Café)
101 East 12th St.

TYLER

People's National Bank
102 N College Ave.

People's National Motor Bank
121 S College Ave.

Tyler Museum of Art
(Tyler Junior College)
1300 S Mahon Ave.

Union Bus Station
311 N Bois D'Arc Ave.

UVALDE

Gymnasium and Music Building
1000 North Getty St.

VAN HORN

Hotel El Capitan
100 E Broadway

VICTORIA

First Church of Christ, Scientist
302 W Stayton Ave.

WACO

American Bank
1601 North I-35 Frontage Rd.

Brazos River Authority Headquarters
4400 Cobbs Dr.

Congregation Rodef Shalom Temple
1717 North 41st St.

Waco-McClennan County Library
1717 Austin Ave.

WAXAHACHIE

Samaria Missionary Baptist Church
508 Dr. Martin Luther King Blvd.

WEST COLUMBIA

Columbia Rosenwald School
247 E Brazos Ave.

West Columbia Elementary School
711 Gray St.

WHARTON

Josephine Traylor Brooking Memorial Nurses Home
215 East University Ave.

Outlar and Blair Clinic
3007-3027 North Richmond St.

Tee Pee Motel
4809 N Richmond Rd.

Index

Page numbers in *italics* refer to photographs.

Aalto, Alvar, 66, 193, 356
Adams, Charles, *160*, 161, 205–206, *206*, *207*
Adams and Adams, 25
Admiral Auto Courts (Houston), 252, *252*
Air Conditioned Village (Austin), 105, *106*, *107*
air-conditioning: Ector County Courthouse, 93; effect on environment of, 91; government buildings, 93; history of, 91; industrial buildings, 271; libraries, 185; pedestrian accessways, 107, 350; shopping malls, 343; single-family homes, 105; skyscrapers, 107; sports buildings, 237; university buildings, 322
Alameda Theater (San Antonio), *220*, 221
Alazán-Apache Courts (San Antonio), 59–60
Albaugh, Ellis F., 60, *61*
Albers, Anni, *138*, 162, *163*
Allen House, Ross L. (Corpus Christi), *40*
All Souls Unitarian Universalist Church (Brownsville), 158, *159*
Ambasz, Emilio, *284*, 285, *286*, 286–287
American Bank (Bellmead), *24*, 133, *135*
American Bank of Commerce (Odessa), *36*, *37*, 123
American Institute of Architects (AIA), 16, 17, 45, 374
Amon Carter Foundation, 107
Amon Carter Museum (Fort Worth), 298, 305–308, *306*, *307*
Anahuac Oil Field, 168
Anderson House, Ralph A., Jr. (Houston), 83, *84*, 85, 87
Angelina County Courthouse (Lufkin), *164*, *172*
Antfarm (art collective), 245; *Cadillac Ranch* (Amarillo), 245, *245*
Antioch Missionary Baptist Church (San Antonio), 154, *156*, 157, *157*
Architectural Forum (magazine): on Harris County Center for the Retarded, 198, 201; on Lamar High School, 11; Temple Emanu-El in, 161; on Trinity University, 318
Art Deco style: advertising and, 246; Alameda Theater, 221; *Austin Daily Tribune* Building, 275; brutalism compared to, 179; coinage of "Art Deco," 227; Fair Park and, 25; Gregg County Community Building, 184–185; Gulf, Colorado, and Santa Fe Railway passenger station, 265; hotels and motels, 252, 254; Houston Municipal Airport Terminal Building, 263; Lamar High School, 11; Love Field, 265; Lubbock County Sheriff's Department and Jail, 184; Lullwood Apartments, 60; People's National Bank, 131, 133; theaters, 218, 221; Tower Station and U-Drop Inn Café, 251; travel-related buildings, 251, 252, 254, 263, 265; Tyler, Texas, buildings, 131; Waco bottling plant, 227
art moderne, 121
Art Museum of South Texas (Corpus Christi), 297–298, *299*
Arts and Crafts movement, 144, 216
Associated Housing Architects of Houston, 52, 58, *58*
Astrodome (Houston), 237, *237*, *238*, *239*, 240
Aubry, Eugene, 147, *148*, 198, *199*, *200*, 353
Austin Daily Tribune Building (Austin), *268*, *275*, 275–277
avant-garde: central preoccupations of, 179; courtyards, 69–70; educational buildings, 329; emancipation potential of, 304–305; Frank Lloyd Wright and, 19; International Style modernism and, 187; oil derricks, 117–118; Philip Johnson and, 32; place and, 78; Walter Gropius and, 12
Avila, Alfredo, 72
Avila, Mateo, 72, 74
Avion Village (Grand Prairie), 338, *339*
Ayres and Ayres, 126, *127*, 267

Bailey, Ray, *186*, 187
Barnes, Edward Larrabee, 31, 298
Barnstone, Howard, 30, 32, 40; Harris County Center for the Retarded, 198, *199*, *200*, 201; Rothko Chapel, 147, *148*, 149–150, 353; University of St. Thomas buildings, 326, *328*
Barragán, Luis, 285
Barthelme, Donald, 25, 102, *102*
Bass, Sid Richardson, 73–78
Bass House, Sid Richardson and Anne (Fort Worth), 31, 69, 73–78, *75*, 380n16
Bauhaus architecture, 12, 20, 78, 162
Beck, John C., 76, 78
Becket, Welton, 31. *See also* Welton Becket and Associates
Beck House, Patricia Davis and John C. (Dallas), 76, 78
Behrens, Peter, 118, 273
Benham-Blair and Affiliates, 129
Bennett, Martin and Solka, 176, *178*
Bennett, Robert S., 373, *373*
Berger, Arthur and Marie, 65, 161, 273, 321
Bertoia, Harry, 146
Bettison, James, 363, *364*
Biggers, John T., 302, 332
Birkerts, Gunnar, 298
Birthday, The (Sterling County), 125–126
Bishop and Walker, 83, 107
Blackwell School (Marfa), 359, *359*

393

Index

Blanton, Annie Webb, 280, 282
Blessed Sacrament School (Laredo), *104*
Bliss and Vaughan, 227, 230, *230*
Boone, Daniel, 121
Boynton, Jack, 304
Braniff International Hostess College (Dallas), 265, *266*, 267
Brants, Cynthia, 79, 81
Brazos River Authority Headquarters (Waco), 372, *373*, 374
Bridges-Campbell and Associates, 88
brises-soleil, 95, 99, 106–107, *109*, 112
Broad & Nelson, 246
Brooks, Barr, Graeber and White, 175, 277, *278*
Brooks, R. Max, 176
Brown, George R., 233
Brown, Richard F., 308
Brown, William R., *250*, 251
Brown & Root, 233, 287, *288*, 289, *290*
Brown Pavilion (Houston), 44, 81, 300, *301*, 302, 303
Brown vs. Board of Education, 13, 15
brutalism, 74, 125, 176, 179
Bunshaft, Gordon, 37, 278–280. *See also* Skidmore, Owings and Merrill
Burgee, John, 110. *See also* Johnson/Burgee
Burkhart, Max, Jr., 99, 99–100
bus stations and shelters, 251; Sears, Roebuck & Company bus shelter (Houston), 246, *247*; Union Bus Station (Tyler), 367, *368*

Cadillac Ranch (Amarillo), 245, *245*
Calhoun County Courthouse (Port Lavaca), *174*, 175
Campbell and White, *114*, *132*, 132–133, *133*
Campbell Centre (Dallas), 38, *38*, *134*, 135, 263
Candela, Félix, 31, 102, 271–273; First Christian Church, 151, *152*; hyperbolic paraboloid roof structures of, 150, 216, 251, 271, 273
Caragonne, Alexander, 30
Carmona, Carina, 372, *372*
Carpenter House, Berthea and Earl (Houston), *225*, 226
Carroll and Daeuble and Associates (later, Carroll, Daeuble, DuSang and Rand), 32, 123, 125
Carson, Chris, 72, 74, *298*
Carter, Amon G., 305. *See also* Amon Carter Museum
Cartier-Bresson, Henri, 40, 43
Case Study House Program, 81
Cathedral of Hope (Dallas), 47
Cato, Lamar Q., 331

Caudill, William, 30
Caudill Rowlett Scott (CRS), 30, 33, 102, *104*, 105, 235, 347, *347*, 349
Centennial Building (Dallas), 25, *27*. *See also* Texas Centennial Exposition
Cerf Ross–Edwin Nicholson Associates, 370, *370*
Chamberlain, John, 356, *357*
Chambers County Courthouse (Anahuac), 168, *169*
Chase, Drucie Raye Rucker, 69, *70*, 71
Chase, John S., 45, 45–46, 69; John S. Chase House, 69–71, *70*, *71*, *72*, 81; Martin Luther King Jr. Humanities Center (TSU), 332, 332–333; Riverside National Bank, 129, *129*; St. James United Methodist Church, 158
Chase House, John S. (Houston), 69–71, *70*, *71*, *72*, 81
Chatham, Hood, Jr., 79, 81
Cherry, Kathryne, 46–47
Childress Optometrists (Longview), 188, 367, *369*, 370
Chillman, James, Jr., 304
Chinati Foundation, 356
Church of the Incarnation (Irving), *150*, 151
Cigarroa Medical Building (Laredo), 99, 99–100
city halls, 271, 341; Dallas, 176, 179, *179*, *180*; Denton, 342; Houston, 169, *170*, *171*; San Angelo, *171*
Civilian Conservation Corps, 167, 216, 254
civil rights movement and legislation, 28, 71, 129, 223, 240
class (economic and social), 14, 59, 60, 65, 69, 70–71, 73, 83, 91, 105, 118, 129, 241, 246, 265, 337, 338
Clovis Heimsath Associates, 331
Cobb, Henry, 111–112, *113*
Cobb, Jack, 260
Coca-Cola Bottling Company (Beeville), 227, *229*
Coca-Cola Bottling Company (Waco), 227, *228*, 230
Cocke, Bartlett, 318, *320*
Cocke, Bowman and York, 40, *41*
Coe, Herring, 92–93, *94*, 96
Coleman County Courthouse (Coleman), *172*, 173
Colley, Richard S., 325; Allen House, *40*; Dos Cruces Gallery, 363, *364*; Texas Instruments Semiconductor Building, 31, 251, 271–273, *272*
Columbia Rosenwald School (West Columbia), 13–15, *14*
Comanche people, 169
Comanche Trail Amphitheater (Big Spring), *215*, 215–216

Congregation B'nai Israel Temple (Galveston), 40, *42*, 43
Congregation Rodef Shalom Temple (Waco), 154, *155*
Conoco Gas Station (Corpus Christi), *250*, 251
Conoco Gas Station (Laredo), *250*, 251
Cook, C. Gale, 101, *101*, 195, *195*
Corgan, Jack, 218, *218*, 246
Cram, Ralph Adams, 146
Cret, Paul, 25, 168
Crim House, Tincy and Liggett N. (Kilgore), 35, *35*
Crim Theater (Kilgore), 218, *218*
Croft, Charles B., 273, *274*
Crow, Trammell, 206, 343
CRS. *See* Caudill Rowlett Scott (CRS)
CRS Sirrine, 179
Cullinan Hall, Museum of Fine Arts (Houston), 43, *44*, 81, 300, *302*, 303, 305, 327
Cunningham Architects, 47
Curtis, Corneil G., 168, *169*
Cynthia Brants Studio (Fort Worth), 79, 81

Dahl, George L., 25, 123, 246, *247*, 367
Dallas City Hall, 176, 179, *179*, *180*
Dallas North Estates (Plano), 38, *38*
Dallas Trade Mart, 206, 343, *344*
Danadjieva, Angela, 110–111
Davis, Foster, Thorpe and Associates, *174*, 175
Davis, Patricia, 76, 78
Dealey Plaza (Dallas), 207
de Blois, Natalie Griffin, 37, 379n32. *See also* Skidmore, Owings and Merrill
Delta Kappa Gamma Society (Austin), 280–282, *281*
de Menil, Dominique and John. *See* Menil, Dominique and John de
Dennis M. O'Connor Public Library (Refugio), 185, *185*
Denton County Civic Center, 341, *342*
Derrah, Robert V., 227
Dewitt, Roscoe P., 338, *339*
d'Harnoncourt, René, 305
Dieste, Eladio, 367
Ding How Chinese Restaurant (Amarillo), 227, *230*, *230*, 232
Dobson, Harmon, *232*, 233
Docomomo International, 48
Donald Barthelme and Associates, 25, 102, *102*
Donald R. Goss Associates, 157–158
Donnelly, Charles P., 185, *185*, 249, *249*
Dos Cruces Gallery (Corpus Christi), 363, *364*
Driscoll, Dan J., 216

Index

Dudley, W. W., 172, *173*
Dupree, Anna and Clarence A., 221

Eames, Charles and Rae, 81
Echo Hotel (Edinburg), *258*, 258–259
École des Beaux-Arts, 133
Ector County Courthouse (Odessa), 93, 95, *95*
E. Davis Wilcox Associates, *132*, 133
Edna Police and Fire Department, 181, *181*
Edna Theatre, 218, *219*
Edward Durrell Stone & Associates, 76, *76, 77*, 298
Egg, Norma, 82, *82*
Egg-Gregory House (El Paso), 82, *82*
Eisenshtat, Sidney, 158, 161
Eldorado Building (Houston), 221, *222*; Eldorado Ballroom, 221
El Lissitzky, 118
Elmo, Hudson J., 337–338, *338*
Entenza, John, 81
Evelyn Motor Inn (Laredo), 102, *103*

Fair Park (Dallas), 25, 65, 121, 167. *See also* Texas Centennial Exposition
Farm Security Administration, 337
Federal Reserve Bank of Dallas, El Paso Branch, *174*, 175
Fehr, Arthur, 25, 28, 203, *204*, 252, *254*
Fehr and Granger, 203, *204*
Field & Clarkson, 127
Filipowski, Richard, 162, *163*
Finger, Joseph, 169, *170*, 263, *264*
Finn, Alfred C., 28, *29*, 114, 131, *132, 133*, 134
First Baptist Church (Longview), 141, *142*
First Christian Church (Denton), 151, *152*, 154
First Church of Christ, Scientist (Victoria), 158, *159*, 161
First National Bank (Corsicana), 126–127, *128*
First National Pioneer Building (Lubbock), 123, *123*
First Presbyterian Church (Raymondville), 141, *142*
First Security National Bank (Beaumont), 92–93, *93, 94*
Fisher, Reynolds, 55, *56*
Fitch and Holcomb, 217, *217*
Fitzgerald, Richard, *294*, 353, *354*
Flavin, Dan, 356
Flores Middle School, Gymnasium and Music Building (Uvalde), 235, *236*
Ford, Lynn, 25, 28, 151, 322, 341
Ford, O'Neil, 25, 28, 32, 35, 37, 45; Denton buildings, 341, *342*; influence on religious buildings, *150*, 151, 154; influences on, 72, 329, 333; Intercontinental Motors, 248, *248*; La Villita Assembly Building, 341; Presbyterian Pan American School, 317–318, 325–326, *326, 327*; Steves House, 69, 72–73, *74, 76*; Texas Instruments Semiconductor Building, 31, 251, 271–273, *272*; Trinity University, *319, 320*, 321–322, *323*, 341. *See also* Ford, Powell and Carson; O'Neil Ford and Associates
Ford, Powell and Carson, 46, 72, 298, 322, *324, 326. See also* Ford, O'Neil
Forest Oil Company building (Midland), *124*, 125–126
Fort D. A. Russell (Marfa), 356, *358*, 359
Fort Worth Water Gardens, 107, 110–111, 126, 381n5 (chap.2); Active Pool, *111*; Quiet Pool, 110
Fountain Place (Dallas), 111–112, *112, 113*, 117, 135, 263, 352
Frank Reese and Associates, *276*, 277
Franzheim, Kenneth, 12, 299–300
Frazer and Benner, 60
Fred Buxton & Associates, 64
Fredonia Hotel (Nacogdoches), 256, *257*, 258
Friedman, Alice T., 32, 47, 82

Gabert, Lenard, 221
Galván Ballroom (Corpus Christi), 223
Galveston Artillery Club, 223, *224*, 225–226
Galvestonian (Galveston), 66, *68*
Garatti, Vittorio, 367
Garland & Hilles, 32, 69, *70*
Garza House, Rafael (McAllen), 55, *57, 58*
George Pierce-Abel B. Pierce, 96, *98, 99*, 107, *108, 109*
Geraldine D. Humphreys Cultural Center (Liberty), 370, *371*, 372
Geren, Preston M., 126–127, *128*, 309, 311, *312*
Goff, Bruce, 30, 339, *340*, 341
Goleman and Rolfe, 107, *108*
Goodhue, Bertram Grosvenor, 168
Good Luck Oil Company gas station #5 (Dallas), *242*, 251
Gordon, Elizabeth, 58
Gothic architecture, 17, 143, 347
Gothic Revival architecture, 62, 143, 158, 360
Gottardi, Roberto, 367
Graf House, Josephine Herbert and Bruno (Dallas), 76, *76–77*, 93, *117*
Great Plains Life Insurance Company (Lubbock), 121, *122*
Green, Dudley, 168
Green, Herbert S., 168
Greenway Plaza (Houston), 346, 350, 352; Greenway Plaza 3 & 5, *351*; Summit Towers North, *352*
Greenwood Memorial Park (Fort Worth), 205–206; Mausoleum, *206, 207*
Gregg County Community Building (Gladewater), *184*, 184–185
Gregory, Gladys, 82, *82*
Gropius, Walter, 12, 19–21, 35, 78, 81
Grossman, Melvin, 260, 263
Grossman House, Max (El Paso), 70, *70*
Gunn, Ralph Ellis, 198, *199, 200*, 201–202
Gunnar Birkerts & Associates, 298

Halprin, Lawrence, 110–111
Hamon, Everett Elijah, 223
Hardin, Benjamin Franklin, 370, 372
Hare, Sid J., 205
Hare & Hare, 170
Harold A. Berry and Associates, *334*, 343, *344, 345*
Harper and Kemp, 176, *180*
Harrington Cancer Center (Amarillo), *201*, 202
Harris, Ethel Wilson, 216
Harris, Harwell Hamilton, 30; Dallas Trade Mart, 206, 343, *344*; Stemmons Towers, *334*, 343, *345*; St. Mary's Episcopal Church, 160, 161
Harris County Center for the Retarded (Houston), 198, *199, 200*, 201–202
Harris County Family Law Center Building (Houston), 176, *177*
Harrison, E. A., 265
Harrison, Wallace K., 78
Harvest Queen Mill and Elevator (Plainview), 19
Haviland, John, 183
Haynes, S. B., 184
Haynes and Kirby, 171, *171*
Haynes & Strange, 185
Haynsworth, Elizabeth Drane, 36, 37, 265
Haywood, Norcell D., 32, 154, 205; Antioch Missionary Baptist Church, 154, *156, 157*, 157; Morris Chapel, Presbyterian Pan American School, 326, *326, 327*; Roseville Apartments, 203, *204*, 205
Haywood Jordan McCowan, 154, 205
Hazel, William A., 13
Hedrick, Wyatt C., 32, 123, 218, 265, 331; American Bank of Commerce (Odessa), 36, 37, 123; Coleman County Courthouse, 172, *173*
Heimsath, Clovis, 28, 30, 331
Hejduk, John, 30
HemisFair '68, 37, 73, 322, 337
Hester, Paul, 39
Hetrick, Richard M., 141, *142*
high modernism, 60, 66, 227, 232, 277

395

Index

Hillier, Bevis, 227
Hines, Gerald D., 120, 346–347
Hitchcock, Henry-Russell, 21, 65
HKS, Inc., *134*, 135
Hofheinz, Roy, 240
Holmes, Dwight C., 263, 265
Hood, Lucian T., Jr., *225*, 225–226
horizontality: of apartment buildings, 59; of medical clinics, 195; of school and university buildings, 11, 92, 235, 318; Wrightian design and, 59
Hotel El Capitan (Van Horn), 252, *253*
House of Mo-Rose (Rancho Viejo), 273, *274*, *276*, *277*
Houston City Hall, 169, *170*, *171*
Houston Municipal Airport Terminal Building, 263, *264*, 265
Houston Port Public Export Elevator, 19–20, *20*
Houston Public Library, Carnegie Branch, *186*, 187
Howe, George, 65–66, 120–121, 135
Howell House, Robert (Austin), 56
Humble Oil and Refining Company, 107, 168, 251; Humble Oil Building (Houston), 107, *108*, *109*; Humble Oil Garage (Houston), 107, *109*
Humpel, Robert, 359
Humphreys, Geraldine Davis, 370, 372
Huxtable, Ada Louise, 149, 280
Hyatt Regency Hotel and Reunion Tower (Dallas), *262*, 263
hyperbolic paraboloid roof structures, 151, 216, 249, 251, 271–273

I. M. Pei and Partners, 111–112, *113*, 176, *180*
Indian Lodge (Fort Davis), 252, *254*, 254–255
Industrial Revolution, 19
Intercontinental Motors (San Antonio), 248, *248*
Interfaith Peace Chapel (Dallas), 47
International Style, 20–21, 37–38, 120–121, 187; Braniff International Hostess College, 265, *266*, *267*; capitalism and, 176; financial buildings, 127; first generation of, 123; government buildings, 175; MoMA exhibit, 20–21, 37–38, 65, 120; second wave of, 106–107, 123
Inwood Manor (Houston), 64–65, *65*, *78*

Jack Corgan and Associates, 246
Jefferson, Thomas, 55, 329
Jefferson Chemical Bank Building (Houston), 347, *348*
Jefferson High School (Port Arthur), 105; Gymnasium, 235, *236*, *237*
Jenkins, William R., 30, 370, *371*
Jenkins and Hoff, 39, *42*, 43

Jewett Arts Center, Wellesley College, 74, 101, 202
J. J. Pickle Federal Building (Austin), 175–176
John F. Kennedy Memorial (Dallas), 206–208, *208*
John G. York and Associates, 55, *57*
John S. Metcalf Company, 19–20, *20*
Johnson, Lady Bird, 69, 216, 280, 287, 374
Johnson, Lyndon Baines, 22, 71, 277–280; Presidential Library and Museum, 277–280, *278*
Johnson, Philip, 21, 31–32, 83, 305–308; anti-Semitism of, 32; Art Museum of South Texas, 297–298, *299*; Beck House, 76, *78*; Fort Worth Water Gardens, 107, *110*, 110–111, *111*, 126; Glass House, 83, 249, 353; Interfaith Peace Chapel, 47; John F. Kennedy Memorial, 206–208, *208*; Ludwig Mies van der Rohe and, 32, 120, 305, 327; Menil House, 353, *355*, *355*; MoMA International Style exhibit organized by, 20–21, 37–38, 65, 120; Pennzoil Place, *119*, 120; Rothko Chapel, 147, *148*, 149, 151, 353; University of St. Thomas, 327, *328*, 329–330. *See also* Amon Carter Museum
Johnson/Burgee, 32, 110–111, *111*, *119*, 120, 297–298, *299*. *See also* Johnson, Philip
Johnson Space Center (Houston), 287, *288*, *289*, *290*, *291*, 297; Mission Control (restoration), 367, *368*
Jones & Kell, *284*, 285, *286*
Josephine Traylor Brooking Memorial Nurses Home (Wharton), 203, *204*
Judd, Donald, 355–359, *358*; Fort D. A. Russell, 356, *358*, *359*; Marfa National Bank and Brite Building, 356, *357*; Marfa Wool and Mohair Building, 356, *357*
Judd Foundation, 355–356

Kahn, Louis I., 28, 30–31, 125, 147, 239; Indian Institute of Management, 317; Kimbell Art Museum, 29–30, 126, 298, 308–313, *309*, *311*, *312*
Kalita Humphreys Theater (Dallas), 30, 372
Kallmann McKinnell and Knowles, 179
KCOR Radio and Television Station (San Antonio), 370, *370*
Keeland, Burdette, 30
Kelly, Marshall & Associates, 125
Kelly, Richard, 310
Kelly, W. L., 60, *62*
Kennedy, John F., 15, 64, 175, 279, 287; John F. Kennedy Memorial, 206–208, *208*; speech at Rice Football Stadium, 233, 235

Kenneth Bentsen Associates, 317, *319*, 350
Kent, Marcellos, and Scott, 318, 329, *330*, *331*
Kent, Wilbur, 34, 35, *164*, 172, *172*
Kepes, György, *138*, 162, *163*
Kessler, George, 66
Ketchum MacLeod & Grove Building (Houston), 347, *349*
Kevin Roche John Dinkeloo and Associates, 135, 179
Kimbell, Kay and Velma, 308
Kimbell Art Museum (Fort Worth), 29–30, 126, 298, 308–313, *309*, *311*, *312*
King, Billie Jean, 240
King, Henrietta Chamberlin, 325
King, Martin Luther, Jr., 130–131, 147, 157; Martin Luther King Jr. Humanities Center (TSU), *332*, 332–333
King, Stewart, 72, 74, 248, 273
King Ranch, 325
Kipp and Winston, 176, *178*
Knipe, Leighton G., 356, *357*
Knoll, Hans, 202
Kraigher, George, 30, *31*
Kraigher House, George (Brownsville), 30–31, *31*
Kuehne, Brooks and Barr, 181, *182*, 280–281, *281*
Kuehne, Hugo Franz, 216–217

Lake Village (Flint), 339, 341; Bruce Plunkett First House, 339, *340*
Lamar, Mirabeau B., 49
Lamar High School (Houston), 8, 11; *Architectural Forum* on, 11; naming of, 49. *See also* map of Texas, limestone (Lamar High School)
Lamar–River Oaks Shopping Center (Houston), 226, *226*
Lamesa Farm Workers Community (Los Ybáñez), 337–338, *338*
Landry, Duane, *150*, 151, 341
Landry, Jane, *150*, 151, 341
Laney, Roland, 341, *342*
Lang and Witchell, 168
Lapidus, Morris, 263
Lasater, Garland, 325
LaSelle, Dorothy Antoinette, 144, 146
Lea, Tom, 25
Le Corbusier, 19, 64–66, 78, 239, 285–286, 329, 342–343; coinage of "brises-soleil," 95; grain silos of, 118; Notre-Dame du Haut, 149; on technical revolution, 17; Unité d'Habitation, 66; verdant landscapes of, 64–65; *Vers une Architecture*, 20; Villa Savoye, 179
Legarreta, Juan, 59–60
Legorreta, Ricardo, 298, *299*

Index

Leinbach, C. H., 184, *184*
Lenarduzzi, Nino, 11, 12
Lerma's Nite Club (San Antonio), *222*, 223
Lescaze, William, 65, 120–121, *121*, 123, 135
LeStourgeon, B. Hough, 252
Lever House (New York City), 37, 106
Lewerentz, Sigurd, 154
Lew Williams Chevrolet City Dealership (Corpus Christi), 249, *249*, 251
Little Chapel in the Woods (Denton), 143–145, *144*, *145*, 146, 151, 322
LLewellyn W. Pitts Medal, 46
Lloyd, Morgan and Jones, 32, 207, 237, *237*, *238*, *239*
Lloyd and Morgan, *212*, 233, *234*
Lloyd Jones Associates, 350
Lloyd Jones Brewer and Associates, 352, *352*
Loggia dei Lanzi (Florence), 307–308
Long, Bert Jr., 363, *364*
Lott, Jesse, 363, *364*
Louis, Morris, 75–76
Lowe, Rick, 363, *364*
Lubbock County Courthouse, 171, *171*
Lucille Halsell Conservatory (San Antonio), *284*, 285, *286*
Lufkin Federal Savings and Loan, *34*, 35
Lullwood Apartments (San Antonio), 60, *61*
Lyndon Baines Johnson Presidential Library and Museum (Austin), 277–280, *278*
Lyndon B. Johnson Space Center. *See* Johnson Space Center (Houston)
Lynn Theatre (Gonzalez), 218, *218*

MacAgy, Jermayne, 329
MacCammon, James N., 256, *257*, 258
MacKie and Kamrath, *34*, 35, 304; Congregation Rodef Shalom Temple, 154, *155*; Edna Police and Fire Department, 181, *181*; Johnson Space Center, 288, *289*, *290*, *368*; Phillis Wheatley High School, *34*, 35; San Felipe Courts (Houston), 52, 58
Magnolia Lounge (Dallas), 65, 120–121, *121*
Manned Spacecraft Center. *See* Johnson Space Center (Houston)
map of Texas, limestone (Lamar High School), *8*, 11–13, 15; stonemason for, 11, 12; Texas history and, 28
Marcellos, Floyd, 35
Marfa National Bank and Brite Building, 356, *357*
Marfa Wool and Mohair Building, 356, *357*
Mariscal, Federico, 17
Martha T. Griffith Hall (Nacogdoches), 330, *330*
Martin Luther King Jr. Humanities Center (TSU, Houston), *332*, 332–333

Matisse, Henri, 76, 149
Mayflower Investment Houses (Dallas), 56, *56*
McDaniels, Ava Jean, 304
McDonald Observatory (Fort Davis), 282, *283*, 284–285
McGinty, Milton, *212*, 233, *234*
McGonigle, Ruth Young, 46
McNay Museum of Art, 297–298, *298*
Mears, Herb, 304
Mease, Quentin, 240
Mendelsohn, Erich, 37, 161, 230, 327, 333, 367
Menil, Dominique and John de, 147, 149, 305, 327, 329; Menil Bungalows, *355*; Menil Collection museum, 39, *294*, 353, *355*; Menil House, 353, 355, *355*
Menil Collection museum (Houston), 39, *294*, 353, *355*
Menil House, Dominique and John de (Houston), 353, 355, *355*
Mercantile National Bank (Corpus Christi), *130*, 131
Mercy Hospital (Laredo), *192*, 192–193
Meyer, Howard R., 32, 321, 341; 3525 Turtle Creek Apartments, 65, 65–66, 67; Lipshy House, 69, *162*, *163*; Temple Emanu-El, *138*, 161, *162*, 163
Miesian characteristics: Brazos River Authority Headquarters, 373; corporate office buildings, 176; Delta Kappa Gamma Society, 280–281; environment and, 373; government buildings, 175, 176; industrial buildings, 248–249; Menil House, 353
Mies van der Rohe, Ludwig, 19, 21, 31, 120, 313; Armour Institute in Chicago, 317; Cullinan Hall, Museum of Fine Arts, 43, *44*, 81, 300, *302*, 303, 305, 327; Philip Johnson and, 32, 120, 305, 327; Seagram Building, 37; Todd House and, 81
MIT (Cambridge, Massachusetts): Baker House dormitory, 66; Kresge Auditorium, 105, 235, *237*; Kresge Chapel, 146; visual design program, 162
Mitchell, George and Cynthia Woods, 66
Mollinary, Louis Lloyd, 60
MoMA (Museum of Modern Art, New York), 20–21, 37–38, 65, 120
Mood, Beaumont, 326, 341
Mood, Martha, 96, 326, 341
Moore, Harvin C., *96*, 146, *147*, 288, *289*, *290*, *368*
Moore, William J., 218
Moore House, Ann Maddox (McAllen), *96*, 97
Mount-Miller, 341

Munson-Williams-Proctor Art Institute (Utica, New York), 305
Museum of Fine Arts (Houston), 298–299; Cullinan Hall, 43, *44*, 81, 300, *302*, 303, 305, 327

Nagel, Chester E., 35, 78, *79*, 81
Nagel House, Lorine and Chester E. (Austin), 78, *79*, 81
National Organization of Minority Architects (NOMA), 45–46
Nayfach, N. Straus, 59, *220*, 221
Negro Motorist Green Book, The, 246
Neuhaus and Taylor, 347; Campbell Centre, 38, *38*, *134*, 135; Inwood Manor, 64–65, *65*; Jefferson Chemical Bank Building, *348*; One Moody Plaza (Galveston), 23
Neutra, Richard, 30, *31*, 338, *339*
New Formalism, 64, 92, 330
Newsum, Floyd, 363, *364*
nightclubs, 76, 221, 226
Nill, J. Sterry, 216
N. J. Clayton and Company, 42
Noonan & Noonan, 235, *236*
Nueces County Courthouse (Corpus Christi), 176, *178*, 179

Oberg, Harold, 241, *241*
O'Daniel, W. Lee "Pappy," 276–277
O'Gorman, Juan, 37, 73
oil derricks, 117–118, *118*; in Kilgore, 118, *118*
One Broadcast Center (Amarillo), 276, 277
O'Neil Ford and Associates, 46, 152, 248, *314*, 323, 326, 327, 341, 342. *See also* Ford, O'Neil
One Moody Plaza (Galveston), 22, *23*
Orange County Courthouse (Orange), 100–101, *101*, 195

Page, Russell, 75, *75*
Page Brothers, 168
Page Southerland Page, 32; *Austin Daily Tribune* Building, 268, 275–277; J. J. Pickle Federal Building, 175–176; Potter County Courthouse, 168–169; Rio House Apartments, 60, *63*, 360
Pan-Americanism, 317–318, *319*, 325
Panhandle-Plains Historical Museum (Canyon), *36*, 37
Park Avenue Medical Center (Orange), 195, *195*
Parker House, Frank G. (Harlingen), 40, *41*
patrons, architectural, 15, 19, 69, 73–74, 187, 367
Pearson, T. Brooks, 227
Pei, I. M., 31, 111, *113*, 176, 179, *180*
Pennzoil Place (Houston), *119*, 120

397

People's National Bank (Tyler), 114, 132, 133, *133*
Permian Basin, 93, 125
Permian Building (Abilene), 88
Peters and Fields, 93, *95*, 96
Peterson, Carolyn, 46, *46*
Phelps, Dewees and Simmons, 126, *127*, *174*, *175*, 216
Philadelphia Savings Fund Society (PSFS), 65–66, 120–121, 135
Philip Johnson & Associates, 31–32, *208*, *306*, *307*, *328*, *355*. See also Johnson, Philip
Philip Willard and Associates, 100
Phillips/Ryburn Associates, 363, *366*
Phillis Wheatley High School (Houston), 34, *35*
Piano, Renzo, *294*, *353*, *354*
Pierce Lacey Partnership, 265, *266*
Pitts, Mebane and Phelps, 91–92, *92*, 135
Pitts, Mebane, Phelps and White, 92, *93*, *94*
planarity, 35, 81, 127, 141, 202, 330, 335
Plaza Theatre (Laredo), 218, *219*
Plunkett, Bruce, 339, *340*, 341
pluralism, 16, 17, 28, 141, 232
Porro, Ricardo, 367
Post, Emily, 58
post offices, 167, 372; Barbara Jordan Post Office (Houston), 365; Post Office Savings Bank (Vienna), 273, 306; US Post Office (San Augustine), 181, 183, *183*
Potter County Courthouse (Amarillo), 168–169
Powell, Boone, 322, *324*, 325
Powell, J. Ellsworth, 185
Pratt, Box and Henderson, 32
Presbyterian Pan American School (Kingsville), 317–318, 325–326, *326*, 327
Presidents-First Lady Health Spa Building (Houston), 240–241, *241*
Press, Hans Jürgen, 359
Price, Thomas M., 223, *224*, 225
Project Row Houses (Houston), 363, *364*
PSFS. *See* Philadelphia Savings Fund Society
Public Works Administration, 143–144, 167, 184
Pucci, Emilio, 265
Pueblo Revival style, 218

race and ethnicity, 12–15, 21, 25, 28, 35, 38, 45, 47, 55, 59–60, 71, 72, 82, 102, 105, 129, 154, 157, 187, 196, 197, 203, 205, 221, 223, 225, 226, 240, 246, 255, 280, 282, 304, 325, 330–331, 341, 359, 370
Ray Sherman Place (El Paso), 60
Reidy, Affonso Eduardo, 66

Reitch House (Mineola), 33, *33*
Rice Football Stadium (Houston), *212*, 233, *234*, 235
Rice University (Houston), 46, 81, 273, 287, 305, 317, 329; Keith-Weiss Geological Laboratories building, 96, *98*, *99*; Rice Memorial Chapel, 146, *147*
Richardson, Sid, 35, 37
Rietveld, Gerrit, 75
Rio House Apartments (Austin), 60, *63*, *360*
Rivera, Diego, 332
Rivera, José de, 260
Riverside National Bank (Houston), 129, *129*
Robsjohn-Gibbings, T. H., 77
Romanesque architecture, 143, 310, 322
Rosenwald, Julius, 13
Rosenwald Schools, 13–15, *14*, 33
Roseville Apartments (San Antonio), 203, *204*, 205
Rothko Chapel (Houston), 147, *148*, 149, 151, 353
Rowe, Colin, 30
Rowlett, John, 30. See also Caudill Rowlett Scott (CRS)
Rudolph, Paul, 31, 47, 202; Bass House, 31, 69, 73–78, *75*; Harrington Cancer Center (Amarillo), *201*, 202; Jewett Arts Center, Wellesley College, 101; One Broadcast Center, 276, 277
Rustay and Martin, *174*, 175
Ruthrauff & Ryan, Inc. Building (Houston), *346*
Ryan, Milton A., 158, *159*, 161

Saarinen, Eero, 135, 217, 265; Idlewild Airport TWA terminal, 246; MIT's Kresge Auditorium, 105, 235, *237*; MIT's Kresge Chapel, 146
Sadler, Luther, 55
Salamone, Francisco, 141
Salmona, Rogelio, 367
Samaria Missionary Baptist Church (Waxahachie), 154, *155*
Samples, Bert, 363, *364*
San Antonio Botanical Garden, *284*, *285*, *286*, 287
San Antonio Riverwalk, 73, 365
San Felipe Cottage (Houston), *96*
San Felipe Courts (Houston), 52, 54, *58*, 58–60, 107
Sanger, Margaret, 82
Sanguinet and Staats, 32
San Jacinto Monument (La Porte), 28, *29*
Savage, Eugene, 25
Schinkel, Karl Friedrich, 297
Schnitzer, Kenneth L., 343, 346, 347

Schocken, Salman, 367
Schoeppl, Carlos B., 256, *257*, 258
Schröder, Truus, 75
Schult, Ernest L., 218, *219*
Scott Brown, Denise, 297
Seagram Building (New York City), 37, 106, 120, 305
sexuality, 46–47, 82–87
Searcy Medical Clinic (Bryan), 43, *44*
Sears, Roebuck & Company bus shelter (Houston), 246, *247*
Sheffield, Weldon, 73, *74*
Shelton and Associates, *152*, *153*, 154
showrooms, car, 248–249
Siesta Motel (Laredo), 259, *259*
silos, grain, 19, 118, 310, *366*
Simms, Carroll, 331–333, *332*
Simons, Shirley, 275, 276
Simpson, Merle A., 96, *97*, 258, *258*
600 Building (Corpus Christi), *42*, 43
Skidmore, Owings and Merrill, 30–31, 37, 176, 277–278, *278*, 280
Smith, George, 363, *364*
Smith, Harvey P., 318, *320*
Smith, Harwood K., 218, *219*
Smithson, Alison and Peter, 327
Smyth and Smyth, 176, *178*
Sobrino, Josephine, 46–47
solar screens, 95, 105, 195, 259
Spanish colonial architecture, 73, 255
Spanish Colonial Revival style, 46, 82, 297
Spear, Morgan, 249, *249*
Spicer, Bush and Witt, 100, *100*
Statler Hilton Hotel (Dallas), 260, *261*
Staub, John F., *8*, *11*, 12, 251
Stearns, Eldrewey, 240
Stein, Edward, 193, *194*
Steinbomer, Henry, 141, *142*
Stell, Tom, 273
Stella, Frank, 75–76
Stemmons, John M., 343
Stemmons Freeway, 262–263, 343
Stemmons Towers (Dallas), *334*, 343, *345*
Stenger, A. D., 55, *56*
Stephen F. Austin State University (Nacogdoches), 317–318, 329–330; East College Cafeteria, 330, *331*
Stephenson, W. C., 227, *229*
Stern and Bucek Architects, *222*, 368
Stevenson, Adlai, 209
Stevenson, Ruth Carter, 305, 313
Steves, Marshall Terrell, 69, 72–76
Steves, Patsy Galt, 69, 72–76
Steves House, Patsy Galt and Marshall Terrell (San Antonio), 69, 72–73, *74*, 76
St. Mary's Episcopal Church (Big Spring), *160*, 161
Stoller, Ezra, 40, *42*, 43, 126

Index

Stone, Edward Durell, 31, 35, 76–77, 77, 96, 218, 298
Stone, Harry, 38
Stone and Pitts, 35, *35*, 218
Stonorov and Hawes, 64
St. Paul Presbyterian Church (San Angelo), 157–158
Strawberry Park Pavilion (Pasadena), 217, *217*
streamline moderne, 184, 227
Stripling, Raiford, 195–196, *196*, *197*
Sullivan, Louis, 35
Swank, Arch B., Jr., 144, *144*, 154, 271, 272, 273, 338, *339*
Sweeney, James Johnson, 40

Taber House, Philip (Amarillo), 55
Tabler, William B., 260, *261*
Taft School (Port Arthur), *104*, 105
Taniguchi, Alan Y., 273–274, *274*
Taniguchi Shefelman Vackar Minter, 273
Tap Restaurant, The (El Paso), 231, *232*
Tatlin, Vladimir, 118
Taylor, Robert R., 13
Taylor and Allen Clinic (Nacogdoches), *196*, *197*
Taylor County Courthouse (Abilene), *178*, 179
Tays Place (El Paso), 60
Tee Pee Motel (Wharton), 255–256, *256*
Temple Emanu-El (Dallas), *138*, 161, *162*, *163*
Terragni, Giuseppe, 241
Texas Centennial Exposition (1936), 25, 28, 246, 331, 337, 367; Centennial Building, 25, *27*; Fair Park, 25, 65, 121, *167*; Magnolia Lounge, 65, 120–121, *121*; Texas Hall of State Building, 25, *26*; Tower Building, 25, *26*
Texas Commerce Tower (Houston), 120
Texas Department of Public Safety Headquarters (Austin), 181, *182*
Texas Hall of State Building (Dallas), 25, *26*
Texas Instruments Semiconductor Building (Dallas), 31, 251, 271–273, *272*
Texas Society of Architects, 16, 22, 25, 45–46, 126
Texas Southern University (Houston), 330–333; Martin Luther King Jr. Humanities Center, *332*, 332–333; *Web of Life* (mural), 332
Texas Tech Library (Lubbock), 91–92, *92*
The Architects Collaborative, 81
Thompson, Ernest O., 277
3800 Main Street/Silos (Dallas), 365, *366*
3525 Turtle Creek Apartments (Dallas), 65, 65–66, *67*
Tittle, Luther, Loving, Lee, *178*, 179
Todd, Anderson and Lucie Wray, *80*, 81

Todd House, Anderson and Lucie Wray (Houston), *80*, 81
Tower Building (Dallas), 25, *26*
Townes, Lightfoot and Funk, 168
trabeation, 133, 241, 343
Trinity University (San Antonio): *Architectural Forum* on, 318; George Storch Memorial Library, *320*; Margarite B. Parker Chapel, 322, *323*; Ruth Taylor Theater, *314*; T. Frank Murchison Memorial Tower, 322, *323*
Trost and Trost, 60, 171, 252, *253*
Tugendhat, Greta and Fritz, 367
Tuskegee Institute, 13, 333
2990 Richmond Ave. (Houston), 347, *348*
T. W. Lee Apartment Building (Gladewater), 60, *62*

Underwood, H. T., 252, *252*
Union Bus Station (Tyler), 367, *368*
Unité d'Habitation, Marseille (France), 66
United Services Automobile Association (USAA), 126–127, *127*, 129
University of Dallas (Irving), 148, *150*, 151, 322, *324*
University of St. Thomas (Houston), 147, 317, 327, *328*, 329–330
University of Texas Pan-American (Edinburg), 319
University of Virginia, 329
Upton, Dell, 18
USAA Building (San Antonio), 126–127, *127*, 129

Vaughan, Arthur, 227, 230
Venturi, Robert, 17, 73, 359
Victor Keidel Memorial Hospital (Fredericksburg), 193, *194*
vigas, 255
Villanueva, Carlos Raúl, 99, 317
Voelcker, Herbert S., 168
Voelcker and Dixon, 168

Waco-McClennan County Public Library, 100, *100*
Wade, Gibson and Martin, 192, *192*
Wagner, Otto, 273, 306
Walsh, Sally, 48, 120, 198, *199*, *200*, 202
Warner & Swasey Company, 283, *284*
Washington, Booker T., 13
Watkin, William Ward, 43, 44, 146, 299–300, 303–304
Welch, Frank D., *124*, 125
Welch, Mabel C., 46, 82, *82*
Welton Becket and Associates, 31, 107, *108*, *109*, 262, 263
West, James M., 276–277
Westbrook, Lawrence, 338

West Columbia Elementary School, 102, *103*
Whataburger, 232–233, 240
White, Robert F., 287, *288*, *289*
Whole Woman's Health Clinic (McAllen), 372, *372*
Wilcox, E. Davis, 32–33, *33*, *132*, 133
Wilder, Mitchell A., 305
Wilkerson, Wallace R., 251
Willard, Philip G., 100
Williams, David R., 28, 338, *339*
Wilson, Morris & Crain, 141, *142*, *190*; Childress Optometrists, *188*, 367, *369*, 370
Wilson, Morris, Crain & Anderson, 33, 176, *177*, 237; Astrodome (Houston), 237, *237*, *238*, *239*, 240; Harris County Family Law Center Building (Houston), 176, *177*
Wilson/Doche, *201*, 202
Windsor Court Apartments (Galveston), 60, *61*
Wisznia and Peterson, *130*, 131, 176, *178*
Withers, Elmer G., 93, *95*
women architects and clients, 31, 37, 46, 69, 72–76, 79, 81–82, 96–97, 144, 147, 149, 193, 203, 205, 216, 265, 280, 282, 305, 329, 353, 355
Wong, Howard, 151, *152*, 248
Works Progress Administration (WPA), 215–216, 255, 372
Wright, Frank Lloyd, 19, 45, 72, 216, 230, 232; apology for radical humanist organicism, 17; Dallas Theater Center, 158; Fallingwater, 35; Kalita Humphreys Theater (Dallas), 30, 372; Prairie houses, 55, 339; Solomon R. Guggenheim Museum, 297; Taliesin West, 126; Usonian houses, 55, 69
Wrightianism, 35, 59, 69, 206, 260, 330
Wurster, William, 31, *138*, 161, *162*, *163*, 321

Yamasaki, Minoru, 64
York, John, 39

Zemanek House, John ("Gaea," Houston), 85, *86*, 87
Zion Lutheran Church (Abilene), 152, *153*, 154, *232*
Zisman, Sam, 271, 272, 273

Book compilation copyright © 2024
by the University of Texas Press

Photographs copyright © 2024
by Ben Koush

All rights reserved

Designed by Ian Searcy

Set in Söhne by Klim and
Fann Grotesque by Colophon

Printed on 100# Anthem Plus Satin

Printed in Canada

First edition, 2024

Requests for permission to
reproduce material from this work
should be sent to
permissions@utpress.utexas.edu

∞The paper used in this book
meets the minimum requirements
of ANSI/NISO Z39.48-1992 (R1997)
(Permanence of Paper).

Library of Congress Cataloging-in-Publication Data

Names
O'Rourke, Kathryn E., author
Koush, Ben, photographer

Title
Home, Heat, Money, God: Texas and Modern Architecture
text by Kathryn E. O'Rourke
photographs by Ben Koush

Description
First edition
Austin: University of Texas Press, 2024
Includes bibliographical references and index

Identifiers
LCCN 2023030199 (print)
LCCN 2023030200 (ebook)
ISBN 978-1-4773-2892-7 (hardcover)
ISBN 978-1-4773-2893-4 (pdf)

Subjects
LCSH: Architecture–Texas–20th century
Architecture–Texas–20th century–Pictorial works
Architecture–Texas–20th century–Case studies
Architecture–20th century–Social aspects–Texas
Architecture–20th century–Political aspects–Texas
LCGFT: Photographs

Classification
LCC NA730.T5 O76 2024 (print)
LCC NA730.T5 (ebook)
DDC 720.9764/0904–dc23/eng/20231204
LC record available at
    https://lccn.loc.gov/2023030199
LC ebook record available at
    https://lccn.loc.gov/2023030200

doi:10.7560/328927